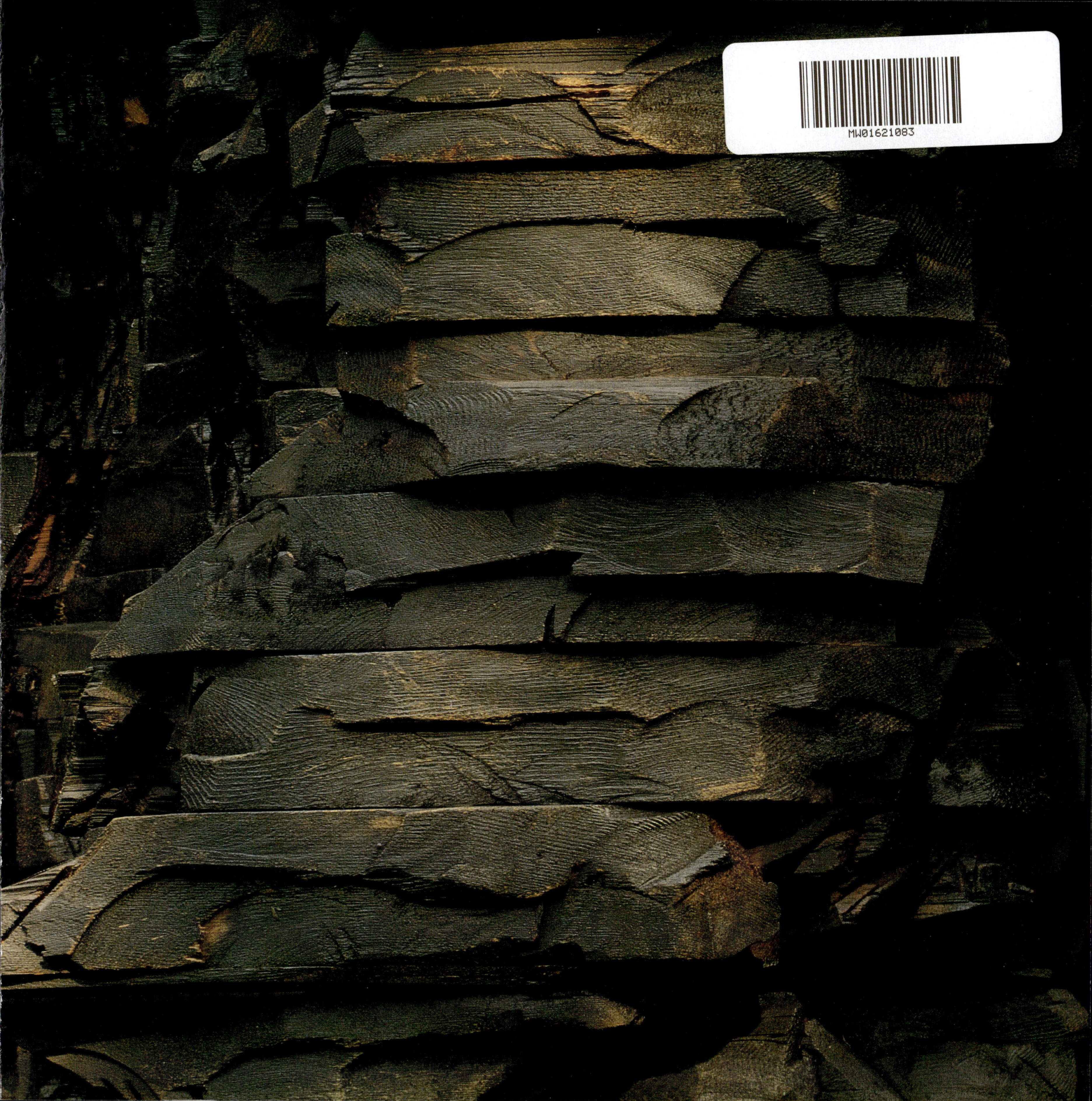

The Sculpture of
URSULA VON RYDINGSVARD

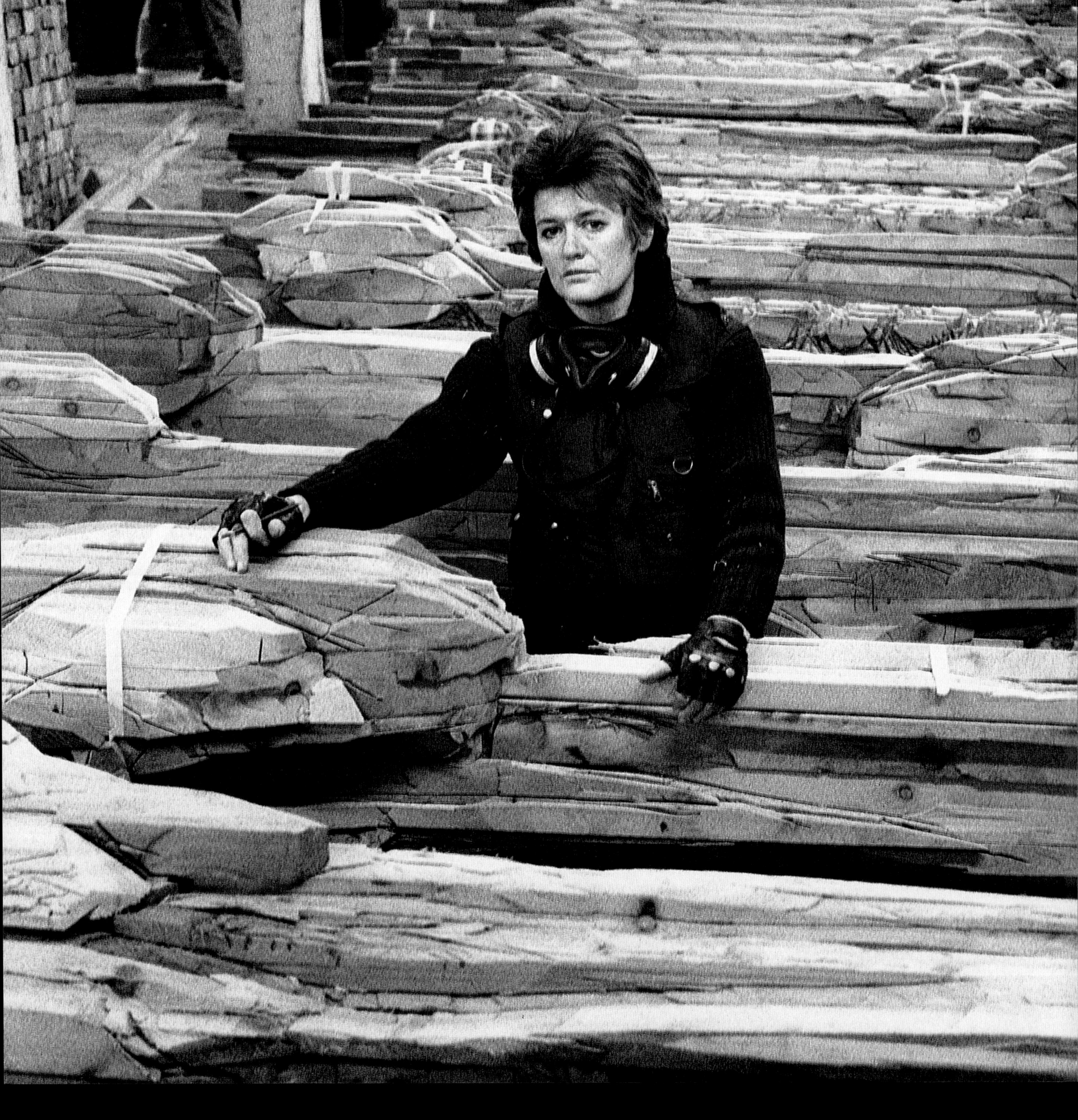

The Sculpture of
URSULA VON RYDINGSVARD

With Essays by Dore Ashton, Marek Bartelik, Matti Megged

HUDSON HILLS PRESS / NEW YORK

First Edition

Published in the United States by Hudson Hills Press, Inc., Suite 1308, 230 Fifth Avenue, New York, NY 10001-7704.

Distributed in the United States, its territories and possessions, Canada, Mexico, and Central and South America by National Book Network.
Distributed in the United Kingdom, Eire, and Europe by Art Books International Ltd.
Exclusive representation in Asia, Australia, and New Zealand by EM International.

Editor and Publisher: Paul Anbinder
Copy Editor: Virginia Wageman
Proofreader: Lydia Edwards
Indexer: Karla J. Knight
Design and Composition: Lorraine Ferguson
Manufactured in Japan by Toppan Printing Company.

Library of Congress Cataloguing-in-Publication Data

Von Rydingsvard, Ursula, 1942–
The Sculpture of Ursula von Rydingsvard / with essays by Dore Ashton, Marek Bartelik, Matti Megged. —1st ed.
p. cm.
Includes bibliographical references and index.
ISBN: 1-55595-122-8 (alk. paper)
1. Von Rydingsvard, Ursula, 1942– —Themes, motives.
2. Ashton, Dore.
I. Bartelik, Marek. II. Megged, Matti, 1923– . III. Title.
NB237.V58A4 1996
730'.92-dc20 96-8209
CIP

Below:
Von Rydingsvard in her Brooklyn studio, 1996.

Endsheets:
For Paul 1990–92, (detail). Storm King Art Center, Mountainville, New York.

Frontispiece, page 3:
Von Rydingsvard in her Brooklyn studio, 1992.

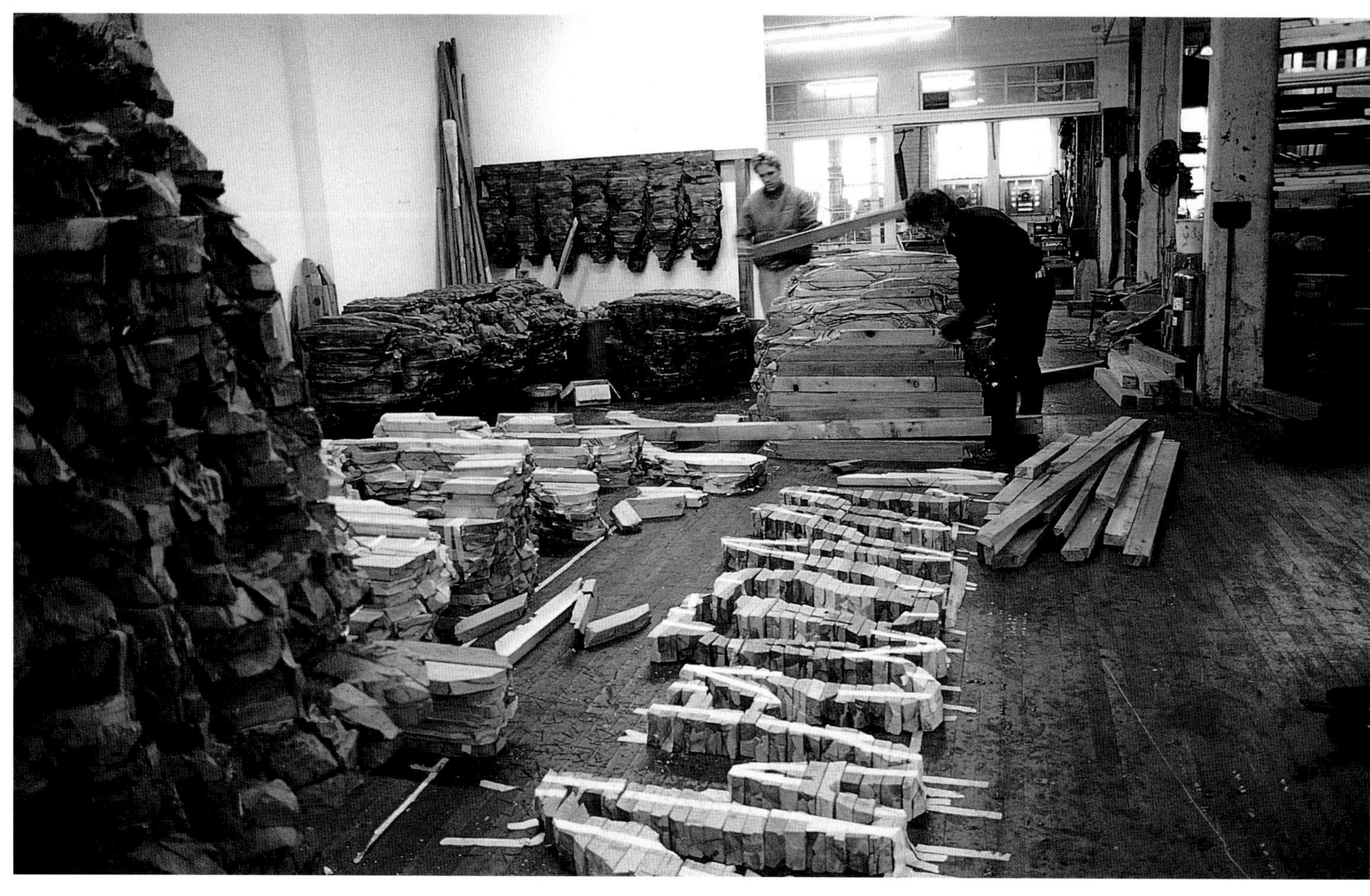

CONTENTS

Installation at Cranbrook Academy of Art Museum, Bloomfield Hills, Michigan, 1989.

From left:

Oj Dana Oj Dana 1989, cedar, graphite, and stain, 144 × 300 × 24 inches. Collection of the artist.

Ignatz Comes Home 1989, cedar, lead, and paint, 48 × 144 × 78 inches. Collection of the artist.

Three Boxes 1986, cedar, graphite, and stain, 36 × 72 × 30 inches each. Collection of Sheldon and Norma Minkowitz, Connecticut.

House of Spoons 1989, cedar, graphite, and stain, 96 × 72 × 48 inches. Collection of the artist.

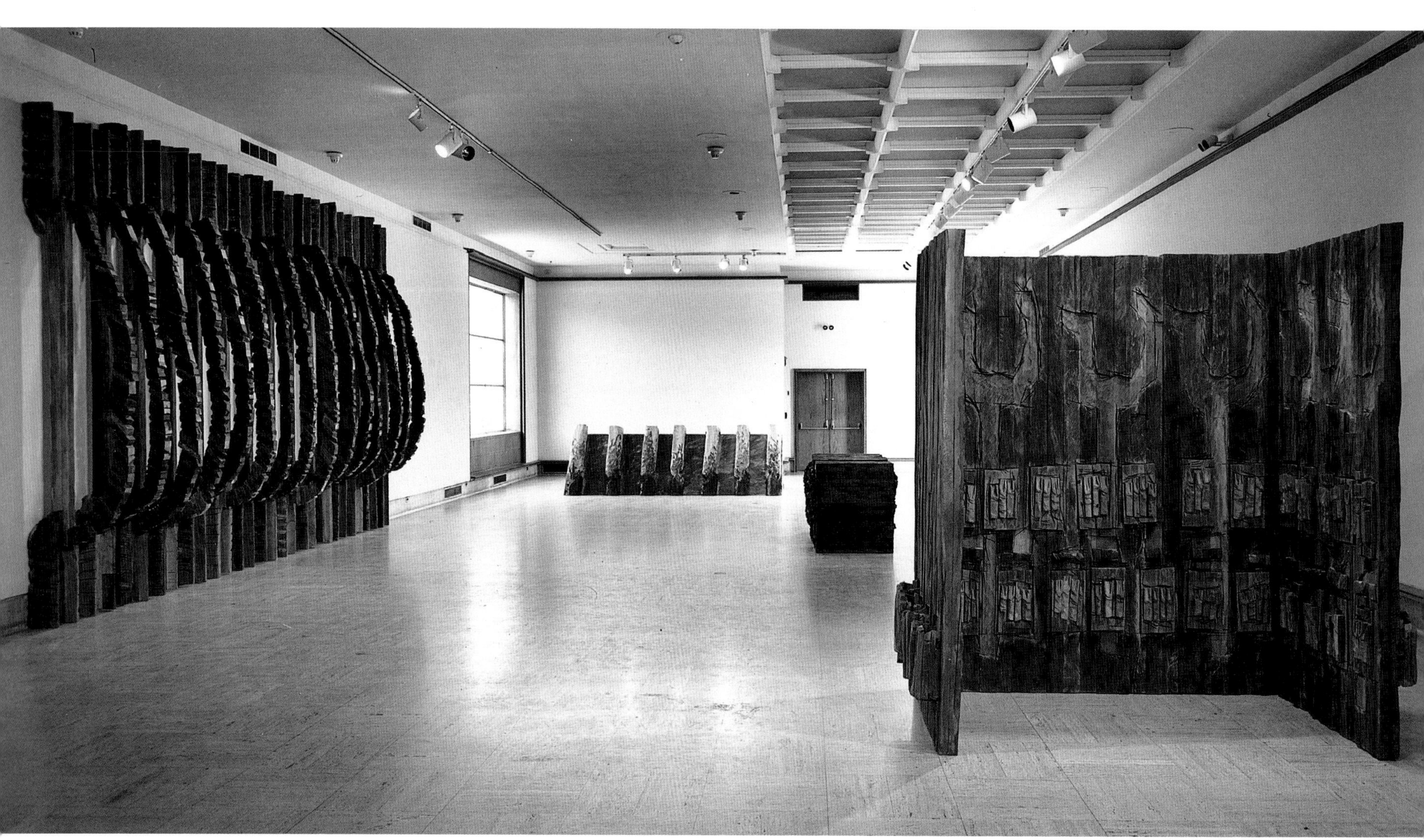

ILLUSTRATED WORKS BY VON RYDINGSVARD

INSTALLATIONS AND WORKS IN PROGRESS

* *Works indicated with an asterisk are illustrated in color.*

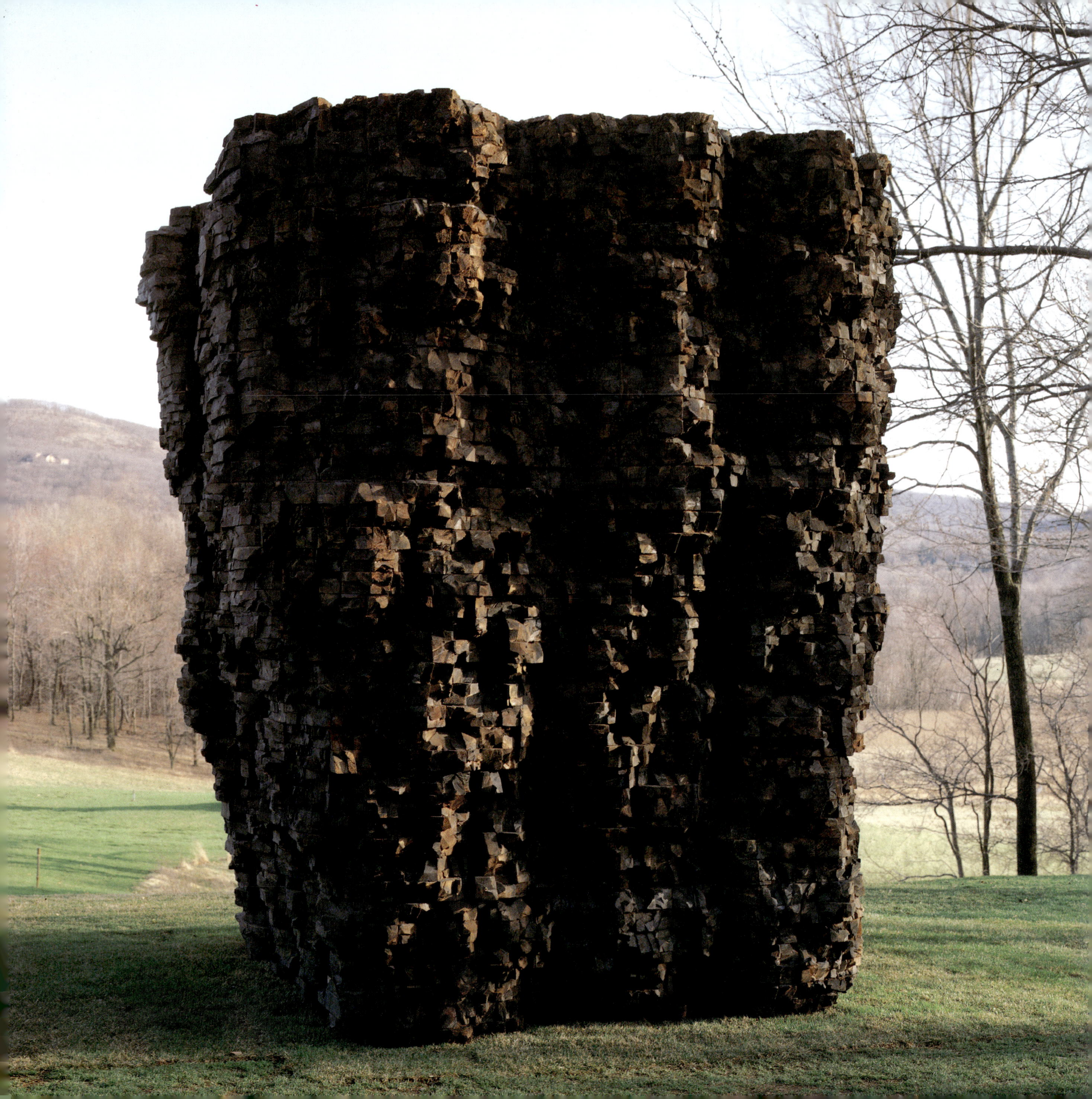

Dore Ashton

URSULA VON RYDINGSVARD

I once asked Ursula von Rydingsvard if she could remember her earliest artistic experience. After a thoughtful pause, she answered: "I remember something about unbleached, coarse linen. It would almost take its own form. I remember its being on me, almost like a nightgown—something about light on my body. Maybe I was three or four . . . outdoors, on the steps." I had expected her to remember some picture she had seen as a child, or perhaps her first drawing. But what she remembered was, in effect, a sculpture. In 1985, when she was already a well-established sculptor, she told an interviewer that she often went to the Metropolitan Museum of Art to see a Greek sculpture of 600 B.C., a "woman shaped like a column particularly in front where veils cling to her body and then they unfurl in the back where forms are more torn apart."[1] I mention these memories from different stages in a sculptor's life in order to talk about sculpture, for there is a fundamental relationship between the perception of sculpture and the presence of the human body. No matter how far afield sculpture has gone since 600 B.C., it has never been able to quit itself of the existence of the first presence each human being knows—his own body as it obeys the laws of gravity, or defies them. It's always there. Sculpture initiates proprioceptive activities. Like any sculptor in any epoch, von Rydingsvard has thought with her body and sensed her presence in the world. The world—that is to say, space—is the raw material in which the sculptor inscribes the human presence.

Von Rydingsvard works, as do all intelligent artists, from out of her culture—the culture she experienced as an artist in a certain place, New York, and the culture she has nurtured for herself from countless sources ranging from poets, to museums, to her personal history. Her way of feeling is largely intuitive, but her means of expressing her feeling are sophisticated. Among the many forces that she has marshaled to get on with her work is memory. In recent years, she has called up early memories, told herself the stories that would incite and explain her imagination. She has dwelled on the childhood years in which she lived with her family in the barracks of a postwar displaced-persons camp. There, in an austere environment, she experienced the sole aesthetic heightening available in the form of the rituals of the barrack designated as a church, "a strict symmetry with a certain kind of performance, and candle light, which was powerful psychologically." There, "I gave myself up to it in a way that was total, unguarded." There, she conceived of the goal of her life, "to be in a state of grace." Perhaps in childhood the state of grace took on ecclesiastical overtones, but as an adult, and an artist, the grace von Rydingsvard still seeks passionately is more nearly related to the ancient Greek myths, to those sister goddesses intimate with the Muses.

The desire to be pure that von Rydingsvard knew as a small child is often one of the tacit goals of artists. That is why we speak of beauty and truth, why sculptors in the earlier part of the century spoke about "truth to materials," and why artists after the Second World War so often referred despairingly (for it is so hard to determine) to "authenticity." Von Rydingsvard grew up as an artist in a milieu where the issue of authenticity was still smoldering and was the prime motor of a quick succession of sculptural groupings—from Abstract Expressionists to Minimalists. All of these groupings were marked by a strong will to get rid of the trappings that obscured the purity of the sculptural gesture. And in this, they were consistent with the patterns of modernism which, ever since the Romantic era, was intent on disembarrassing art of the unexamined freight it had borne for centuries. This was a principle deeply enshrined in the modern psyche. Even seemingly baroque sculptures, teeming with forms, such as some of the

opposite:
For Paul 1990–92, cedar and graphite, 172 × 108 × 164 inches.
Storm King Art Center, Mountainville, New York, gift of Sherry and Joel Mallin, The Horace W. Goldsmith Foundation, Vera G. List, Ann M. Hatch, and Steven and Nancy Oliver (1994.1).

Robert Smithson
Ninth Mirror Displacement 1969, Yucatan.
Estate of Robert Smithson. Courtesy John Weber Gallery.

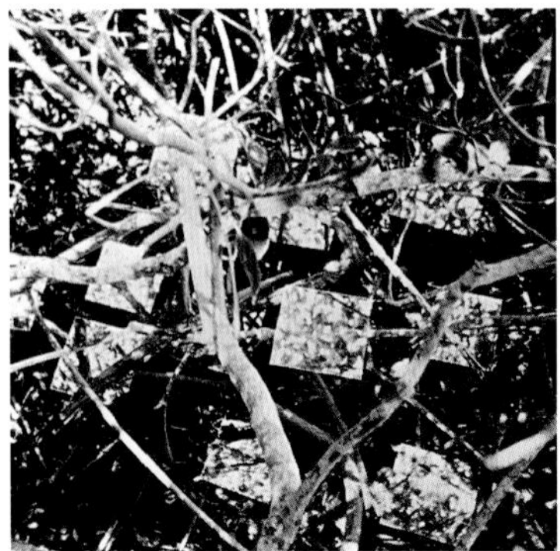

Eva Hesse
Sans II 1968, fiberglass, 38 × 170¾ × 6⅛ inches.
Whitney Museum of American Art, New York, purchase with funds from Ethelyn and Lester J. Honig and the Albert A. List Family.

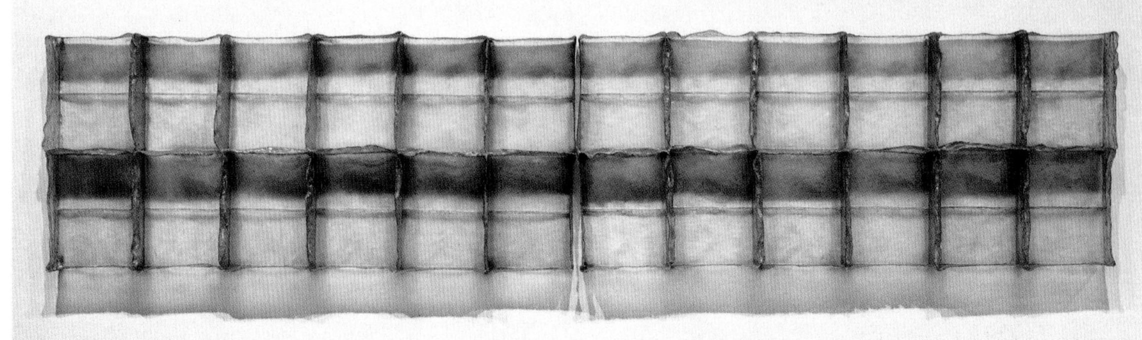

bricoleur works of Pablo Picasso — his playful constructions of cardboard guitars and costumes for *Parade* — or of Alexander Archipenko, with his coats of many colors arrayed on complicated sculptural shapes, were driven by the will to shed stale sculptural conventions and render the gesture of the maker pure. When sculptors of the generation immediately before von Rydingsvard's put forward new departing points and assimilated principles of psychology and perception to their practice, as did Robert Morris when he utilized gestalt psychology for a "holistic" view of the world, they, too, sought to establish the truth, both about the way the human being navigates the world (or space) and the way the world is ordered.

"Authentic" comes from *authentes* in Greek: one who does anything with his own hand. But the hand, as so many poets and aestheticians have remarked, is the compliant servant of a whole complex of impulses and mental decisions. Sometimes it seems to have its own life, but that life, like the life of an artist, has been conditioned, shaped, rendered potent by so many subtle forces that no one has ever been able to describe exactly what happens when the artistic hand becomes a shaper.

Still, some of the incidents in the formation of a sculptor can be more or less objectively described — the outer events, for instance, such as schooling. Von Rydingsvard, the immigrant child, arrived in the United States in time for fourth grade, went through high school in a small town where there were "no teachers with a deep involvement," and spent a few semesters at the University of New Hampshire, where she took a course with an Abstract Expressionist painter, Christopher Cook, whose passion impressed her, but whose explanations she never understood. It was with an art history professor, Jim Fasanelli, that she discovered aesthetic amazement, and it is significant that the two lectures she recalls best were about Greek temples and the Hagia Sofia. What impressed her, she recalls, was the amount of detail. "I felt amazed by details," she says, and that amazement would almost certainly be carried into her mature sculptures, where, despite their overall simple conformation, there are myriad small details. There were other schooling years—at the University of Miami, where she did a lot of painting, and at the University of California at Berkeley, where she was, as she says, "carried by the tide of flower children and rebellion" but had little memorable response. Meanwhile there was a marriage and a child, and finally, a flight to New York in 1973, where she enrolled in Columbia University's graduate program, and where she situates "the date of my birth—it was as if nobody ever heard anything I said before that time."

She had already tried her hand at sculpture, relief sculptures made of muslin. (Did they evoke her early memory of coarse linen, shaped? Or was it the other way around?) The permission to use unorthodox materials had long been implicit in modern art history. Picasso, after all, had used upholstery fringe as part of a wood relief early in the century, and a decade before von Rydingsvard's arrival in New York, Claes Oldenburg had soaked muslin in plaster to make giant ice-cream cones and hamburgers. But when she muses about her formation, von Rydingsvard refers animatedly to her exposure to the painters of the Abstract

Untitled (Steel and Thread) (detail) 1974, steel and thread, 50 × 40 × 3 inches.
Collection of the artist.

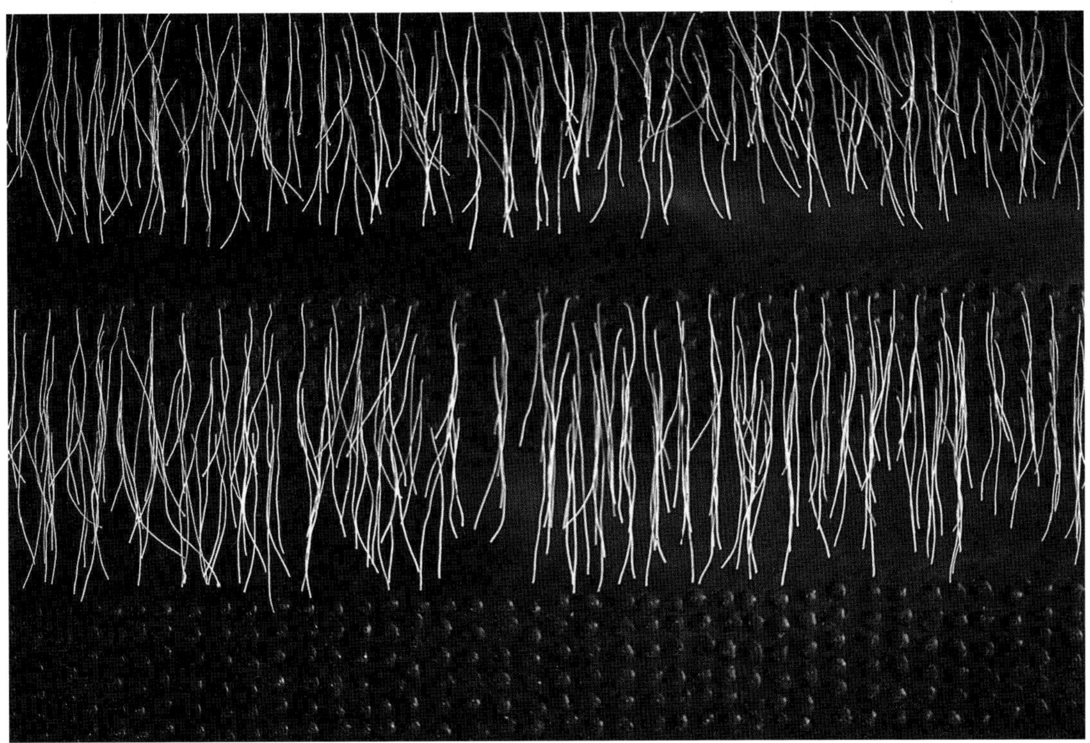

Expressionist movement and, most particularly, to the work of Willem de Kooning and Arshile Gorky, who "had a real link to life, and it was the *real* link. I wanted it."

What von Rydingsvard saw in Gorky's work was undoubtedly the seemingly contradictory method—first of careful preliminary thinking and preparatory sketches, then of improvisatory gestures. The expressive value of free association was explicit in Gorky's work, where each form was poised to metamorphose, and where line flowed away from form and back, enunciating the memory of impulse. Gorky was also an immigrant in his adolescent years, and later in his life he also scoured his early memories and created a mythology (if one accepts the basic definition of myth as the stories human beings tell themselves to enable them to exist in the incomprehensible outer world) that he utilized in his working process. He rediscovered a rural past, with its agricultural tools and its peasant lore—something von Rydingsvard has also resurrected in her various discussions of her work, and in the work itself. Gorky thought of the primitive plough, while von Rydingsvard thought of shovels and hand instruments used in the ritual of farming. The air of improvisation enlightened the work of de Kooning as well, whose broad use of material—in his case, paint — always bespoke a leaping free of convention, a sense of life as implicitly motile, in which stasis occurs only when an ensemble of vivid forms has exhausted the impulse of their author.

But on the other side, and somewhat in defiance of Abstract Expressionist principle, were the sculptural experiments of the 1960s and early 1970s, grouped under various labels, such as "primary structures," the title of an exhibition at the Jewish Museum in 1966; "Minimal art"; "process art"; and "earthworks." Any student in sculpture at Columbia in the years von Rydingsvard attended, 1973–75, would have had to take the radical departures of such artists as Robert Morris, Carl Andre, Ronald Bladen, Tony Smith, Sol LeWitt, Robert Smithson, and Eva Hesse into account. And indeed, von Rydingsvard reports that she was "in awe of them—their philosophies seemed so clear, so pure." Purity was a deep need for her. She admired LeWitt for the

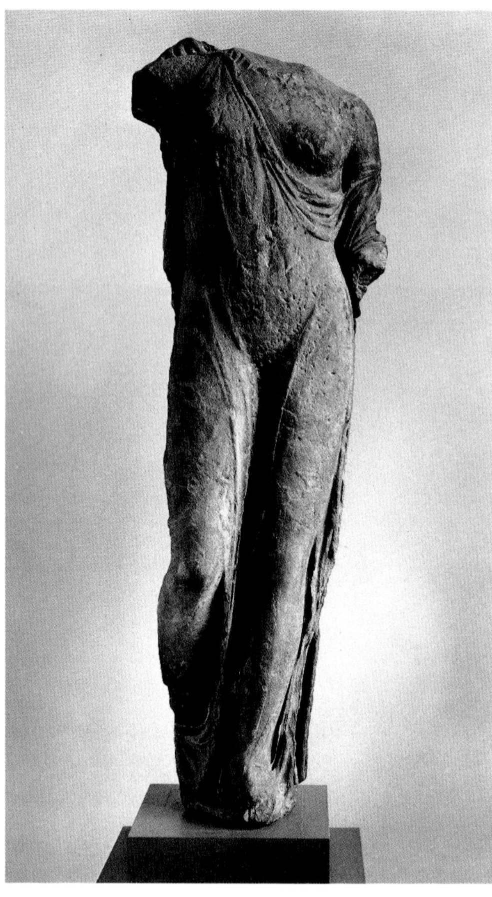

Aphrodite
Roman copy of a 5th-century-B.C. Greek original, marble, 59½ inches high. The Metropolitan Museum of Art, New York, funds from various donors, 1932 (32.11.3).

"almost pragmatic base of his logic," and she was "bowled over" by the physical aspects of Smithson's work, citing the celebrated piece *Spiral Jetty.* She describes this innovative step of Smithson's as a "single-handed invasion that was brilliant—an appendage to nature that made a lot of sense." "Simple, clean, and decisive," she says admiringly. But she also mentions temperamental differences with the Minimalists that would emerge as she groped her way to her own territory. The symmetries so pervasive in Minimalist sculpture were echoed in her memories of the wooden barracks of her childhood home, but that childhood had become a source of emotional darkness and light that transpired far from the cool, objective place so many Minimalists inhabited.

In fact, her language, when she discusses the art historical sources of her vision, is always the language of emotion. She admires sixth-century-B.C. Greek sculpture because it is "contained, and very rich emotionally." She likes medieval sculpture for its "tone," so different from Renaissance sculpture—a tone based "on their unwavering beliefs." And of all the twentieth-century artists who touched upon her deepest feelings, she admires most of all Alberto Giacometti, not, as she hastens to add, for his content, but for the depth of his feeling, for the way "he would rake deep psychologically," and for the visible relationship between him and his studio. "He bowls me over not in what he says directly, but in an indirect way—there is a gripping thing in his work . . . the process of groping, the maybe, maybe," she says. If her attention was called to the tidy "anaxial symmetry," as he called it, of Carl Andre's floor pieces, in which any part would replace any other part, or to the permutations of geometry of LeWitt, or to the endless additive possibilities suggested by Robert Morris in his early work, von Rydingsvard was still seeking, or, as she says of Giacometti, "groping" toward a fusion of feeling and form, closer probably to the sensibility of Eva Hesse, who, like her, was born in Germany and later spent an important year there, and whose attitudes were more in line with the Abstract Expressionists than with the Minimalists. "I want to allow myself," Hesse said in an interview in 1970, "to get involved in what is happening and what can happen and be completely free to let that go and change."[2] Von Rydingsvard, despite the unitary nature of much of her sculpture, also works without the a priori, planned, or "conceptual," attitude of the Minimalists. She rarely makes preliminary drawings—or at least, not specific drawings for given pieces—and she works more like a painter, stroke by stroke. "The reality of what actually happens always changes the original fantasy," she says.

By the time she left Columbia, von Rydingsvard was fortified with a rich variety of possible sculptural approaches and by the habit of challenging her own assumptions. Unquestionably, the energetic activities of her immediate predecessors, the so-called Minimalists and process artists, tempered her views. It was not so much their tendency to think of environment as the decisive force in the making of sculpture, as it was their emphatic use of unaccustomed spaces such as floors, ceilings, fields, and in the case of Smithson, water and volcanoes. The surveyor's view of the world

Alberto Giacometti
Bust of Diego (Diego, Study from Life) 1954, bronze (edition 2/6), 15¼ × 13¼ × 8 inches.
Hirshhorn Museum and Sculpture Garden, Smithsonian Institution, gift of Joseph H. Hirshhorn, 1966.

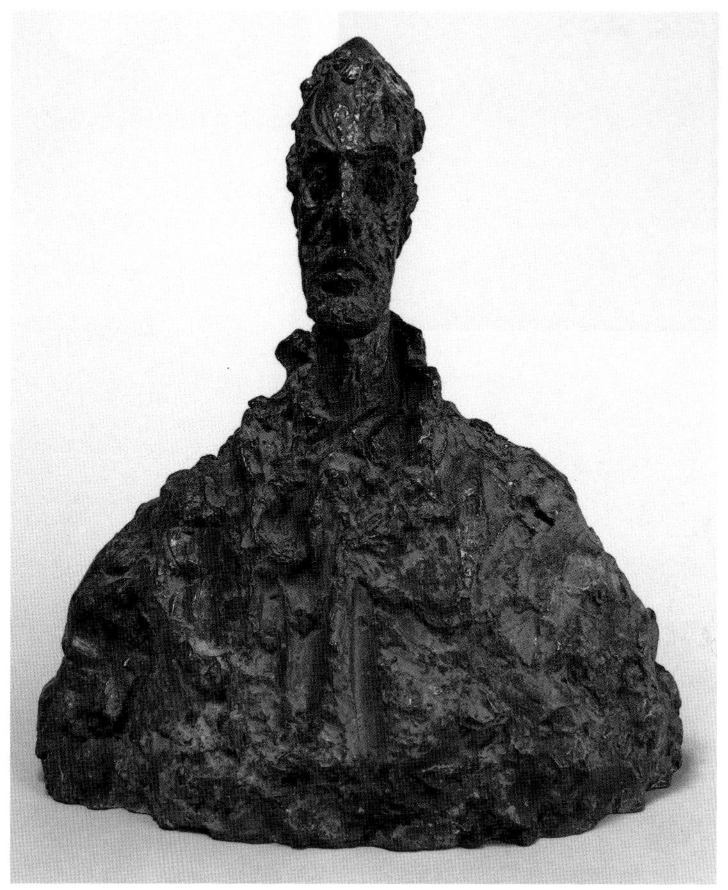

had invaded the world of sculpture. Artists measured off their spaces in the outdoors, but also in the confines of the gallery. A viewer was no longer required to focus on a single object and circumnavigate it, but was asked to enter a total space to which individual units contributed while never forming a central axis. The single object was not the central locus, and often horizontality, rather than the vertical monolith reminiscent of *homo erectus,* prevailed. Still, the break with sculptural tradition was never as complete as contemporary criticism willed it to be. Von Rydingsvard knew that instinctively.

The idea of a sculpture incorporating its environment has turned up again and again in the history of sculpture. When the Japanese carved the small netsuke, the human hand meant to cradle it was implicit in its shape. When Michelangelo designed the Medici Chapel, he created a total environment. Gianlorenzo Bernini was the master of the entire oval space that constituted the Piazza Navona. And in recent American sculpture history there were precedents. The idea of converting the cubic space of a room into an element of sculpture, perhaps first broached by Kurt Schwitters in his *Merzbau,* was extended by Louise Bourgeois in 1949 when she installed an exhibition of carved wooden sentinels throughout the room, and when she created the strange walk-in sculpture, *The Blind Leading the Blind,* with its many rickety legs carved unevenly out of planks of wood. Soon after, Louise Nevelson began assembling bits and pieces of found wood into ensembles, installed in the late 1950s, complete with thematic continuities, and lighted deliberately to suggest the total configuration as a single work.

Von Rydingsvard embarked on her professional life in New York soon after graduating from Columbia, having a succession of one-person exhibitions at an artists' cooperative gallery, 55 Mercer, and at the Robert Friedus Gallery, between 1977 and 1980. She established her studio with the intention of creating carved wood sculpture, using the traditional carver's tools—mallet and assorted chisels. But she quickly discovered an antipathy for the retrieved tree stump and its inescapable associations with traditional views of nature. According to her, a friend appeared with a gift of cedar four-by-fours, milled to a sharp-edged perfection, and perfectly neutral in her eyes. She has described her initial steps in converting these machined elements into hand-fashioned objects:

> My first instinct of how to alter them was to see if I could get rid of these edges. I carved away to make them round. Then I glued two hunks onto the bottom, because it needed to stand up, and that roundness needed some kind of break. It was too monotonous, so I gave it a bulge at the bottom which also got it to stand up. I repeated that form a number of times, and that was my first piece in cedar and my first lamination.[3]

And it was her first journey into the realm of ambiguities that has characterized her work ever since. Her works, which so often announce themselves in orderly groups of forms, as though pacing

Untitled (Steel and Wooden Uprights) 1976, wood and steel, 72 × 37 × 12 inches. Private collection.

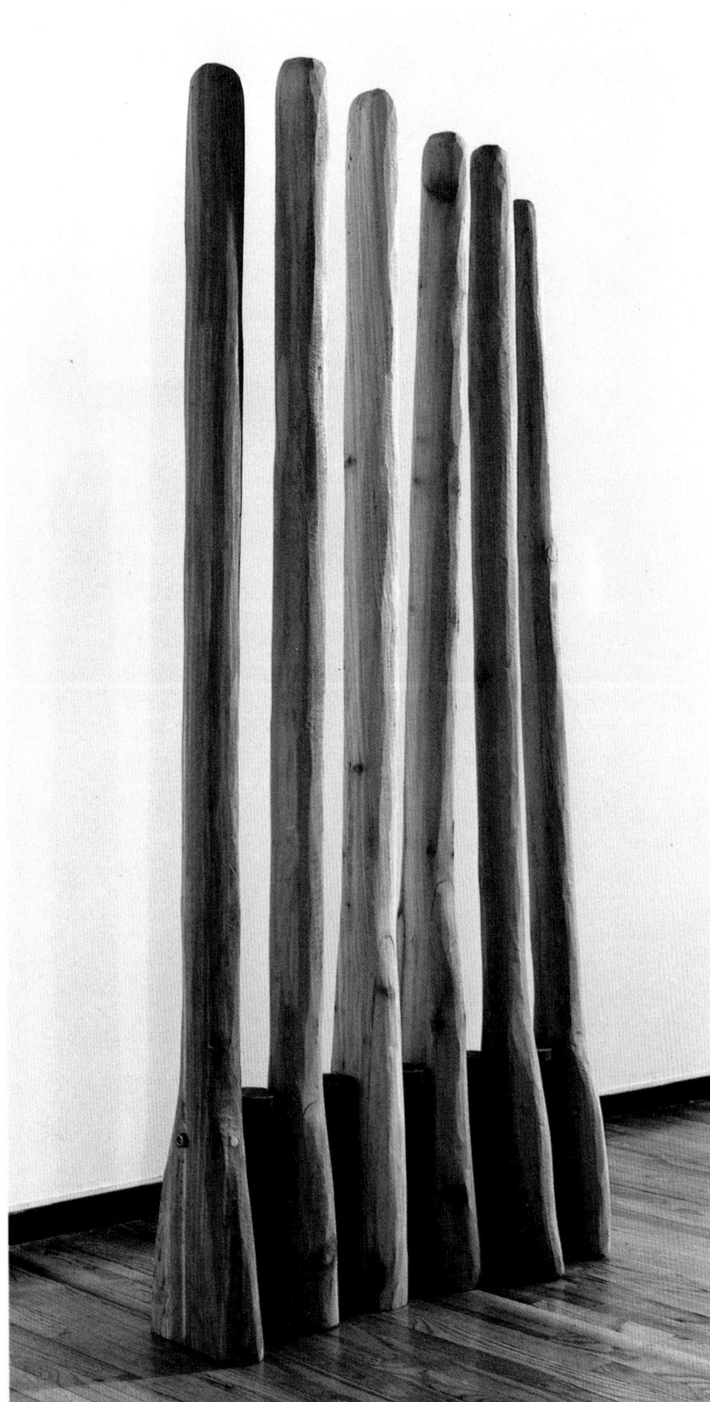

Untitled (Nine Cones) 1977, cedar, 42 × 156 × 180 inches.
Installation at Battery Park City landfill, New York, 1977.
Collection of the artist.

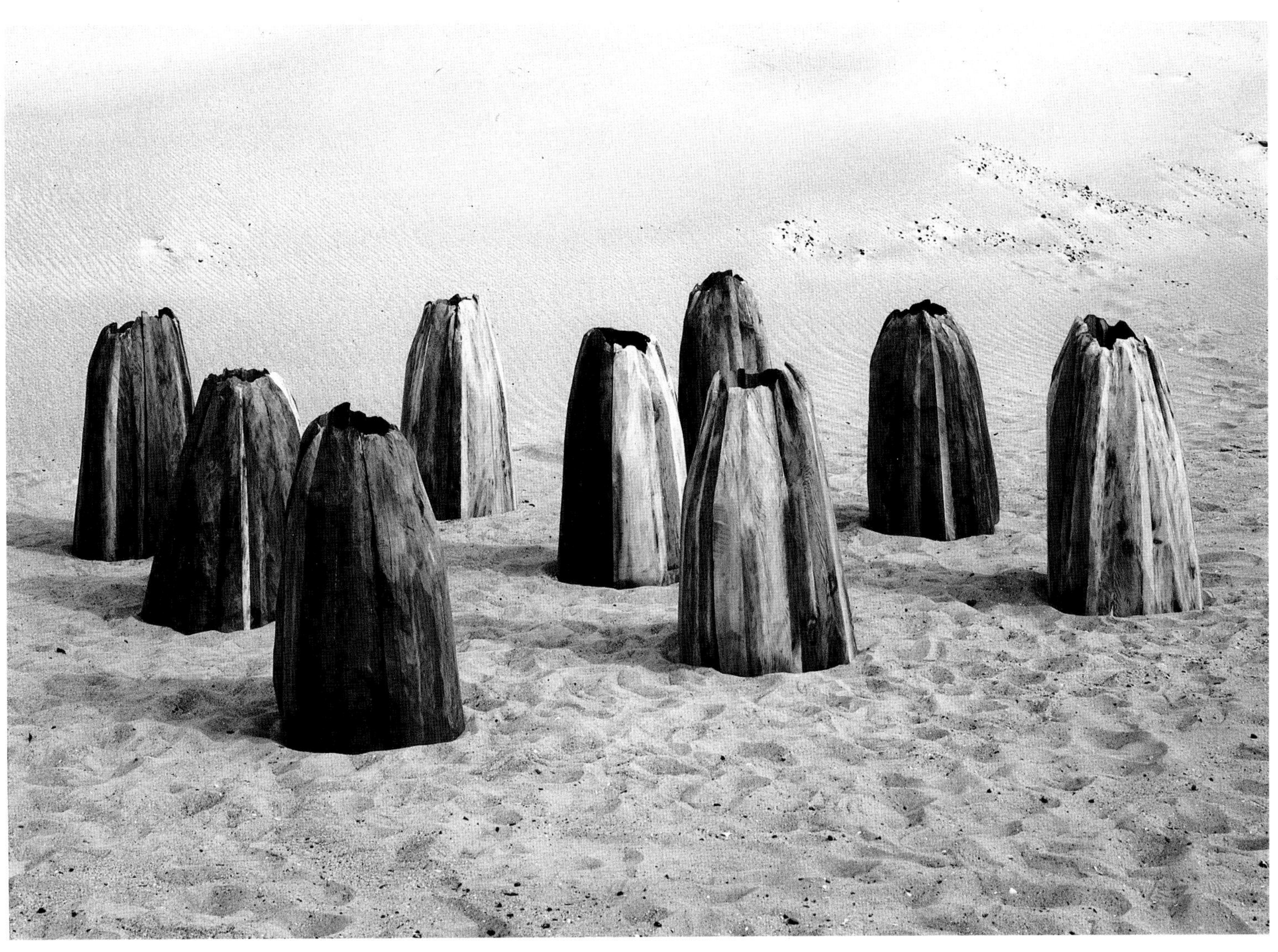

off the spaces as does the human gait, are never exactly conceived with a single meaning in mind. Rather, von Rydingsvard's impulse to repeat general forms but never specific details resides entirely in her deeply hidden need for repletion, fulfilled, as she has so often declared, purely intuitively. Repetition serves what she sometimes has called a ritual function. It also serves to emphasize the distinctiveness of details, always freely shaped and never identical. Ambiguity becomes a device to open opportunities for a variety of meaning. As William Empson once so elegantly demonstrated in his book *Seven Types of Ambiguity,* the poet, who like the artist works with certain fixed conventional structures, opens out his imaginative prospects by means of ambiguity, as when Shakespeare so often used a series of negatives, such as not and nor, that instantly evoked both his objects and that which they were not: "Since brass, nor stone, nor earth, nor boundless sea . . ." (Sonnet 65). By means of conjugation, in the grammatical sense of the word, von Rydingsvard incorporates different moods and tenses within a single multipartite work and achieves finally what a musician might call consonance.

Already in her early experiments with sawing, planing, gluing, and carving beams of cedar, von Rydingsvard was establishing a rhythm she could recognize as emanating from herself, although it was, and is still, mysterious, unfathomable. The arrival at certain groupings—three roughly similar shapes, or nine shapes, or seven in a row—was never preordained, but seemed to her to emerge as she worked form after form. The repetition of small units then takes on a kind of allegorical function, just as it did for Piet Mondrian, when he went from tracking the horizon through the final contour of a sand dune, to describing the inherent nature of the sea (not how it actually looked, but rather as it felt when its structures were analyzed into rhythms of plus and minus).

In those early works, von Rydingsvard accepted the modern convention of the floor- or ground-based perspective. Her composed, or rather, constructed shapes were never presented on a plinth, but were always directly on the floor, or on the ground outdoors. Giacometti had already worked with discrete parts arrayed on the floor in the 1930s, as in his *Woman with Her Throat Slit,* and the ancient Japanese had always known the possibilities inherent in the forms at our feet, into and onto which we peer. Something of the Japanese paradox involving miniaturization in order to suggest a cosmic order was already present in von Rydingsvard's earliest exhibitions. Certain characteristic forms appeared that would later be amplified and made powerful even in those smallish ensembles of the 1970s. For instance, there were several ensembles of shapes that were barely knee-high, with sloping, gourdlike walls and narrow openings that suggested some sheltering enclosure—the snug interior hollow barely visible, as in a deep bird's nest—or, handled slightly differently, and with closer placement, mountains or cliffs.

In 1978, for example, von Rydingsvard showed a cluster of richly carved forms, in which the work of her chisel created the bosses and hollows of traditional woodcarving. The title of one piece, *For Weston,* might suggest an association with the sharply defined landscape photographs in which Edward Weston sought sculptural contrasts of light and shadow. But von Rydingsvard was not thinking of the photographer at all, but of a friend named Weston McDaniels. Using the same technique of gluing and carving lengths of cedar beams, von Rydingsvard developed at the same time an alternate way of presenting forms that are closed solids arrayed on a grid. These works were intended to be seen outdoors and are composed of closely serried slabs that suggest primitive structures, "vernacular" architecture such as that seen in tiny settlements or villages in exotic places. Von Rydingsvard's imagination in these early ensembles has already staked out one area of its psychological territory: feelings that evoke the functions of dwelling, or sheltering.

A year later she was sufficiently well known to be asked to present several outdoor works, or as they were clumsily called,

For Weston 1978, cedar, 48 × 66 × 18 inches.
Collection of Vera List.

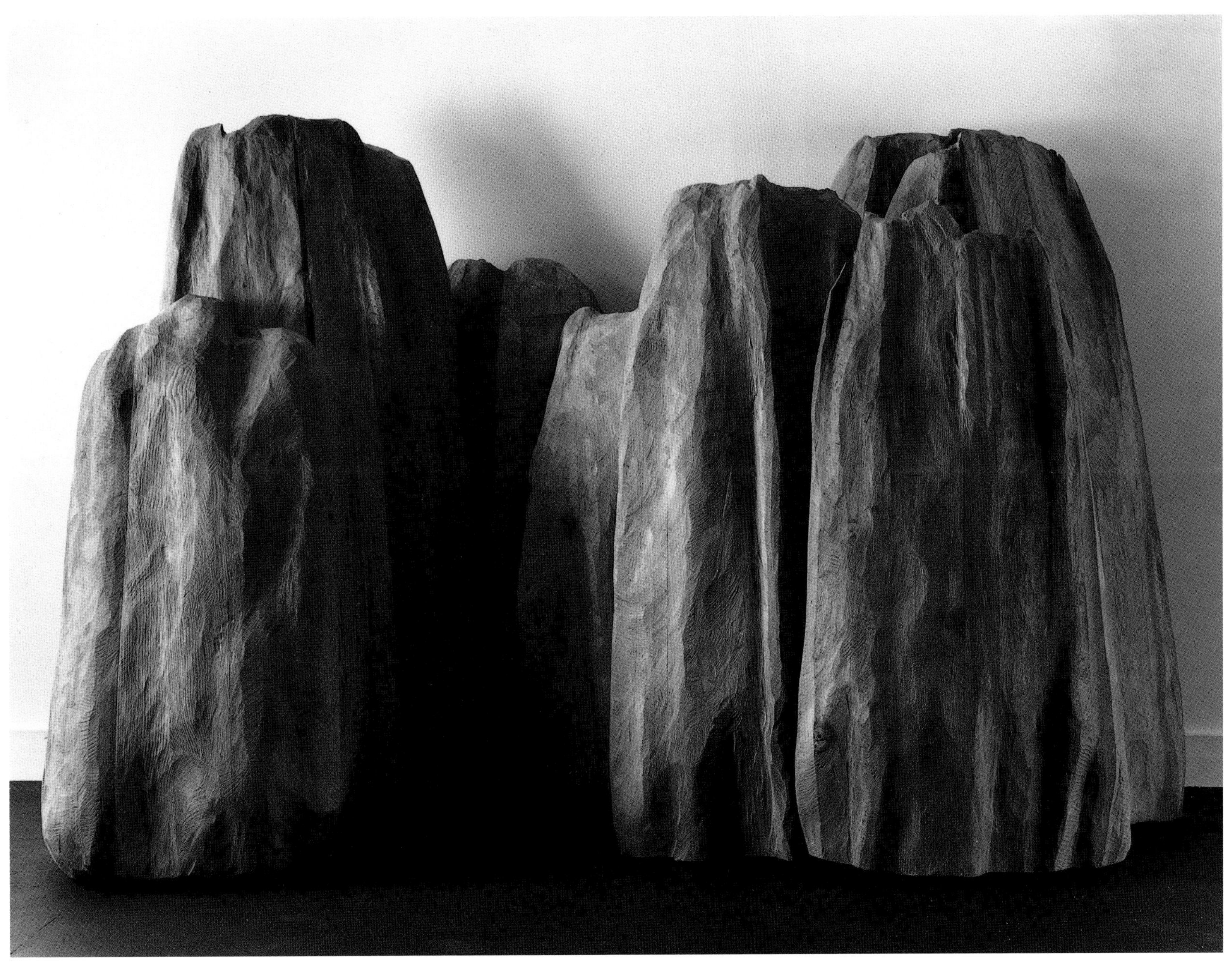

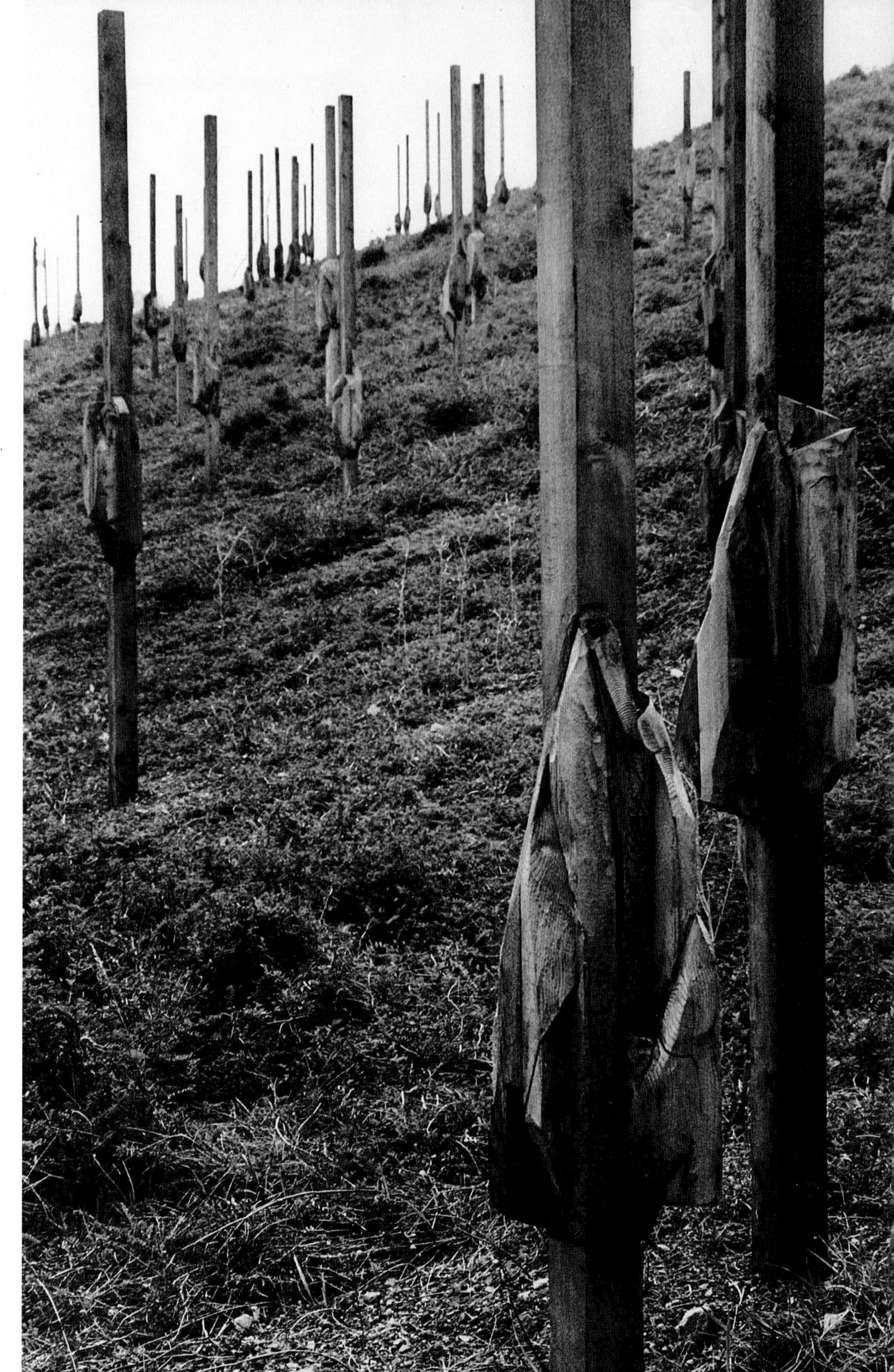

Song of a Saint (Saint Eulalia) 1979, cedar,
12 × 330 × 160 feet.
Installation at Artpark, Lewiston, New York, 1979.
Destroyed.

Koszarawa 1979, cedar, 2½ × 150 × 30 feet.
Installation at Wave Hill, Bronx, New York, 1979.
Destroyed.

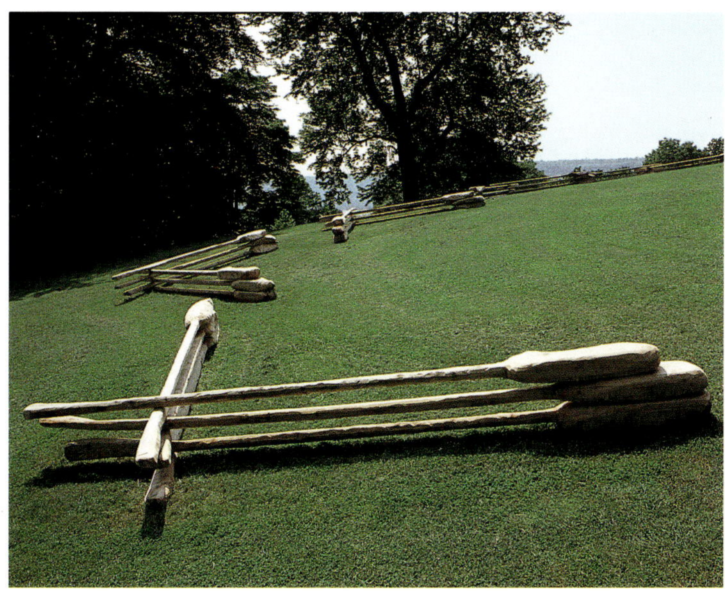

Song of a Saint 1979, cedar, 17 × 38 × 23 inches.
Collection of Martin Sklar.

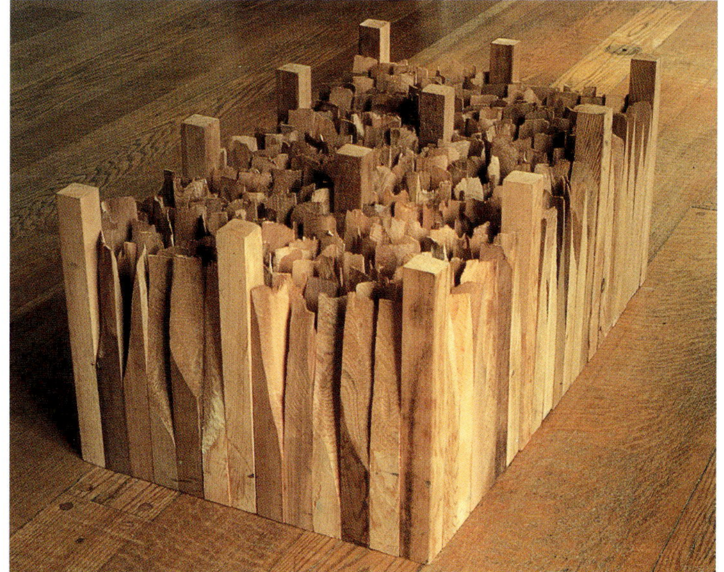

"site-specific" sculptures. Now she could stretch out, bring sweeping vistas under her control. At Artpark, in Lewiston, New York, she chose a grassy slope in a gully into which she installed 180 totemlike stakes adorned with carved appendages at varying heights. Her title, *Song of a Saint,* included "Saint Eulalia" in parentheses. The parenthetic reference is one of the indirect clues von Rydingsvard sometimes provides. In this case, Saint Eulalia is an apparition von Rydingsvard divined from a poem by Federico García Lorca, and she associated it, vaguely, with fire and female flesh. Certainly the curving appendages on the blunt-edged four-by-fours are organically suggestive. One of von Rydingsvard's most perceptive admirers wrote that the "laminated pods . . . produced a striking proscenium for the rising and setting sun" and said that the artist meant to evoke "the sounds of wind blowing inside the bell tower of a cathedral."[4] This synesthetic intention with its romantic, poetic allusion, recurs in von Rydingsvard's work and must be considered an endemic property of her oeuvre.

In another piece of the same year, also titled *Song of a Saint,* the "song" is more harsh and brings in a note of savagery that recurs from time to time in later works. This work, a rectangular floor piece of tightly packed two-by-fours with jagged edges, marked off by twelve towerlike beams and wholly self-contained, is also a prototype for later works. Its general form is suitably ambiguous, suggesting anything from a bed of nails to a medieval village to a sarcophagus. Its "song" is arcane, probably even to the artist herself.

The following year, 1980, von Rydingsvard was still caught up with the idea of saints, perhaps fortified by a trip to Europe in which she visited many sacred places, among them the churches housing Giotto's murals and the town of Orvieto, which rises like a great ship from the Italian plain and remains powerfully present in the artist's memory. Invited to create something for the Battery Park City landfill in Manhattan, von Rydingsvard developed a suite of diminishing forms that emphasized the gen-

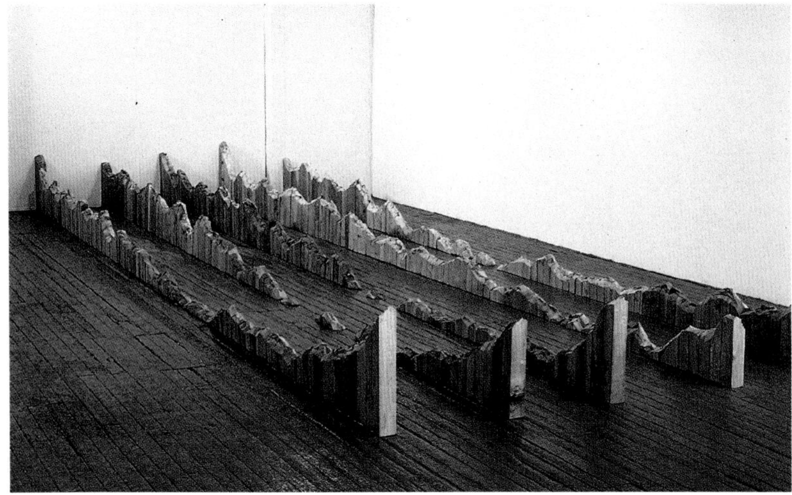

Untitled (Worn Walls) 1980, cedar, 36 × 348 × 108 inches. Collection of the artist.

tle slope of the site, a sand dune. The hue of the sand, changing as it is swept by light from dawn to dusk, had intimate affinities with the pinkish hue of the cedar posts, climbing and descending the dune. Here von Rydingsvard, who has a special feeling for the last light of day, and has described how deeply she has been affected by the aureole of gold edging objects with the light of the sinking sun, was able to express her most lyrical feelings toward the landscape, and in cresting the dune with arching members—winglike shapes, or echoes of the organic curve of the dune—she moves into the space of the work's title, *Saint Martin's Dream.* Although these flying members are rare in her work, the arch is often implied in later works. In the visual arts, the form of the arch often suggests a dreamlike, romantic vision as the arch-romantic Giorgio de Chirico emphasized in both his paintings and his writings. He quoted Otto Weininger's 1919 essay, "On Metaphysical Art": "In an arc there is still something incomplete, that needs to be and can be completed—this makes for a presentiment," to which de Chirico adds that the idea "clarified for me the eminently metaphysical impression that porticoes and arches in general have always made on me."[5]

The period in which von Rydingsvard fancifully titled works with saints' names is rich in presentiments, perhaps the most specific being an installation at the Rosa Esman Gallery in 1982 titled *Stations for Santa Clara.* Whatever associations von Rydingsvard may have had with the saint whose name means light, her installation was full of what de Chirico would have called enigma. In one wall of the tall compartments, or niches, she constructed, von Rydingsvard installed mysterious shapes—two large, monolithic, Stonehenge-like shapes huddle within one niche, while two low, benchlike shapes dwell next door, and six pillowlike or rocklike shapes spill out from the fourth and final niche. Whatever the saint's trials may have been, her stations, as created by the sculptor, reveal only mystery.

Finally, the ecclesiastical allusions, although no longer to saints, appear once again in an outdoor piece titled *16 Handrests,* 1984. This self-enclosed construction, with its wall and gateway, is a place, a built place that is like nothing so much as a church—perhaps the raw barrack that was the first church von Rydingsvard knew—with strangely magnified altars, or pews. As one walks into the interior space, the sculptured extrusions from the giant lecterns are like cloths used in some religious ritual. This walk-in structure was among the last von Rydingsvard created using the four-by-fours bluntly, as the building members they were intended to be.

But the fence in its honest function of framing and excluding was to be modified in many ways as von Rydingsvard became increasingly confident both of her technical capacity and of her range of expression. There were to be many sculptures that played upon the idea of a wall and expanded the wall's basic definition. There were, for example, several works in which von Rydingsvard aligned two or three freestanding walls, echoing the very technique of lamination at the base of her approach to sculpture. But in their expression, these carved walls, aligned in parallel formation, were distinctive. In an untitled work of 1984, for instance, two eye-level walls, rudely carved to give a tough but worn look, constrain and close an interior in which spiked forms are revealed. Around the same time, there were the almost animistic suggestions, with their hint of cruelty, in the works titled

Saint Martin's Dream 1980, cedar, 20 × 260 × 35 feet.
Installation at Battery Park City landfill, New York, 1980.
Collection of the artist.

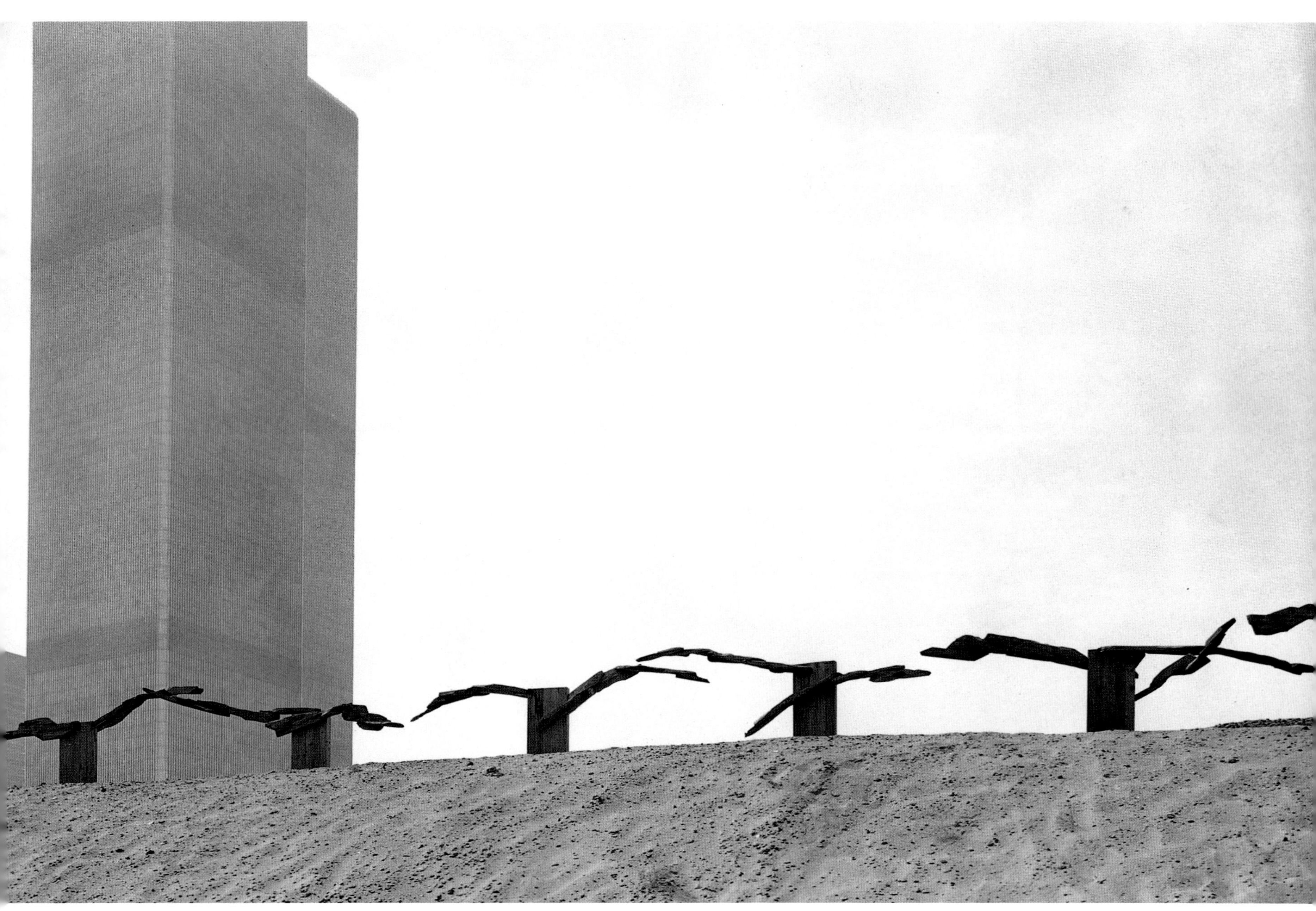

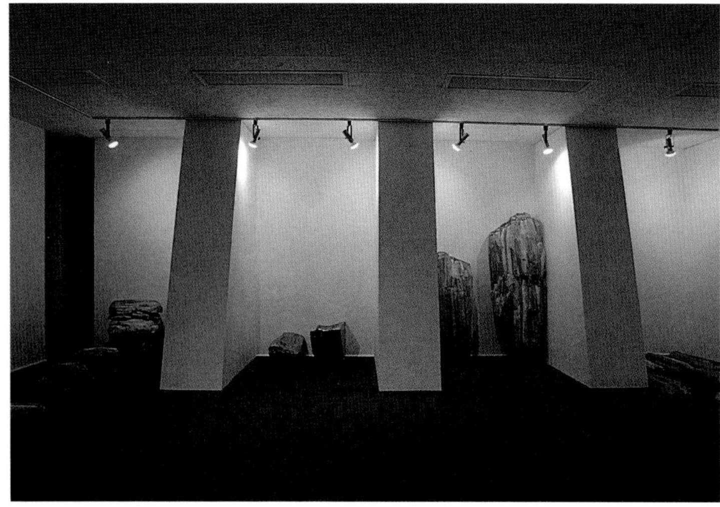

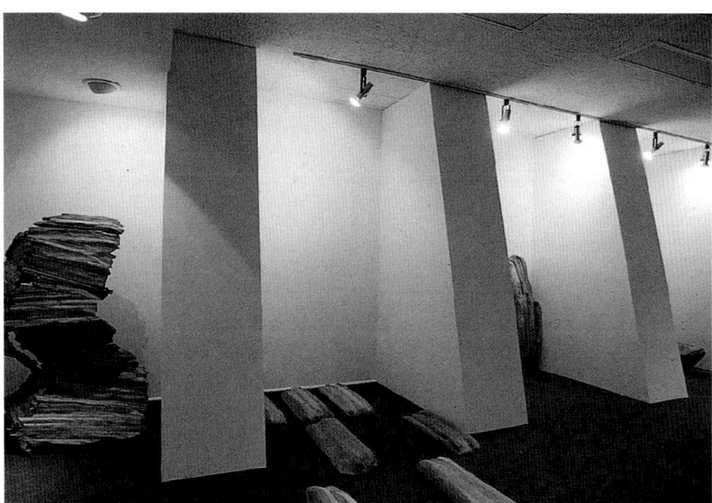

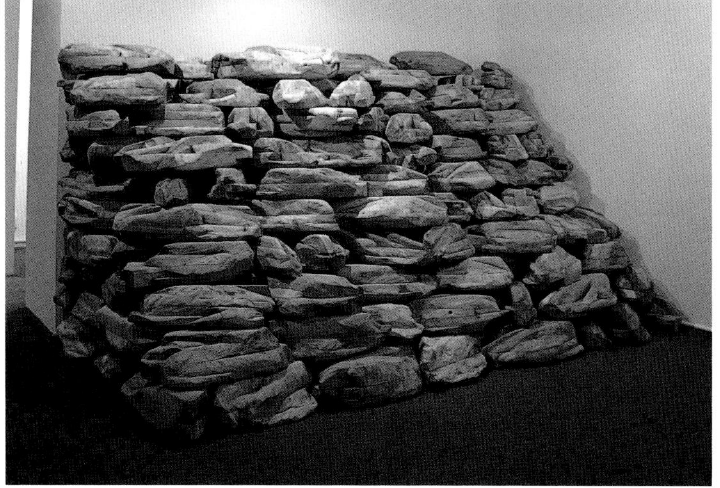

Stations for Santa Clara 1982, cedar, 6 elements, varying in size from 72 × 26 × 12 inches to 60 × 180 × 48 inches, installed in a room 32 × 22 feet. Installation at Rosa Esman Gallery, New York, 1982.
Collection of the artist.

Lucretia's Wall I and *II,* 1984 (cedar, 54 × 157¾ × 39 inches and 53½ × 139½ × 8½ inches, both collection of the artist), the latter evoking biological skeletons in its jointed, leglike surface, and the former—a tripartite wall with spiky members protruding within, above, and without its upper edge—menacing in its ambiguous compilation of regular and irregular forms. Von Rydingsvard's wall metaphors increasingly referred to states of feeling. Whether they functioned as barriers, as enclosures, as ramparts, as measurements of an indeterminate space, as bas-relief freestanding sculptures, or as slightly sinister fences (with occasional hints of barbed wire), they bore with them varying emotional intensities. Sometimes they were carved to suggest worn and benign ancient things, and sometimes, in the raw, hacking attack of the sculptor's tools, they carried a fearful contemporary intensity.

Toward 1986 von Rydingsvard began to emphasize the enigmatic weights of her sculptures by rubbing into the warm-hued cedar elements rich deposits of pitchy graphite. Now, the faceted surfaces of her laminated shapes took on a new dimension in the coruscating lights and shadows of the surfaces. More than ever, her delight in profuse detail, which she had first discovered as an art history novice, served her expressive needs. It is around the later 1980s that the works really take on the absolute presence that is at once wholly prepossessing in its thingness and, at the same time, wholly allusive. Her most powerful works would be those that were least available to a single description, but rather could be described as "looming." Things that "loom," says Webster's, come into sight, especially above the surface of sea or land, in enlarged, distorted, and indistinct form, often because of atmospheric conditions; "hence, figuratively, to appear . . . in an exaggerated or an impressively great form." Or, as a noun, "an appearance of exaggerated elevation or size of anything, as of land or of a ship, seen in fog or darkness."

Naturally, looming has always been a possible quality of sculpture, particularly sculpture that emphasizes mass and volume

Tunnels on the Levee 1983, cedar, 42 × 600 × 240 inches.
Installation at Deweese Park, Dayton, Ohio, 1983. Destroyed.

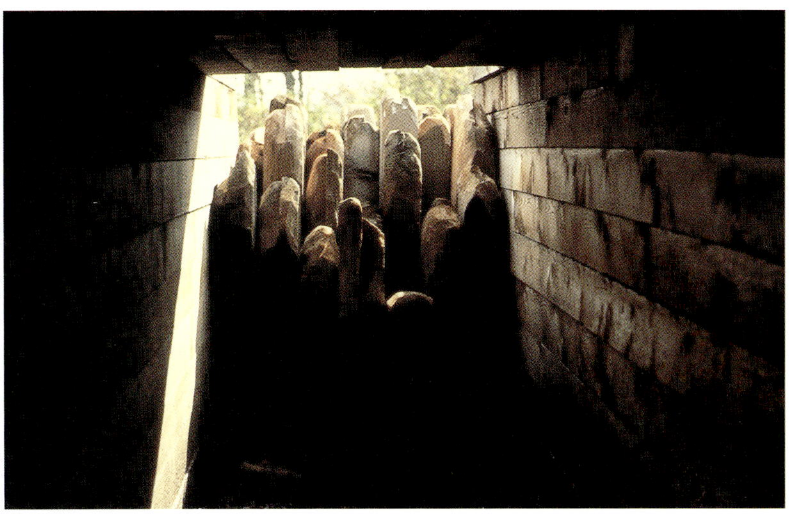

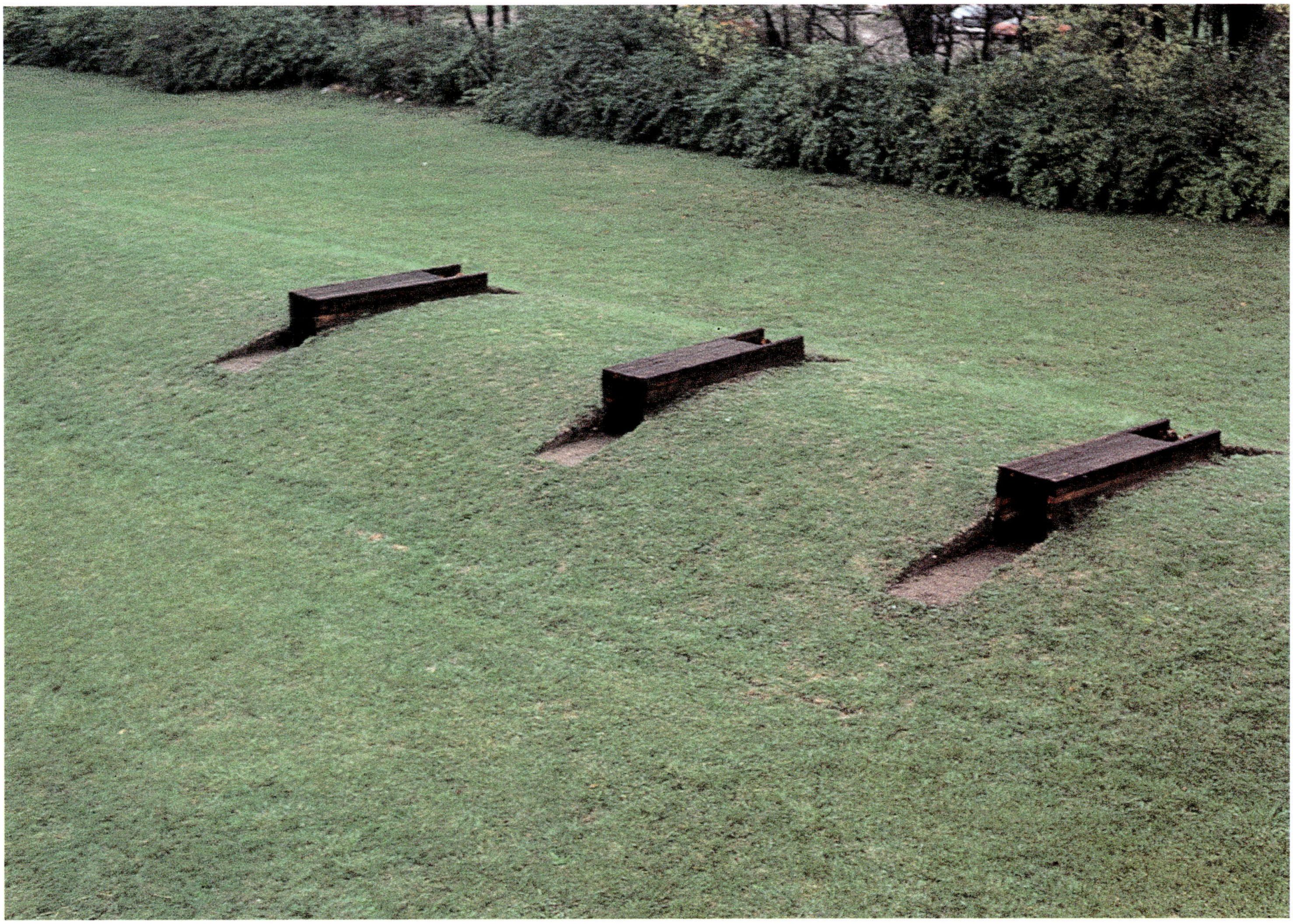

16 Handrests 1984, cedar, 56 × 228 × 204 inches.
Installation at Queens College, Queens, New York, 1984.
Collection of the artist.

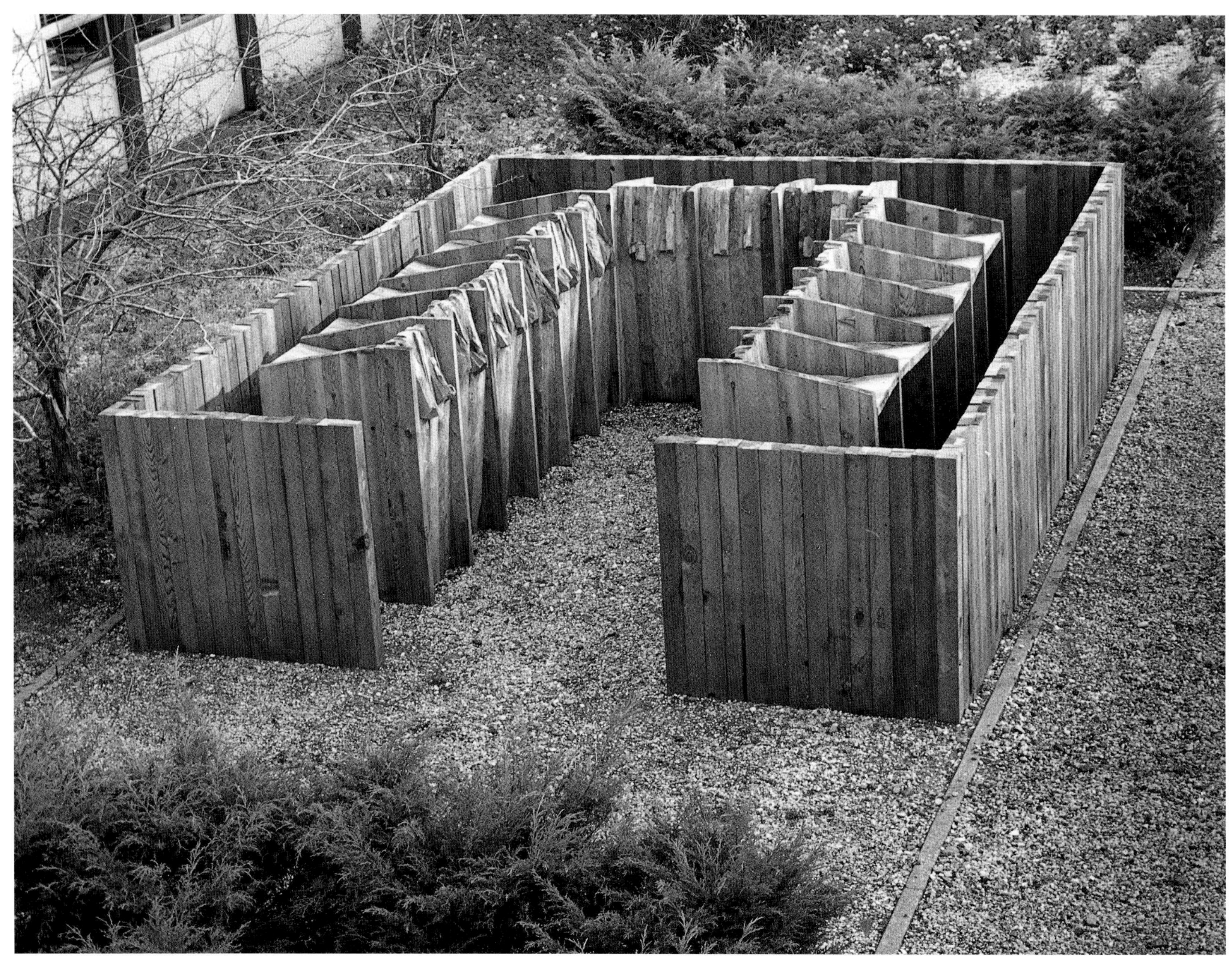

and that either rears up from the ground or seems ineffably planted there. Moreover, it is in the great traditional sculptural practice of exaggeration that the issue of scale is addressed in so many cultures. Scale, as every artist knows, is not a matter of size. Grand scale can be achieved by many cunning artistic tactics. One means is to take a vaguely familiar, relatively small object in the world, such as a cup, or a human head, and to render it in disproportionally large dimensions, such as the Roman colossi or the Easter Island heads. Another is to take a phenomenally large mass, such as a mountain, and reduce it. The unaccustomed adjustments the eye and mind must make to such feints on the part of the artist add drama, enigma, sometimes uneasiness, sometimes delight to the aesthetic experience. Then the "loomingness" of a figure in space becomes an object for contemplation. Once the feeling of a strange and large configuration is stabilized, the various details that add up to the overwhelming impression can be assimilated and make way for still further impressions. The history of art is full of looming presences and absences: grottoes, tunnels, spirals, secret niches; menhirs, sculptured walls, grouped figures in monuments, towers, wells, lookouts, massive gods. Much of the aesthetic satisfaction available in the world's history of sculpture lies in the age-old artistic impulse to create impermeable presences that loom in familiar spaces with such aplomb that space is transformed into the stuff of poetry.

Von Rydingsvard registered all the modern diversions from the power of the monolith — the use of transparent materials, the movement from mass to line, the use of accretion rather than carving, the tendency toward horizontals — and instinctively moved back to the old vision of the dense, unmovable, but moving presence. Her sculptural sense is to discipline solid matter, and in many ways her work can be defined in the quip of Barnett Newman, who defined sculpture as what you bump into when you step back to look at a painting.

Von Rydingsvard relies on our innate capacity to locate ourselves, and then she dislocates us in both sweeping and subtle terms. Each human is endowed with the ability to make a lightning decision of locus. A thousand or more neural activities cooperate in such a simple gesture as walking up a flight of stairs. Most individuals nonetheless have the innate capacity to locate the shapes and rhythms of objects called steps, and know instantly how to negotiate them. The artist is often an expert at interrupting the automatic activities of normal human behavior, bidding us to relearn, to reconsider the habitual. When von Rydingsvard moved audaciously into large-scale works, and when she emphasized the equivocal nature of surface and depth by means of the shadowing of graphite, she challenged visual and proprioceptive habits and awakened feelings long dormant in aesthetic experience. She worked, perhaps not consciously, for the restoration of *things, presences.* And she understood that things, or objects, even if they are not easily identified, are primers of the elementary imagination.

By the late 1980s von Rydingsvard had assembled a vocabulary of basic forms, some of which had been present from the beginning of her works in laminated cedar elements. For instance, there is the recurrent shape she refers to as a cone, which sometimes metamorphoses into a vessel, and sometimes into a cliff. There are hollow shapes that take on the lineaments of ancient amphorae, great jars, sometimes with rudimentary handles, sometimes with purely billowing walls. There are also less readily identifiable shapes that suggest the symmetries of nature — that is to say, the irregular symmetries that one might find in a bird's nest or a beaver's dam or a fir tree. Then there are rectangular shapes, sometimes rounded off, that are like sarcophagi, or like giant horse troughs. There are recumbent pieces, gouged out, that are reminiscent of dugout canoes or ancient litters. And there are the caves and tunnels, the ramparts, and the homely walls. Now, in full command of her process, von Rydingsvard begins to make

Untitled 1984, cedar, 44 × 13 × 42 inches.
Collection of the artist.

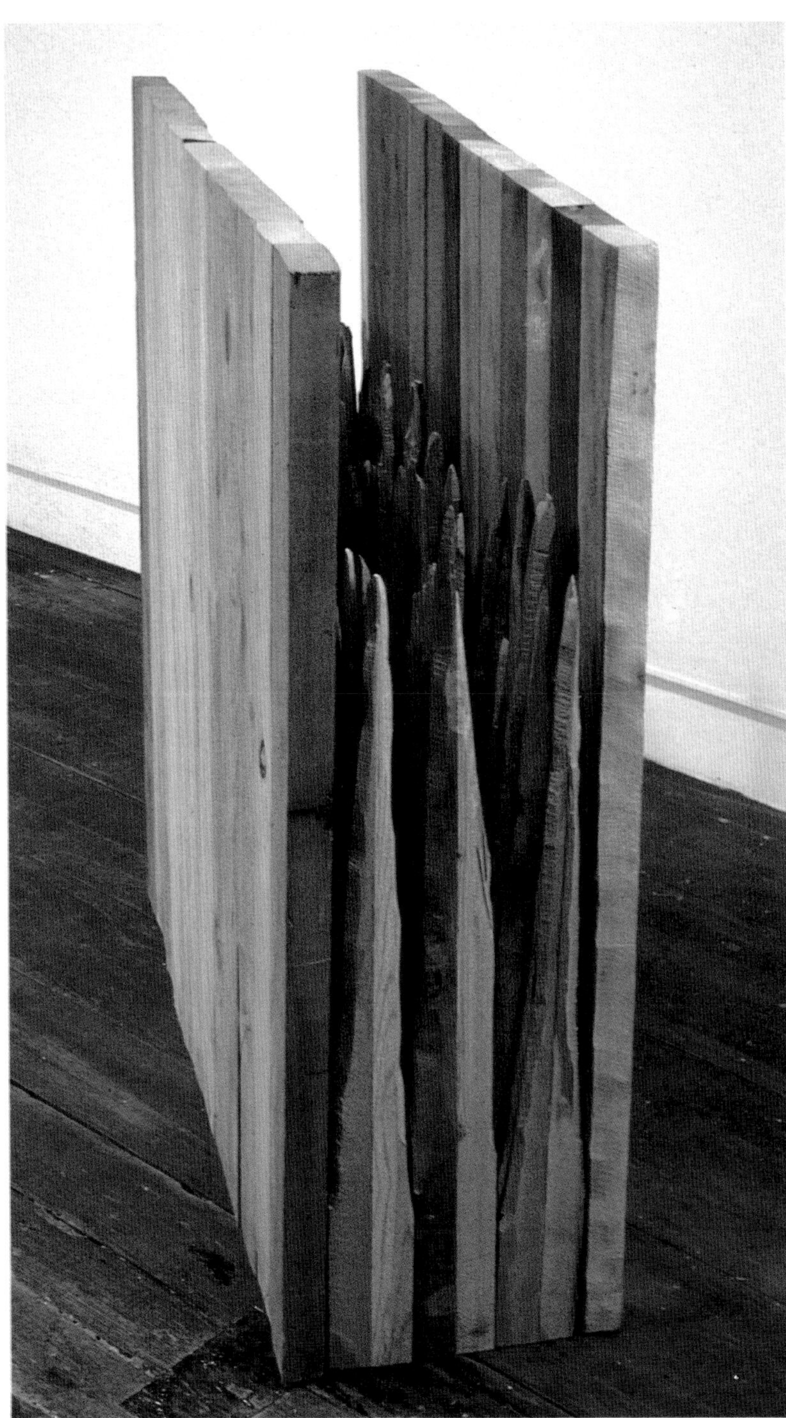

Untitled (Felt Box) 1986, cedar, graphite, and felt, 24 × 54 × 24 inches. Collection of Eileen and Peter Norton, Santa Monica.

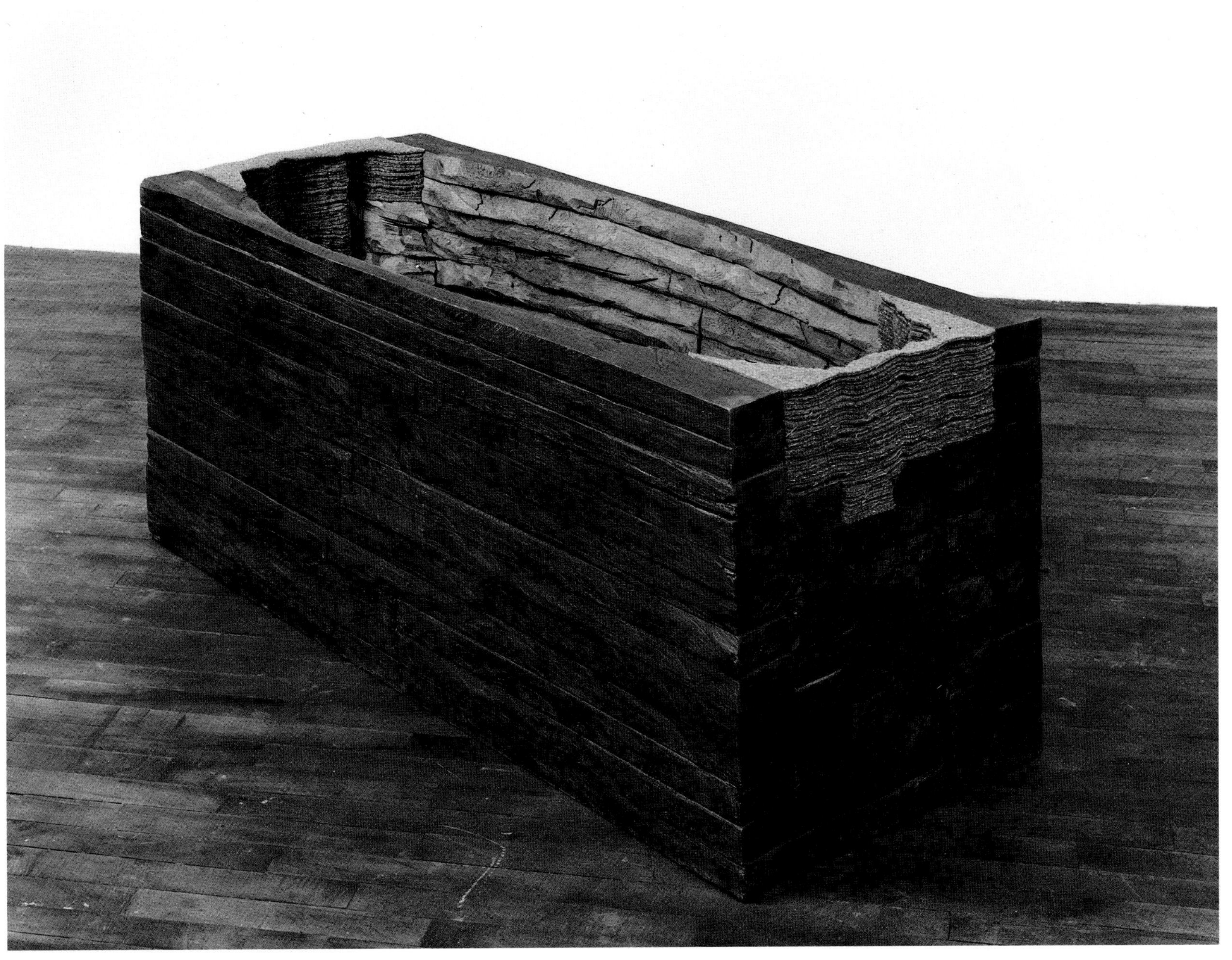

Ignatz Comes Home 1986, cedar, lead, and paint, 48 × 144 × 78 inches.
Collection of the artist.

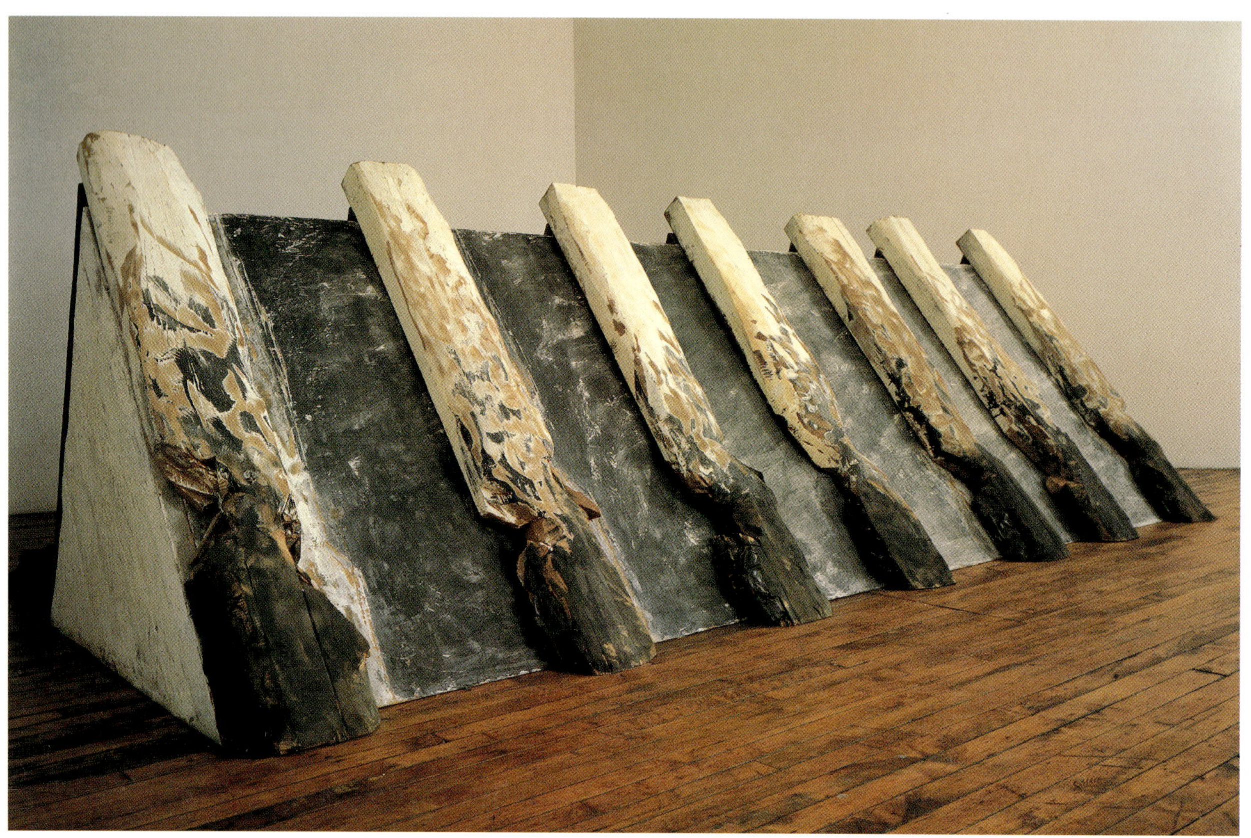

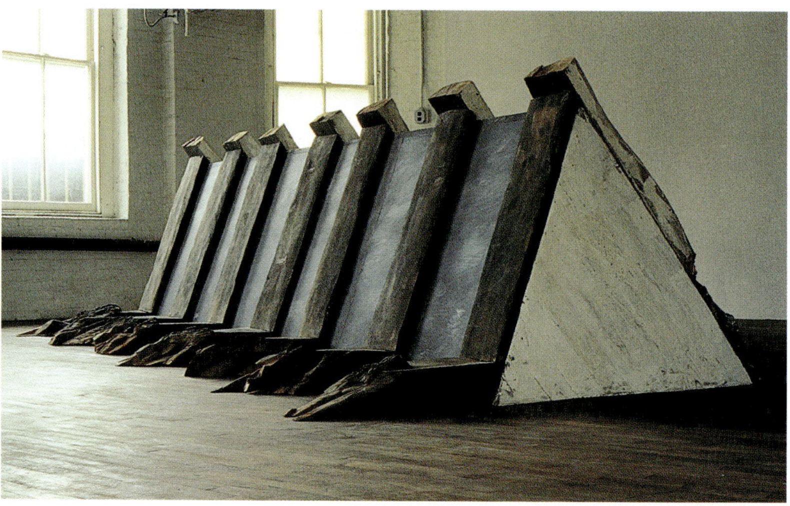

Polish Wing 1987, cedar, lead, and paint, 42 × 156 × 4 inches.
Donatella and Jay Chiat Collection.

Untitled (Shovel) 1987, cedar and stain, 88 × 11 × 11 inches.
Collection of Bette Ziegler.

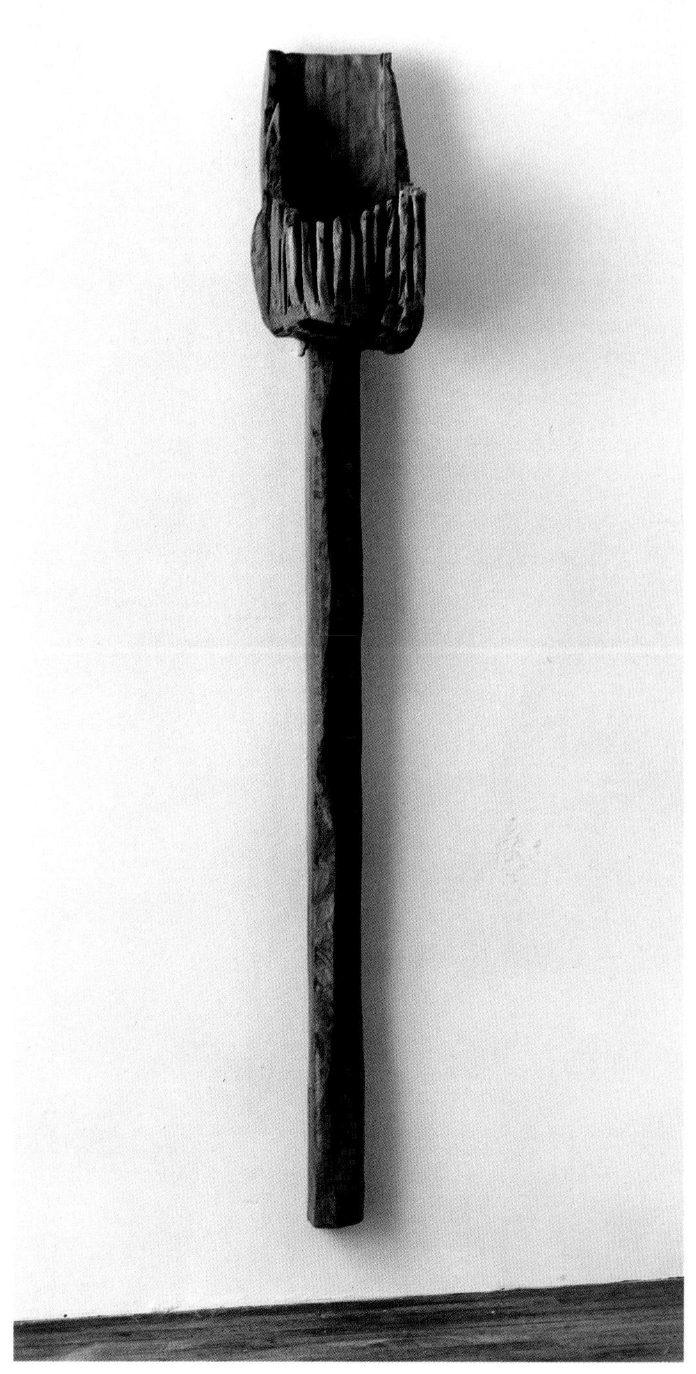

Paul's Shovel 1987, cedar, 83 × 13 × 5 inches.
Collection of the artist.

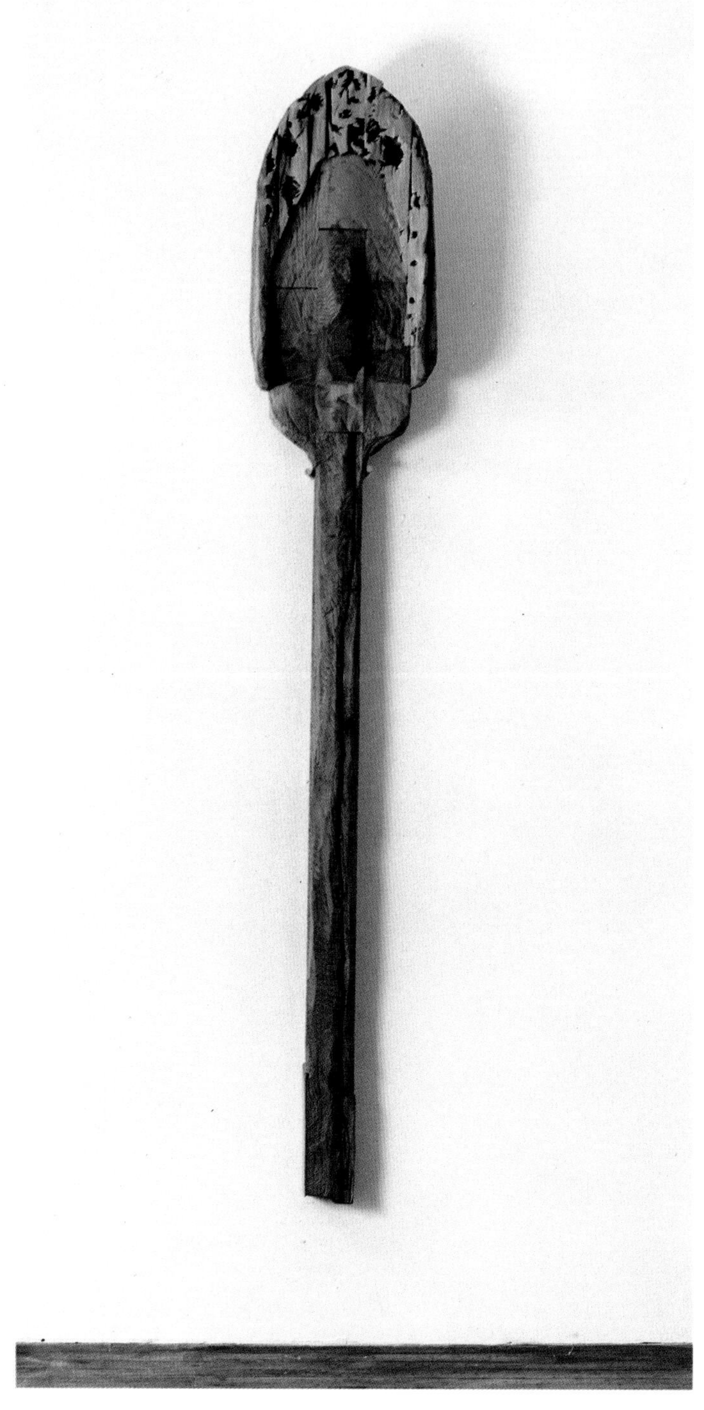

Grzebyk II (Comb II) 1987, cedar and stain, 70 × 38 × 7 inches.
Collection of Vera List.

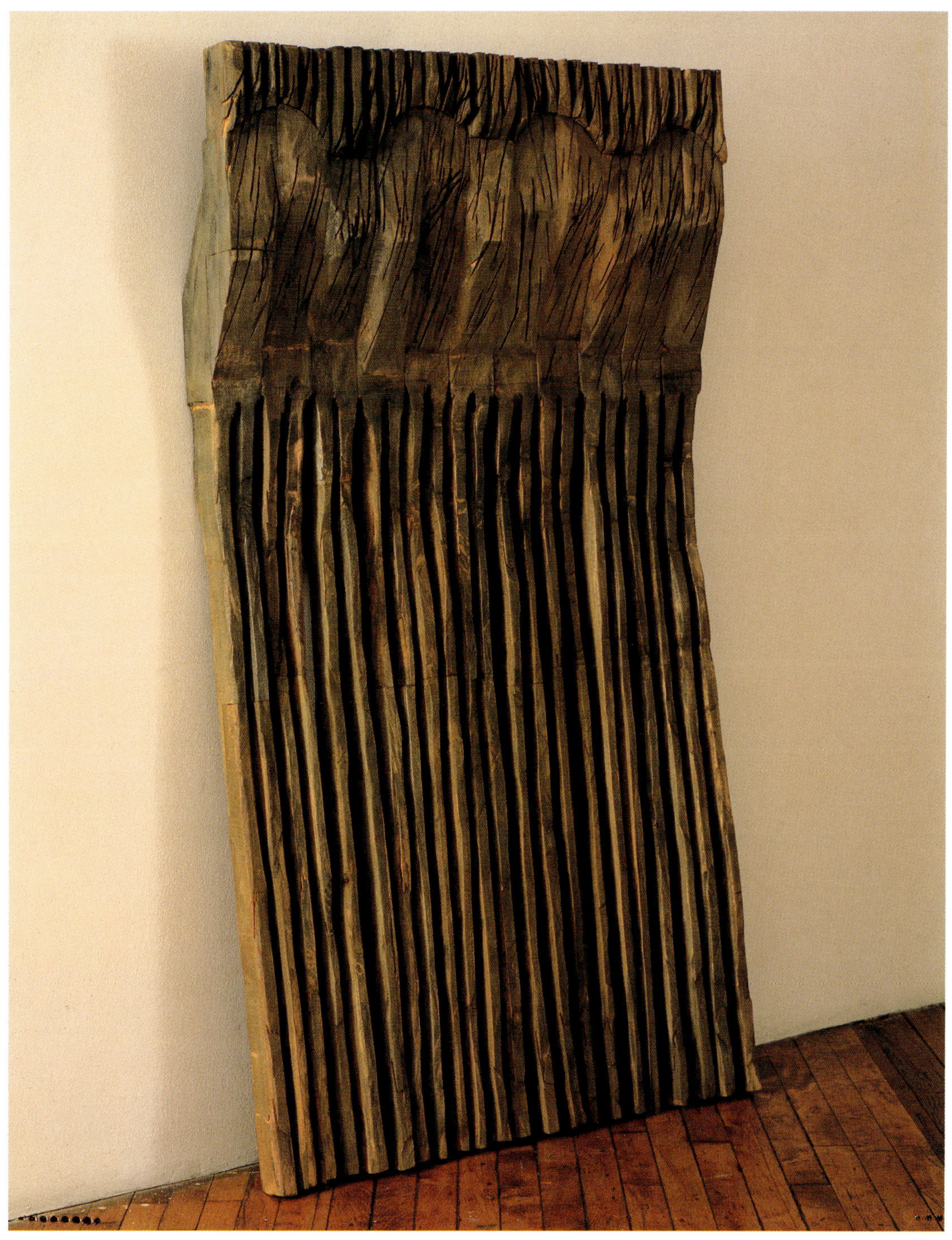

Untitled (Seven Mountains) 1986–87, cedar and graphite, 62 × 201 × 42 inches. The Metropolitan Museum of Art, New York, purchase, Lila Acheson Wallace Gift, 1988 (1988.257.a–u).

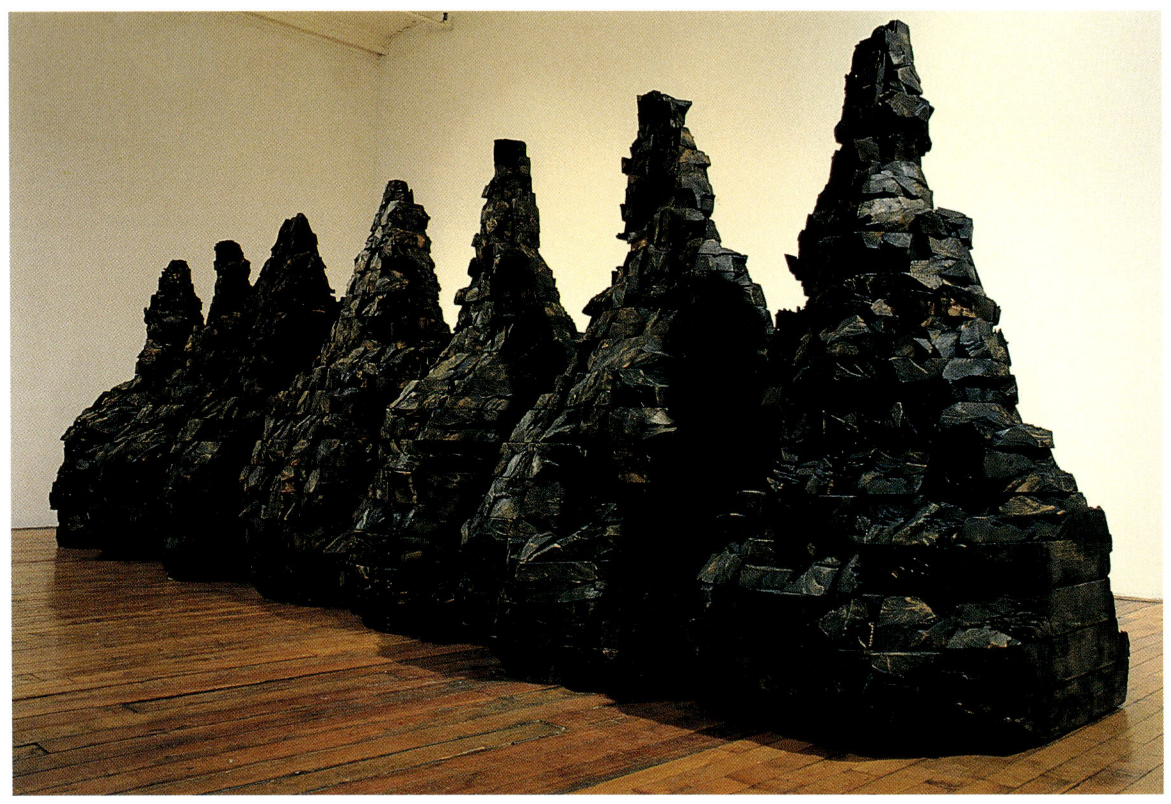

strange objects and to mix her metaphors in provocative ways. A work such as *Untitled (Seven Mountains)* of 1986–87 uses the cedar units in such a way that there appear to be lateral striations that would incorporate geological time. It suggests the constructions of ancient peoples, such as the piled-up stones forming Sardinian *nuraghe* that punctuate the landscape, which to this day remain mysteries to the art historians who have studied them. The worn surfaces are, so to speak, edged by time as well as light—an effect that von Rydingsvard prizes, and that she admired in the Yucatan Maya monuments, which, although they might have been structured with trued, rectilinear stones, have assumed through time the soft and irregular contours imposed by the forces of nature.

A prominent example of the new way of combining and mixing metaphors is a wall work of 1987, *Zakopane.* In this work of twenty-two fused vertical units, von Rydingsvard created diagonal members at its crest that from certain views suggest eaves, and from others are more like Gothic flying gargoyles, casting the two-by-four supports below into shadow. At the base of this strange wall are twenty-two hollow extrusions — vessels of some sort, although not resting on the ground. These are carved and scarred, and they are conspicuously different in size and shape, although they march down the line of upright planks quite evenly, as in some kind of Brechtian drama. The nature of the piece is wholly mystifying. And yet von Rydingsvard has provided a governing metaphor in the title. Zakopane is a rustic town in the mountain-

Zakopane 1987, cedar and paint, 138 × 264 × 36 inches.
Collection of the artist, courtesy Galerie Lelong, New York.

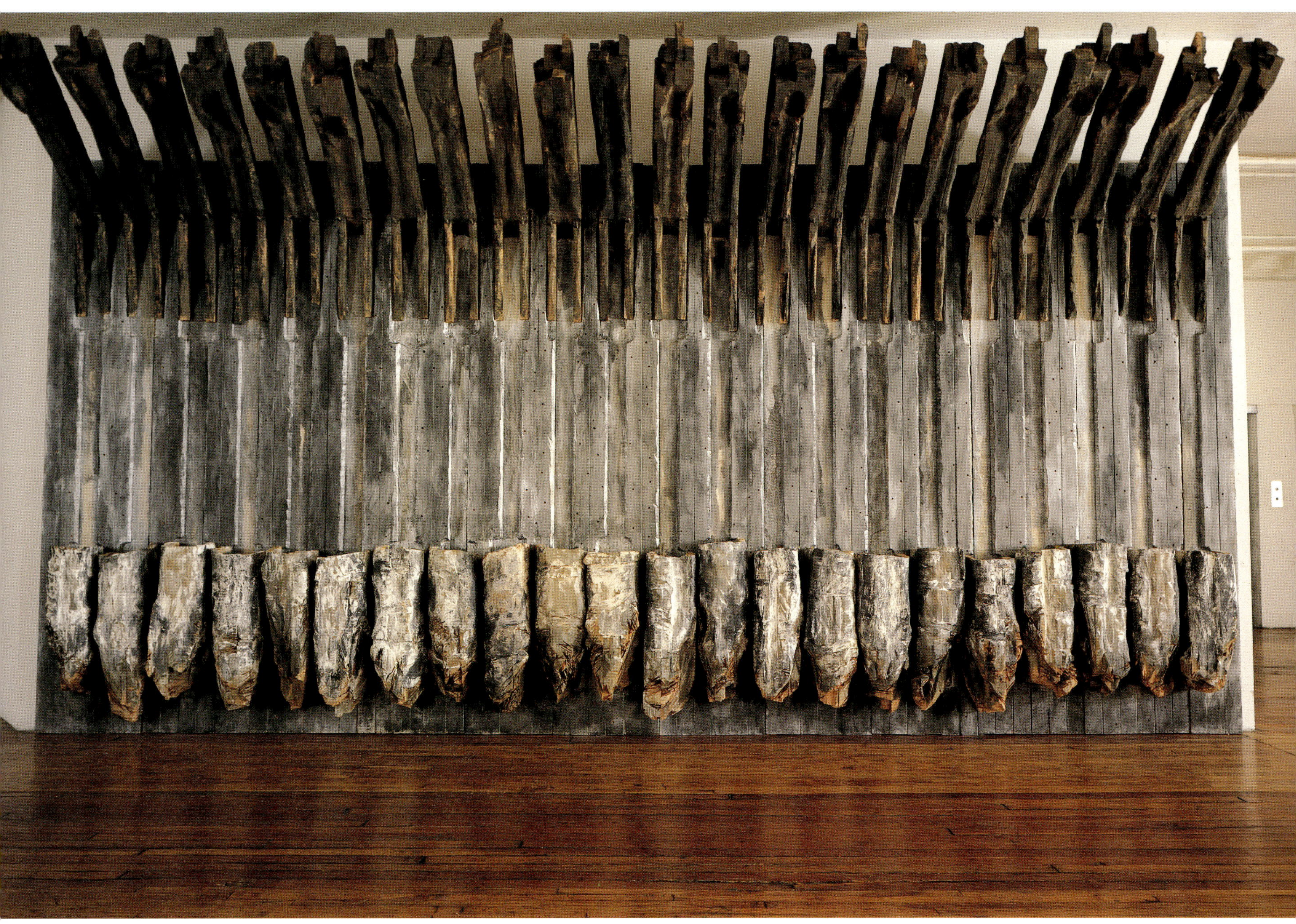

Umarles (you went and died) 1987–88, cedar and stain, 78 × 128 × 12 inches. The Brooklyn Museum, New York, purchase, Gift of The Contemporary Art Council (1989.5 A–N).

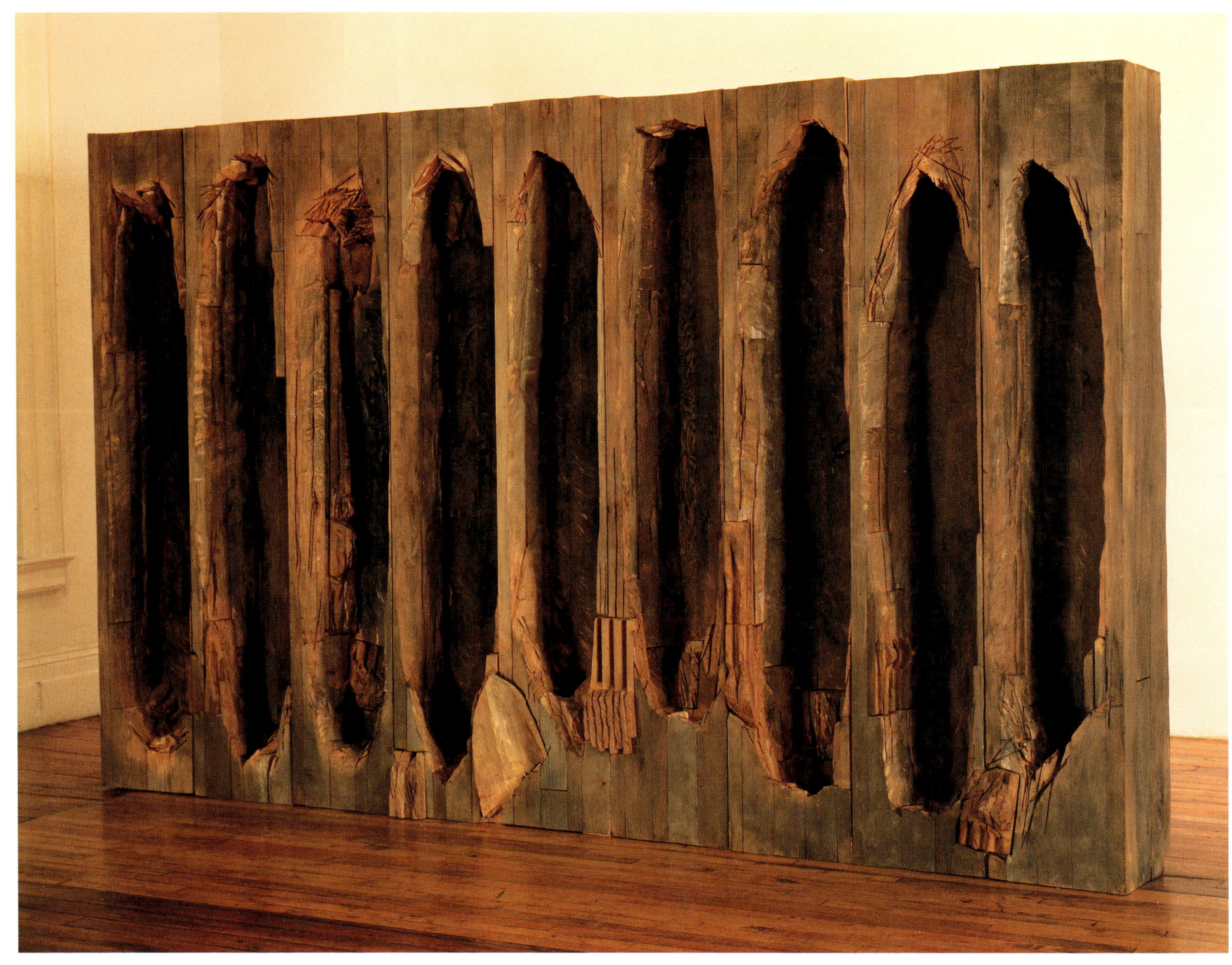

Umarles (you went and died) (back view).

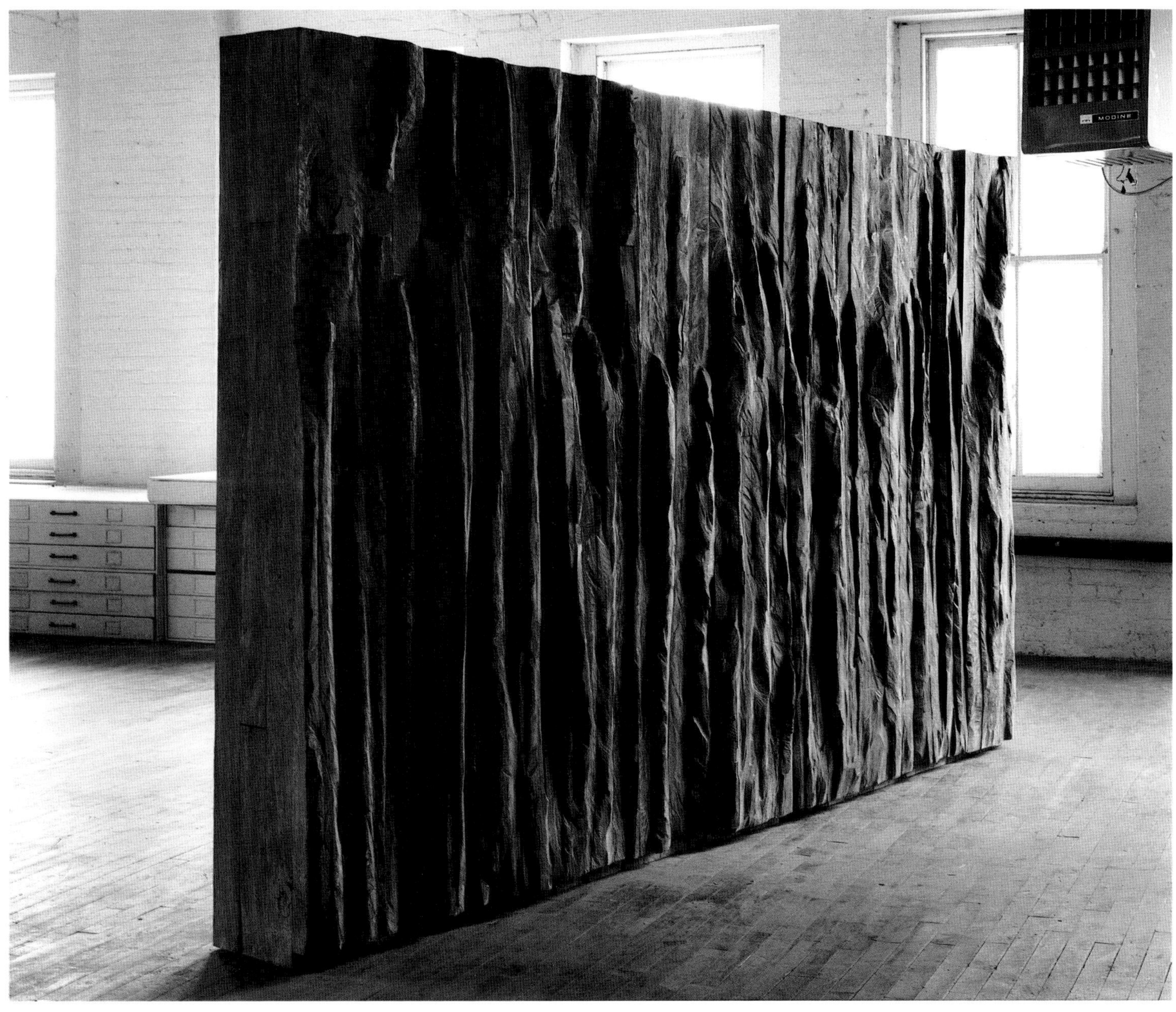

Oj Dana Oj Dana 1989, cedar, graphite, and stain, 144 × 300 × 24 inches. Collection of the artist.

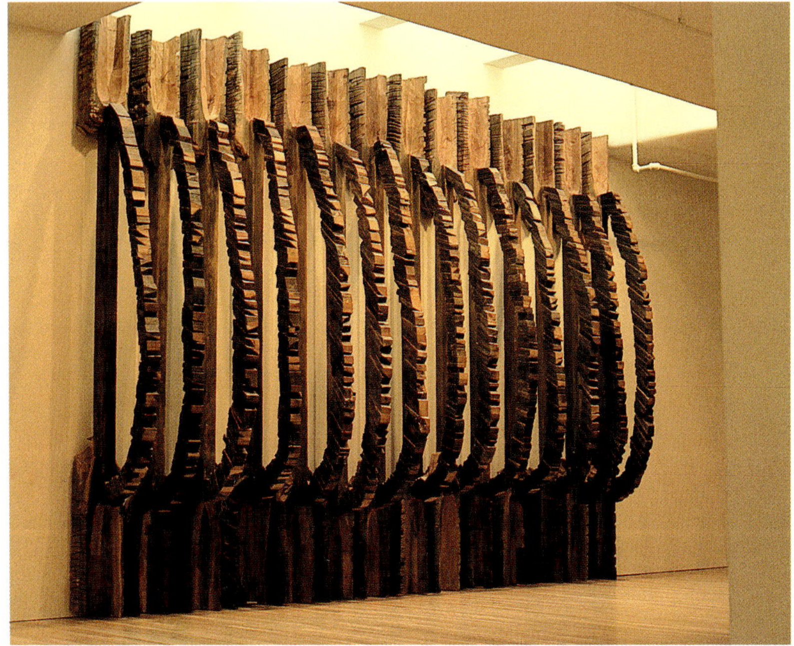

ous area of Poland used as a ski resort. Its dwellings are (or at least were when I visited some thirty years ago) built of stout wooden planks and logs, and its storerooms house such rudimentary instruments of rural life as pitchforks and shovels. In her sculpture, von Rydingsvard stresses the man-made character of her forms and at the same time suggests the reiteration, through generations, of fundamental tools.

Those hollow shapes in *Zakopane* are easily transformed metaphorically, as an impressive work of 1988 demonstrates. *Ursie A's Dream* brings together seven shapes—like sconces or niches or containers—that use the sharp-cut ends of the cedar beam like building blocks. There are no worn or rounded surfaces, yet the effect is similarly confounding. These are containers of darkness, and they stand upon a platform of darkness—a great terrace of planed, ground, chiseled planks that are neither floor nor earth, on which the surface is darkened with graphite and emits a strange, crepuscular light. Mood and feeling, essential ambiguity, establish this sculpture despite the clearly geometric elements and the methodical demands of von Rydingsvard's process.

There would be further eccentric and daring plays upon the basic forms of her vocabulary. In 1990 von Rydingsvard returned to the cone, this time inverting nine elongated cones in a precarious, barrierlike structure. *Nine Cones* displays the quixotic, additive impulse that is characteristic of her work, but it also suggests an amplification of her imaginative process that borders on the surreal. It is more like the mad impulse of the Catalan sculptor-architect Antoni Gaudí than it is like anything that greeted her when she embarked on her adult life as a sculptor and encountered Minimalism.

Along with the large-scale indoor and outdoor pieces, von Rydingsvard continues to fashion smaller works, often designed to hang on walls. From around the mid-1980s there is an ongoing group of objects that seem to fetch up childhood memories. Increasingly von Rydingsvard sought out aspects of her past, as the

Ursie A's Dream 1988, cedar and graphite, 72 × 144 × 156 inches. Installation at "Home Show," organized by Contemporary Arts Forum, Santa Barbara, California, 1988. Private collection.

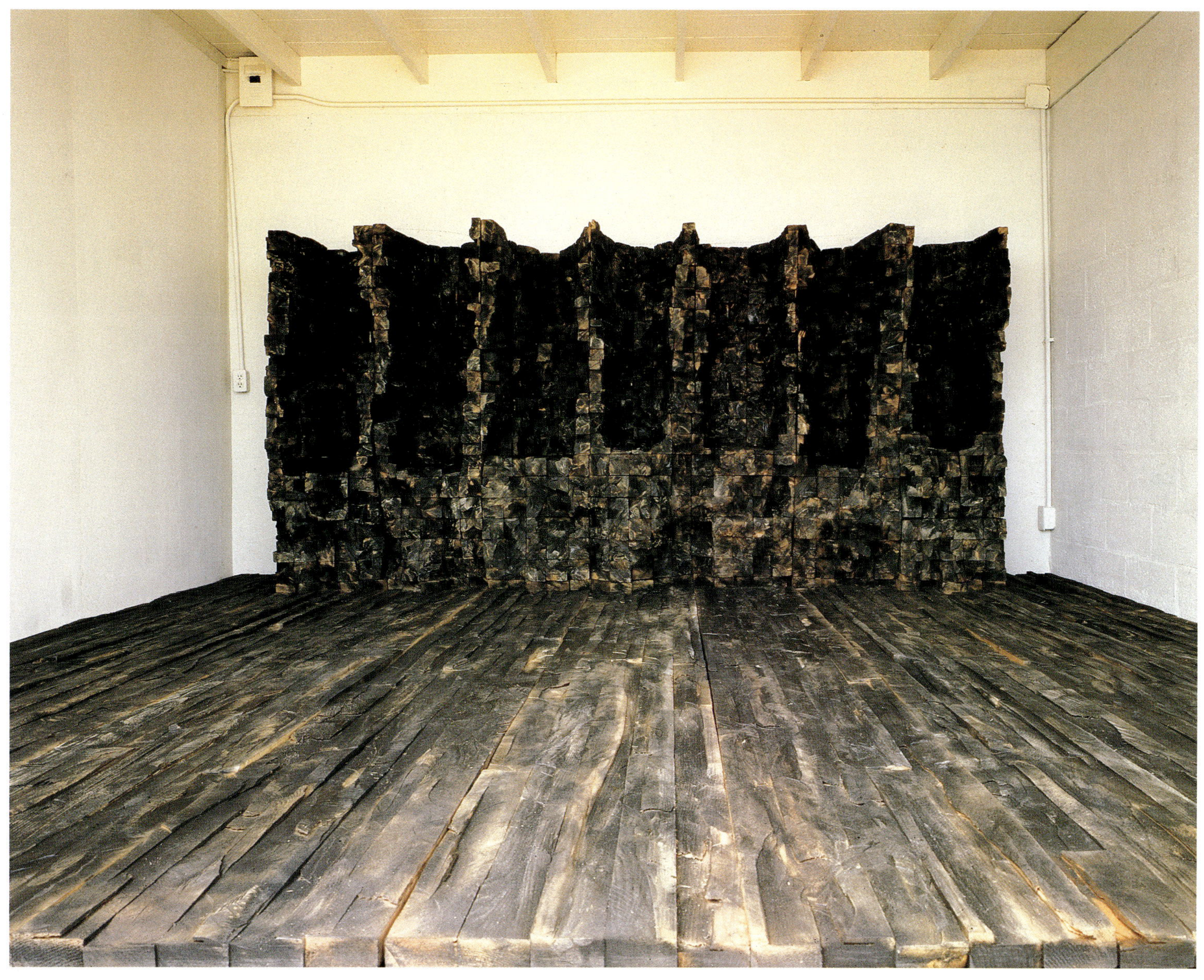

Untitled (45 Tubs) 1988–89, cedar and rubber, 24 × 792 × 360 inches.
Laumeier Sculpture Park, Saint Louis, Missouri.

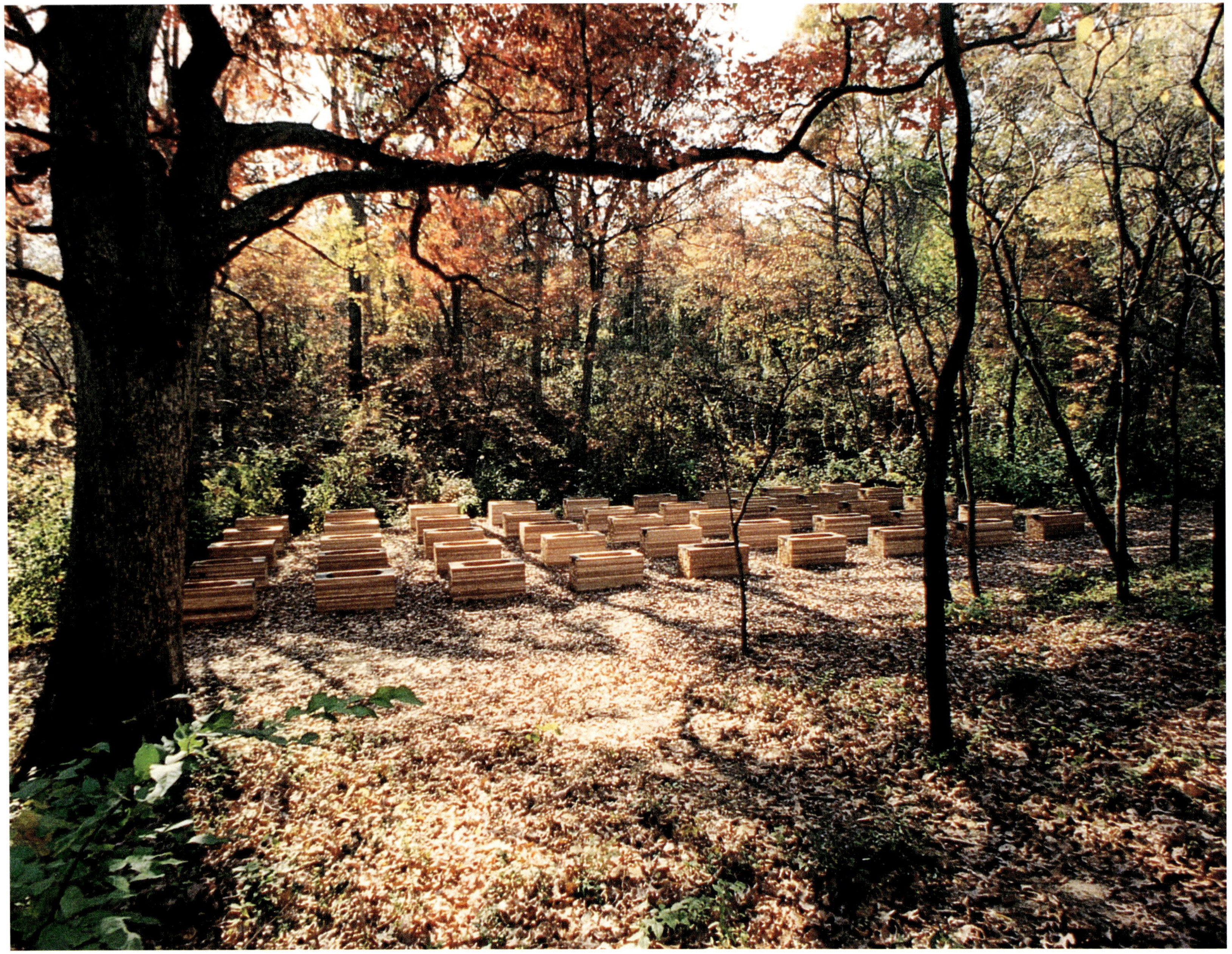

Nine Cones 1990, cedar and graphite, 69½ × 160 × 34 inches.
Fisher Landau Center, Long Island City, New York.

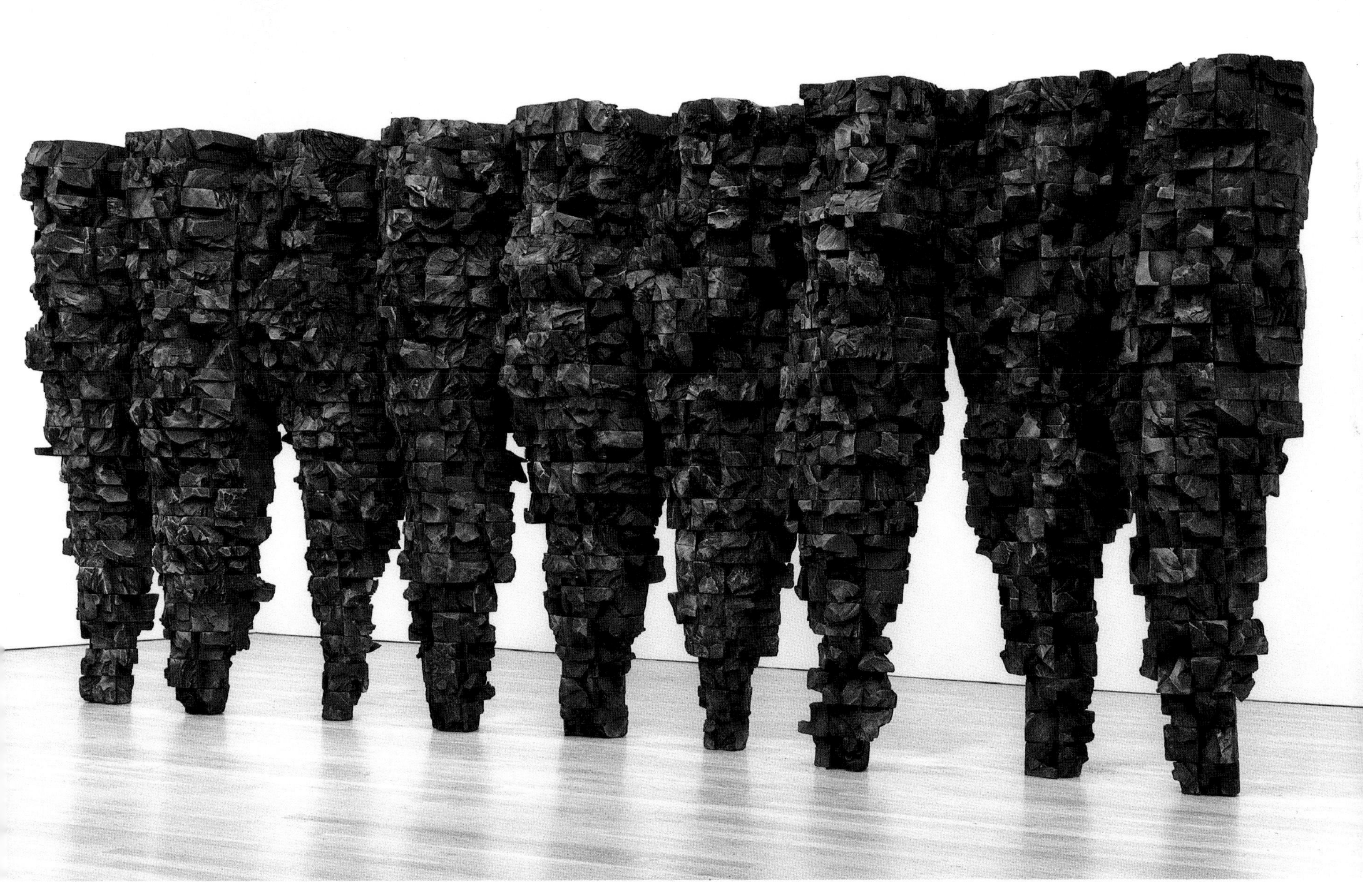

Schwitters's Shovel 1989, cedar and stain, 84 × 12 × 12 inches.
Courtesy Greenberg Van Doren Gallery, Saint Louis.

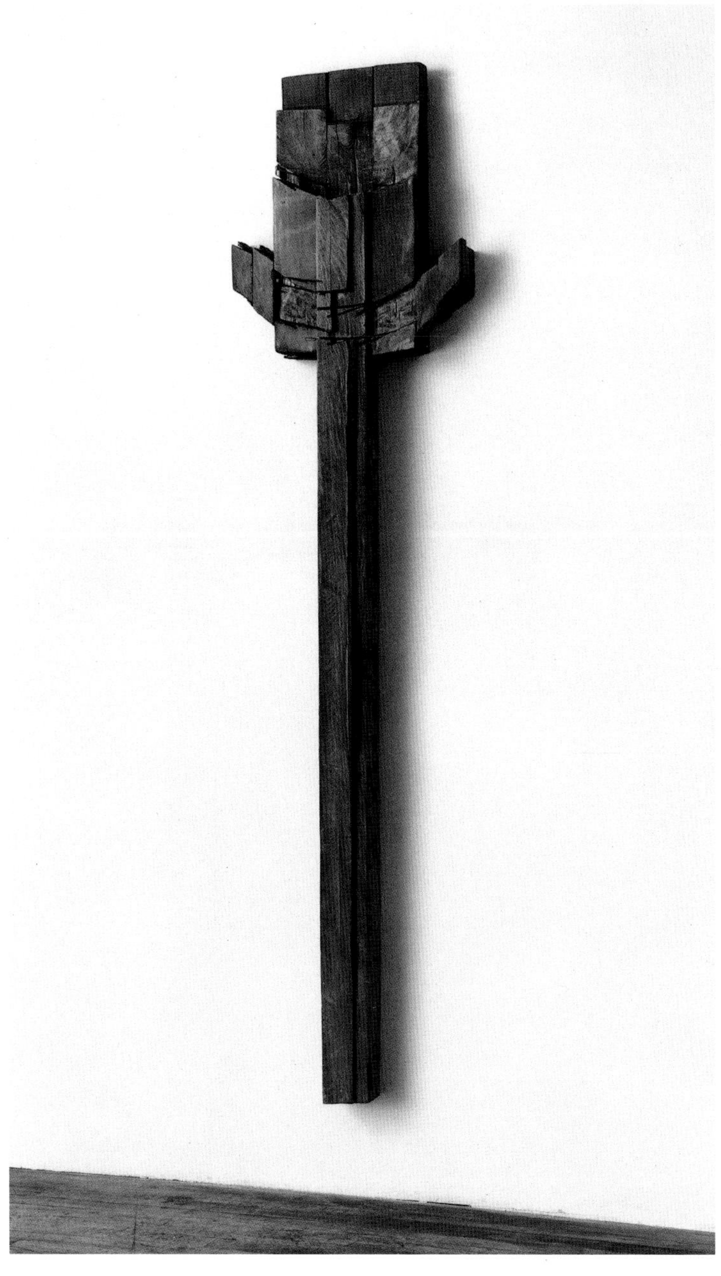

daughter of generations of farmers, building a personal mythology that would nourish her working imagination. Shapes reminiscent of working tools of the tiller recur, as do objects recalling kitchen utensils such as rolling pins, washboards, bowls, spoons, and ladles. But von Rydingsvard's pitchforks and shovels and wooden spoons are rarely mimetic. To the basic form she brings her culture, altering , exaggerating, and making multivalent the meanings of these wall reliefs. A good example is *Schwitters's Shovel,* 1989, an abstract relief of wittily arrayed Cubist planes invoking modern art history, emphasized by von Rydingsvard's delicate application of stain. Nearly always, von Rydingsvard's motifs move out of their designated meanings. The tools she remembers, or imagines she remembers, from her early childhood, are frequently transformed into objects that have metaphoric expansions.

In one of her wall pieces, *Dreadful Sorry,* 1987–88, the squat shape of a farmer's knife transforms itself into the flame of a votive candle, which is a rare instance of von Rydingsvard's use of paint to add meaning. Similarly, *Untitled (Whitewash Shovel),* 1988 (cedar and whitewash, 82 × 10 × 9 inches), almost seven feet tall, hanging on the wall, takes on a strange, apparitional character, its rhythmically designed carved washboard pattern delicately etherealized by a thin layer of whitewash. Even a piece of 1990, pointedly titled *Three Bowls,* begins with the conceit of being a utensil and grows far beyond the bounds of that identification. These huge vessels, which the viewer senses contain an interior void, play richly upon the contraries called up by the title.

Gaston Bachelard elucidated the phenomenal aspect of such containing forms with their dialectic of inside and outside, and remarked the paradox that we cannot imagine emptiness of such images as drawers, cupboards, and, he might have added, bowls. There is something of that paradox implicit in certain of von Rydingsvard's freestanding pieces, such as the 1991 *Pink Companion.* This splendid, intricately fashioned rectangular piece is utterly confounding in its secondary associations, but its imme-

Dreadful Sorry 1987–88, cedar and paint, 96 × 105 × 17 inches.
Collection of Richard Ekstract.

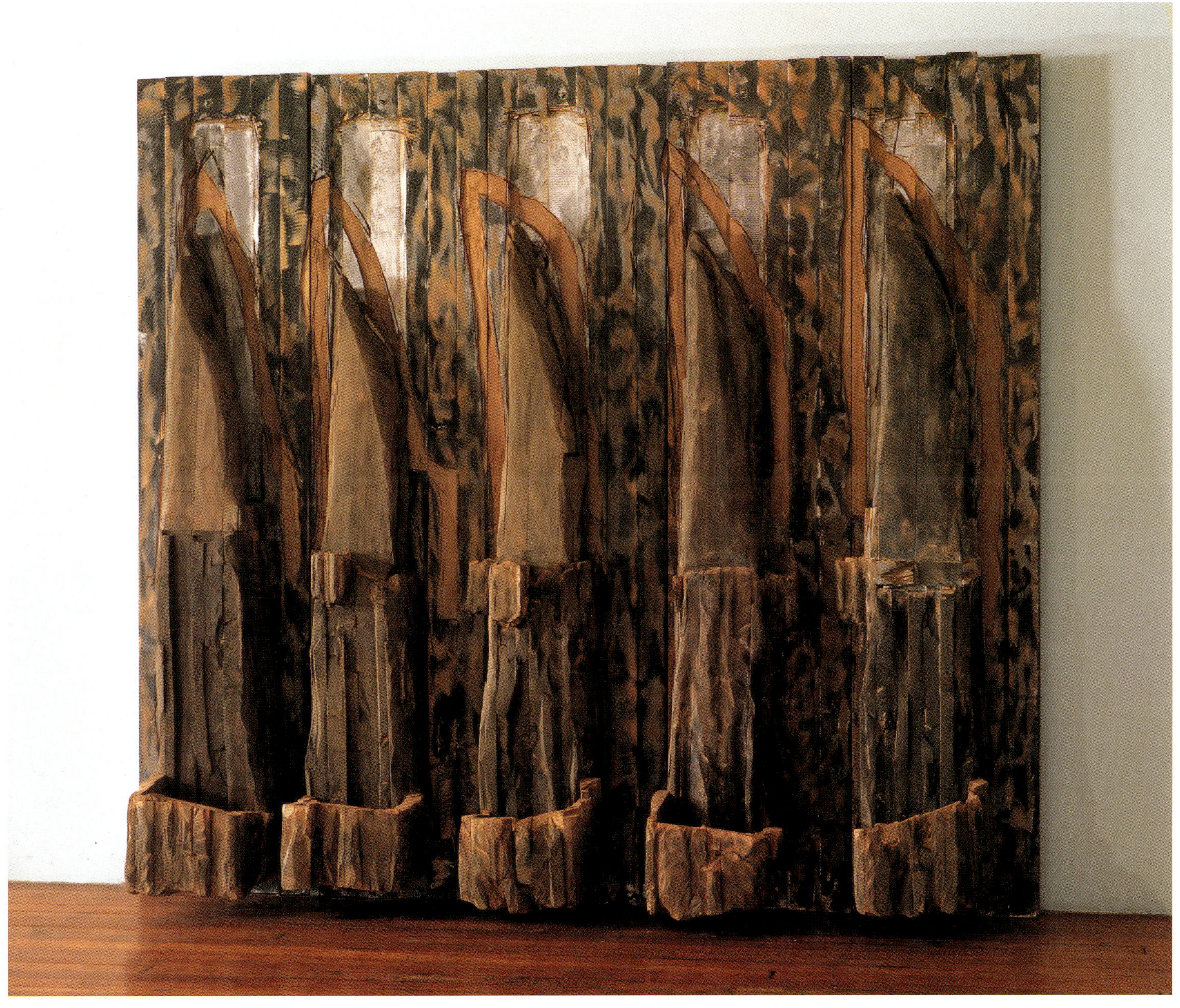

Three Bowls 1990, cedar and graphite, 112 ½ × 190 × 96 inches.
Installation at Walker Art Center, Minneapolis, Minnesota 1990.
Collection of the artist, courtesy Galerie Lelong, New York.

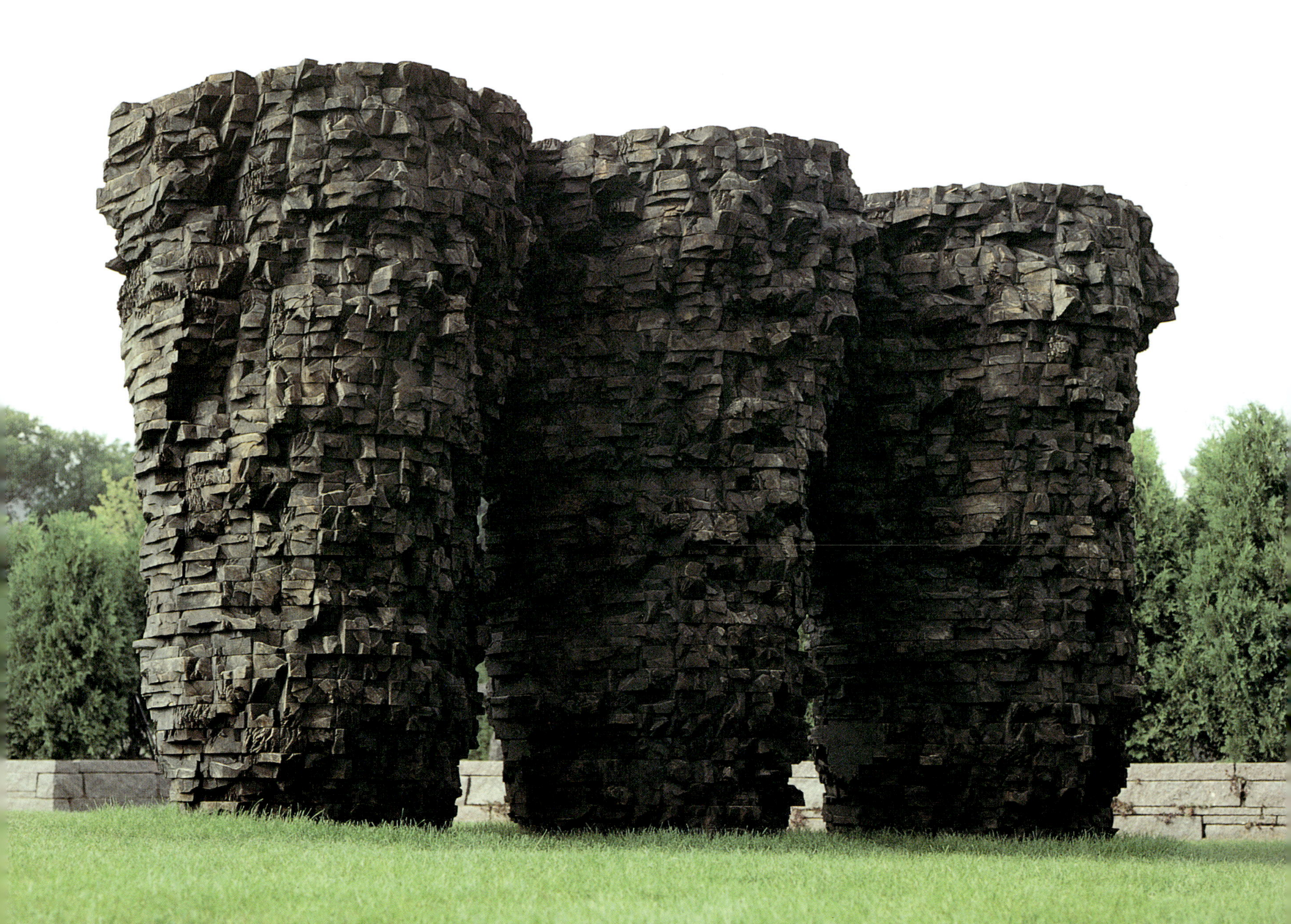

Lace Mountains 1989, cedar and graphite, 96 × 96 × 36 inches.
Collection of the artist, courtesy Galerie Lelong, New York.

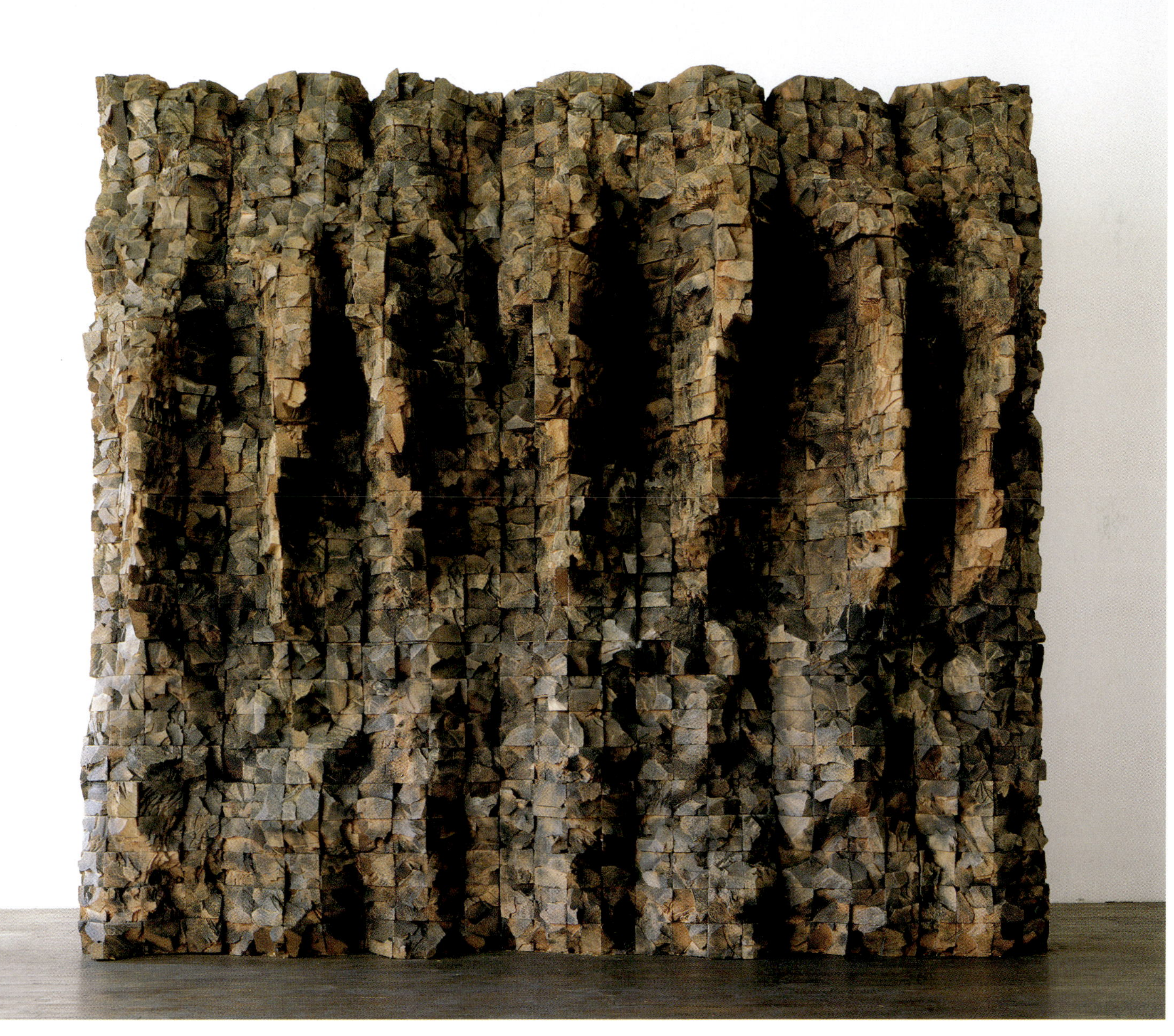

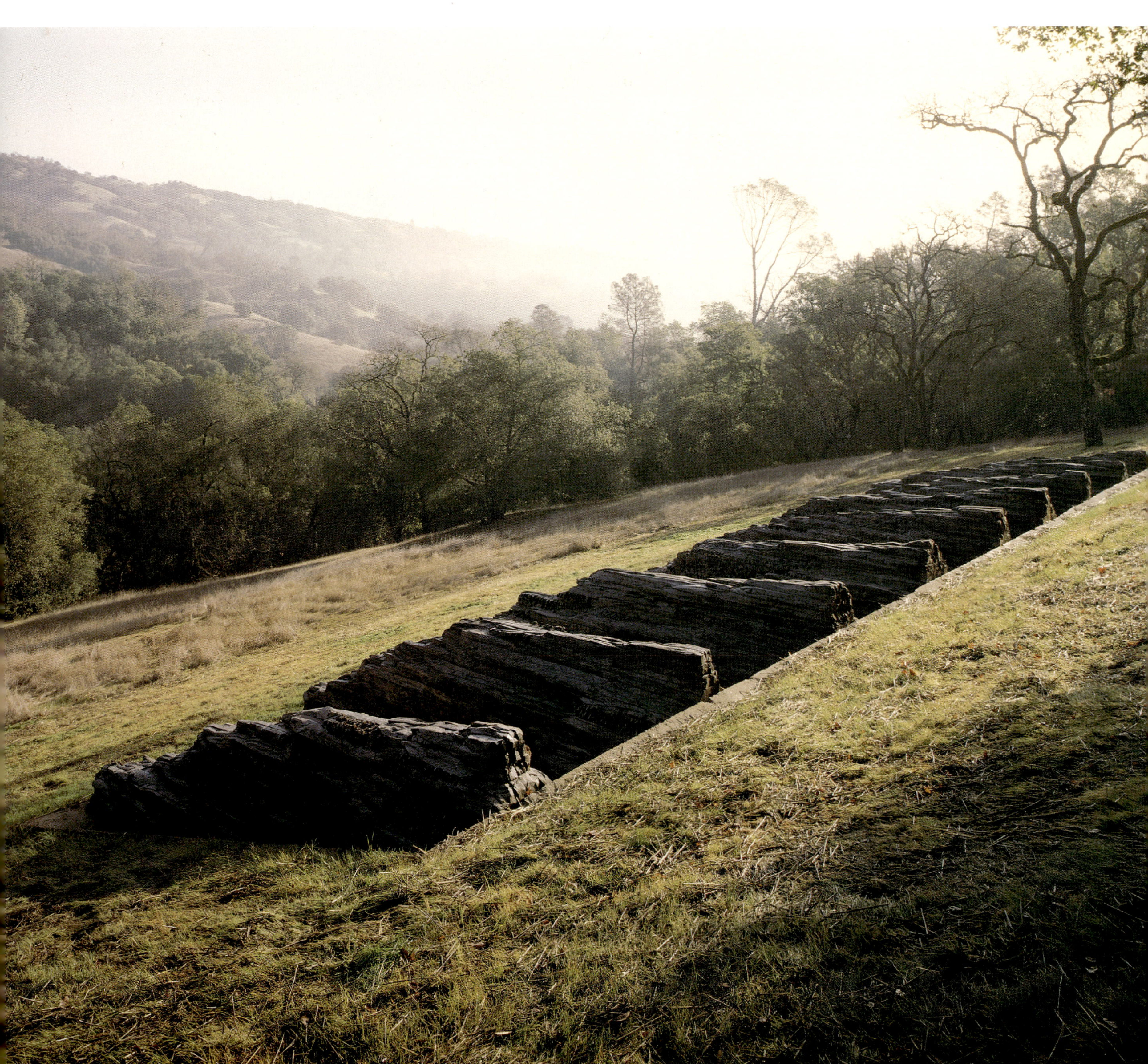

opposite and below:
Iggy's Pride 1990, cedar and graphite, 84 × 924 × 210 inches.
Steven and Nancy Oliver, Oliver Ranch, Geyserville, California.

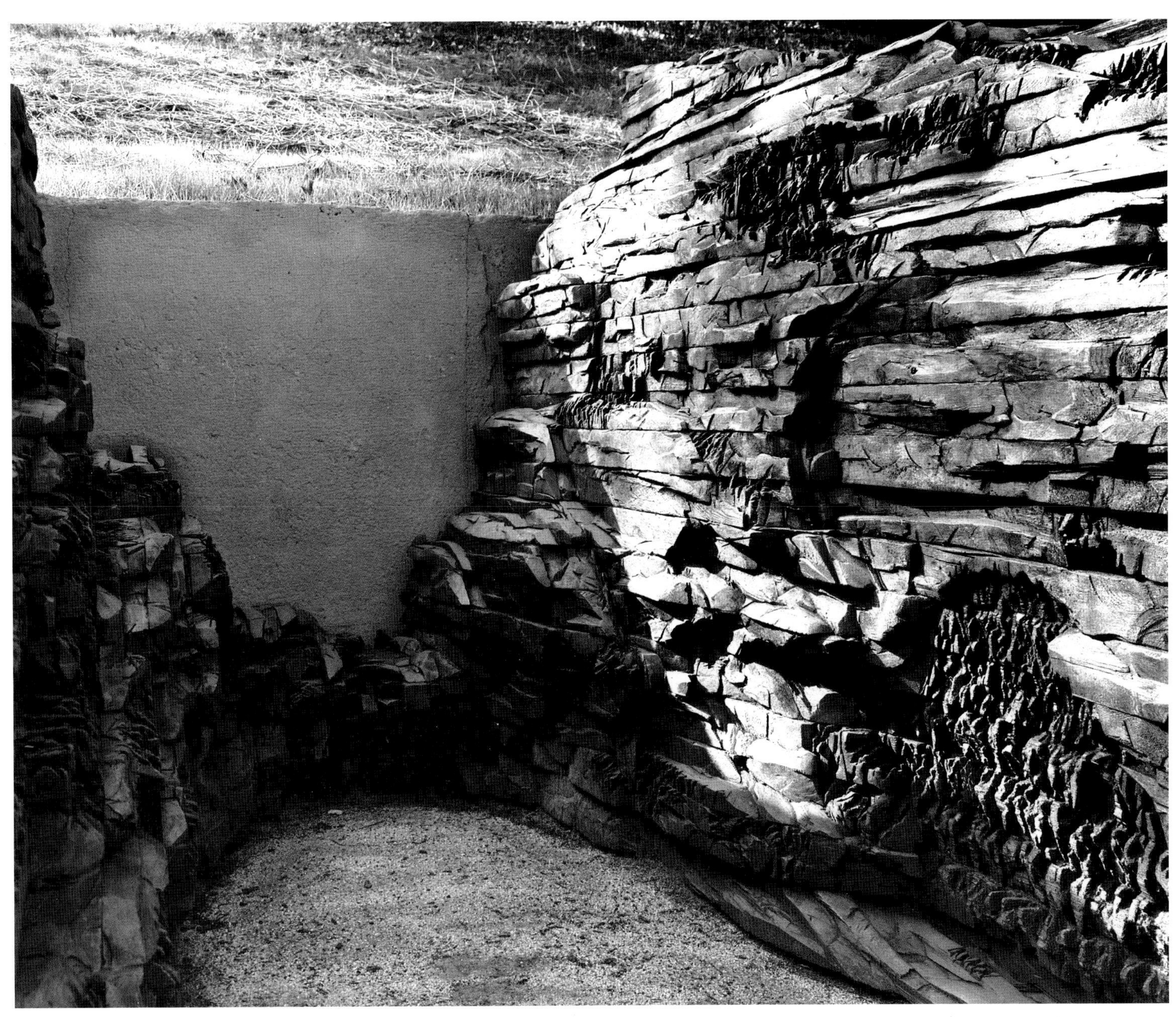

opposite:
Pink Companion 1991, cedar and graphite, 46½ × 61 × 21½ inches. Collection of the artist, courtesy Galerie Lelong, New York.

diate presence speaks of solidity, impermeability, a hermetic being. Yet, association with things that have hidden interior voids are also at work, things such as Italian *cassoni* or Etruscan sarcophagi. Then there are the disquieting reversals: von Rydingsvard's basic rectangle, which is almost exactly equal to that posed above it, is a rhythmic flow of rippling cuts that are nothing so much like water, while above, the vertical beams form a solid as heavy and dependable as a kitchen chopping block. Is this real mass as opposed to the illusionary mass below? The tension of opposing qualities, fluidity and solidity, endows this sculpture with its commanding and somewhat disturbing existence, not at all companionable despite its title.

Since 1990 von Rydingsvard has had many opportunities to develop large-scale projects proposing singularly ambitious ideas. In these works, it becomes clear that her desire is to reach the epic and to subordinate the lyric, while still sustaining its intimate character within individual elements. If I use the term "epic," I am using it in its fundamental meaning. For the ancient Greeks, *epos* was a tale, most probably sung and usually in some poetic sequence, as in Homer's *Iliad.* It is measured off, and many ancient epics are rhythmically linked with passage phrases such as "and then," "and then," and "and then." The grandeur of the epic lies not only in its heroic content, but in the sustained, attenuated rhythms. It is spoken or sung, no matter how loosely, in expansive units.

One of von Rydingsvard's most astonishing feats on an epic scale occurred in 1990 when she was invited by the Capp Street Project in San Francisco to create a large work in situ. She chose a huge warehouse space that had once been an automobile detailing garage, and conceived of a floor piece that would all but fill the space. Her normal practice of building from the ground up, as would a potter, had to be rationalized because of the limited time—six weeks—she had to create the piece. Von Rydingsvard enlisted dozens of assistants, with whom she worked both as foreman and impresario. David Levi Strauss described the piece in the catalogue as "a 43-foot-long, 17-foot-wide, 2-foot-deep expanse of cedar, with 98 rough-hewn cup-like receptacles cut into it in an irregular honeycomb grid. The piece filled and overwhelmed the Capp Street atrium, seeming to move over the floor like a great barge or ark."[6] Levi Strauss remarked on the laborious working process of layer-by-layer marking, sawing, and grinding, noting that "at each stage of the process, hundreds and thousands of marks were inscribed on the mass with pencil, saw, grinder and a variety of hand tools, adding up to a wearing down." This "adding up to a wearing down" Levi Strauss saw as "the back and forth of actual time, the time taken to 'mean it,'" and he added:

> Though this sculptor does not practice mimesis (her
> humility precludes it), these human inscriptions
> of eventfulness are echoed in the formation of tidepools,
> tree stumps, and river beds—minute quotidian world-
> formative acts.
>
> Thousands of marks made consciously,
> leavened with kind cuts and cruel, then leaded
> down, blackened to absorb the light. A topology of
> chambered need. An apparition in the Dark.[7]

Levi Strauss's associations, inspired by watching the complicated process the artist employed and then appraising the final work, are steeped in romantic associations with nature. Yet this piece was confined in a man-made and impersonal interior space. The writer responded with appropriate poetic license by speaking of "a topology of chambered need" and invoking its mysteriousness as "an apparition in the Dark." Two years later the piece would be presented in quite other circumstances, and endowed with a Polish title, *Ene, Due, Rabe*—an allusion to a Polish children's counting game. The shift into another voice, using the same unitary epic

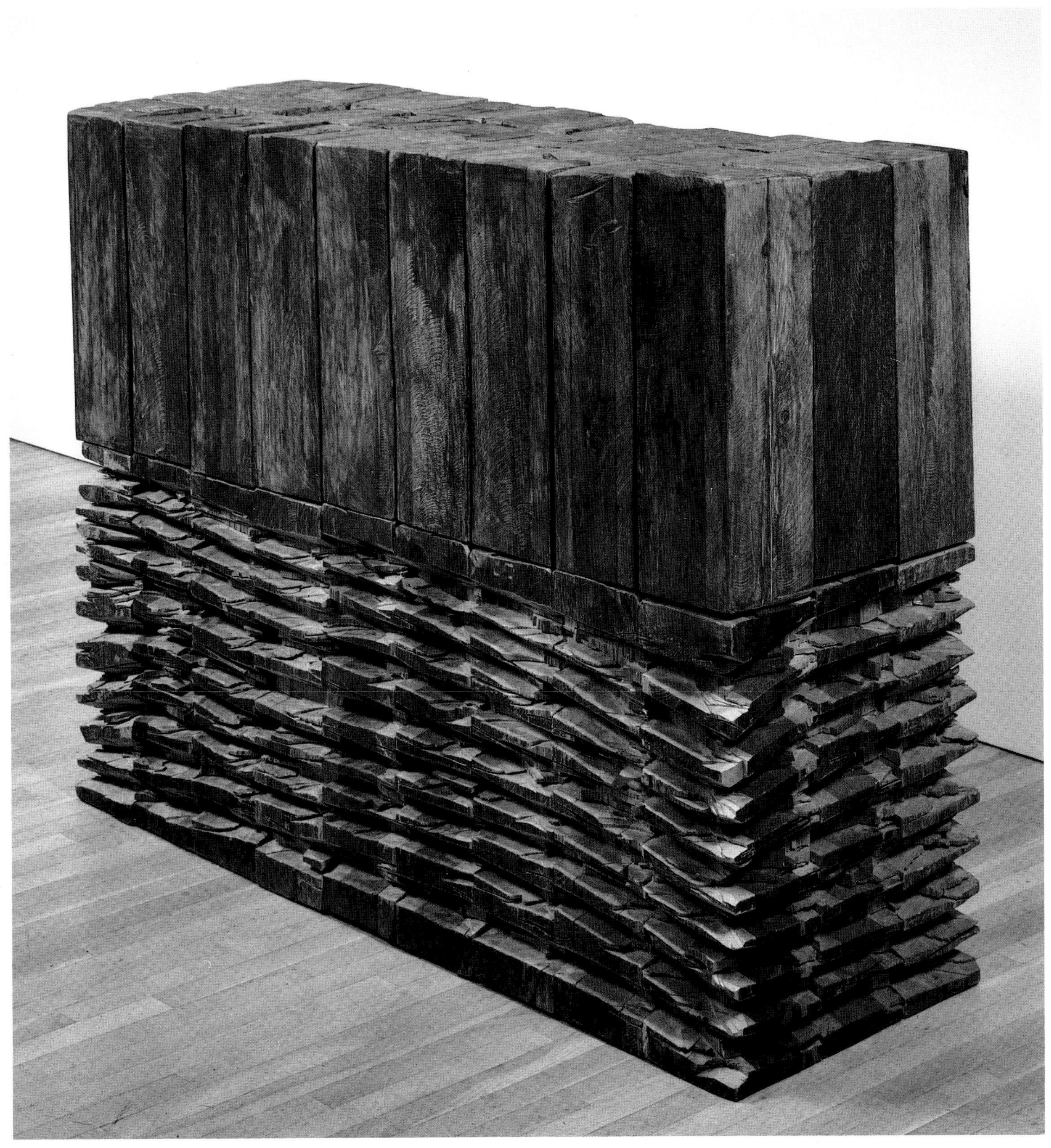

work, is characteristic of von Rydingsvard, whose emphasis on psychological values permits her great imaginative latitude and infuses her work with its metamorphic mobility.

Two years after this major foray, von Rydingsvard was offered a retrospective exhibition, which offered the opportunity to create outdoor pieces in the exceptionally beautiful rolling hills of the sculpture garden at the Storm King Art Center in Mountainville, New York. All of her attempts to make connections with the earth, to "take some sort of control of a space as a farmer does when he tills the soil," and "to take a linear hold of a mountainside so that part of nature becomes really understandable to you" found fulfillment in the ideal conditions of Storm King. Pacing the terrain, memorizing the feel of hollows, the dips and rises of the cultured land (for this was no wilderness), von Rydingsvard put together an ensemble of huge pieces that uncannily filled the ambient spaces with her brooding sense of time and personal history. Her mark on the land was dramatic, and various readings of the outdoor pieces, at different times of day, and in radically differing light circumstances, did not dispel the almost theatrical emotional tone binding the group of unlike and widely spaced looming presences.

Earlier von Rydingsvard had experimented with burrowing into the land, sometimes with harsh cuts, as in *Tunnels on the Levee,* 1983, where three low tunnels slice into the earth and, with their vaguely anthropomorphic contents of carved posts huddling together, augur something violent and emphatically unnatural. Later, in 1988, she discovered a World War II bunker high on the bluffs of the Pacific coast at Santa Barbara, which also seemed a menacingly unnatural cut in the natural contours of the high escarpment. In *Ursie A's Dream* she treated the interior of the bunker as a site that in its dark and crowded space contrasted almost violently with the great sweep of the sea and the earth-and-sand matrix into which the bunker was thrust. At Storm King, however, there were no savage assaults on the terrain. Rather, like garden architects and sculptors throughout art history, she used the natural topography of the site to enhance her sculptures, while at the same time suggesting new relationships with the ground itself.

Certainly one of the most impressive inventions at Storm King was a ground sculpture called *Land Rollers,* 1992. The technical description does it little justice: there are seventeen elements that from a distance might be telephone poles, tarred and scarred, laid side by side on a plateaulike space at the crest of a hill. Each element is about fifteen feet long and is bounded by smooth forms (like the handles of a rolling pin?) that contrast with the unsmooth, lumpy, deep-cut forms of the poles. Naturally, their roundness invokes a sense of movement, and since this configuration, like a viewing platform, sat on the edge of a rise, the incipient movement would be, as the title suggests, a rolling down into the proverbial rolling countryside. But there is an added spatial ingredient here suggested to von Rydingsvard by the *allée* of cultivated trees in the valley beneath the rise. Here the principle of borrowed scenery, used to such great effect by ancient Japanese gardeners in the Zen temples of Kyoto, is activated. The stroller at Storm King would see in the immediate foreground the strange platform of rounded poles, while registering in the distance the parallel rows of trees that become a part of the sculpture, extending it into infinity.

The two horizontal creations—*Land Rollers* and the transported Capp Street accretion of honeycombed hollows, now called *Ene, Due, Rabe*—were complemented at Storm King by massive vertical elements scattered just far enough in the landscape to be apprehended by viewers by means of peripheral vision. The huge gathering of cones in *Five Cones,* 1990–92, formed a barrier-like screen from afar. But from close standpoints, they echoed faintly the shapes of the horizontal pieces. They were further related by their cloak of graphite that both hides and reveals the intricately patterned and shaped surface.

Five Columns 1991, cedar and graphite, 105 × 123 × 63 inches.
Collection of the artist, courtesy Galerie Lelong, New York.

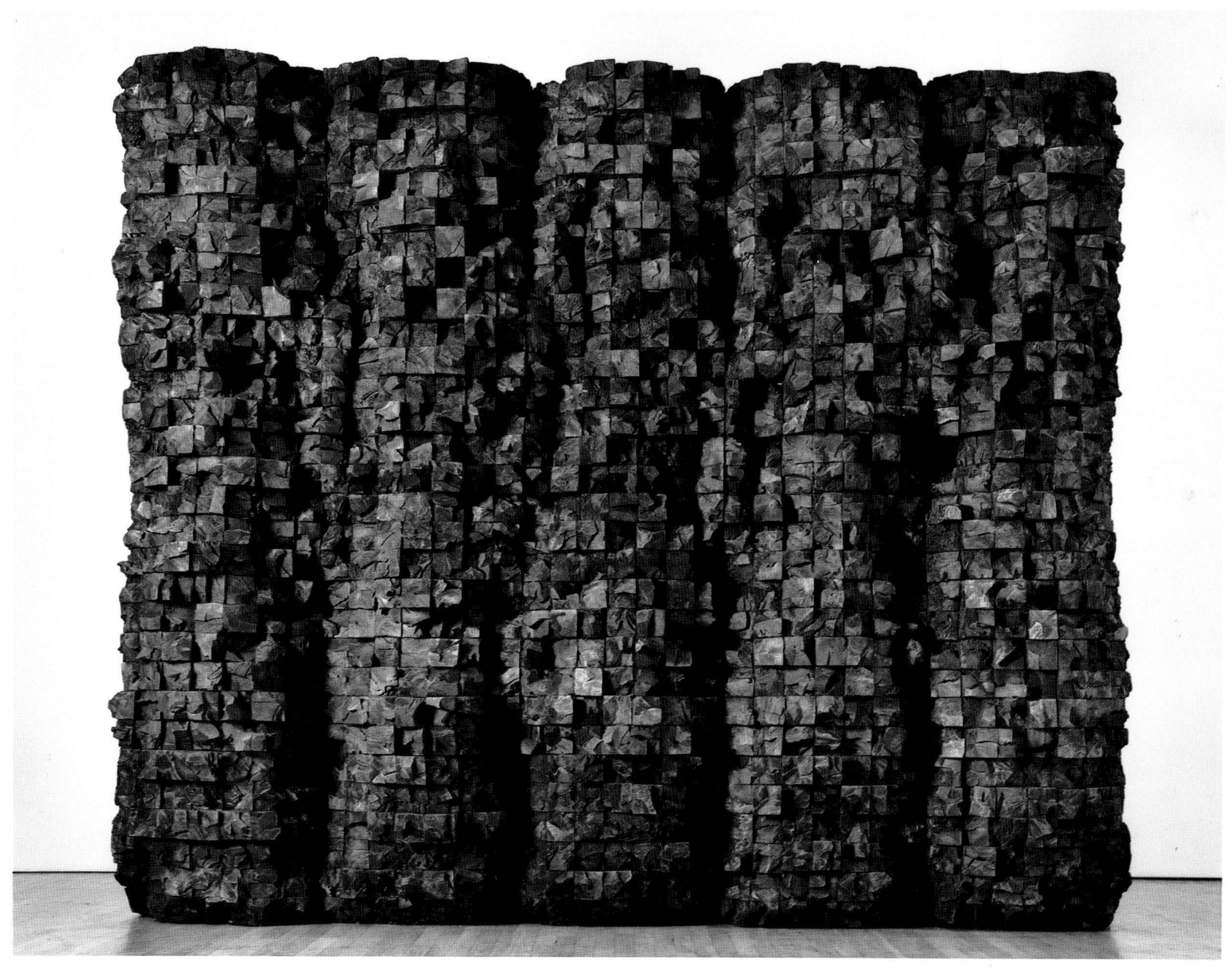

opposite:
Five Cones 1990–92, cedar and graphite, 98 × 108 × 60 inches.
Installation at Storm King Art Center, Mountainville, New York, 1992–93.
Private collection, New York.

Set off at a distance, another vertical element in the total landscape composition, *For Paul,* 1990–92, functioned as would a stand of trees, their contours molded by distance, their details indistinct. As the stroller in this distinctive garden approached *For Paul,* however, the generalized, almost naturalistic form was transformed into a massive sculpture rising up, looming in great majesty, from the ground. It is a commanding piece with powerful contours and skillfully toned, coruscating surfaces that bespeak enormous energy barely contained within. Negotiating these considered and reordered outdoor spaces, the viewer gradually assimilates and rhymes the individual parts, creating, as he moves, a psychological space—an imaginary garden that is the mirror of the sculptor's poetic impulse. For here, as in other situations von Rydingsvard has created, there is an elegiac quality that calls up associations with Romantic poetry from Shakespeare's bare ruined choirs to Coleridge's and Wordsworth's evocations of past and ruined landscapes and the melancholy reflections they instigate. Her *Land Rollers,* which from a vulgar point of view might be described as the foundation for a corduroy road, is completely transformed in the landscape into a dark and mysterious experience, accessible only to those vague reaches of the spirit that have to do with meditative, lingering feelings—hardly defined metaphors for the passage of time and the sad deposits of partial memory.

Perhaps von Rydingsvard's invention of an outdoor space at Storm King owes something to her serious consideration of the work of Constantin Brancusi, who, among precursors, seems to have held her attention unwaveringly. Brancusi, after all, was the first modern artist to see the potential in the modular unit. His first endless column, built of carved wood elements (nine rhomboids in diminishing perspective), was created in 1919 for Edward Steichen's garden and was conceived to be a metaphysical object—a link of earth with sky that for Brancusi fulfilled a mystical craving fed by his reading of the eleventh-century Tibetan monk, Milarepa. Years later Brancusi created his park, Tirgu Jiu, in Romania, using the concept of the endless column as the *centrum mundi,* the cosmic rood holding up the tent of the sky and growing from the ground. The scheme Brancusi invented for integrating far-flung sculptures in the large park, making use of the surrounding urban vistas, was at once complex in detail and simple in its overall design. Those who have visited and moved through Brancusi's creation have always reported on the exceptional feeling of hidden relationships among parts, and the overall feeling of total cohesion. For von Rydingsvard, the works dispersed among the vistas at Storm King, where the boles of trees in a distance mark off irregular spaces, and the sloping swards lead always to delicate visual climaxes, seemed to fulfill psychological intimations similar to those of the great Romanian master.

A quite different order of psychological space reigns in the piece *Slepa Gienia (Blind Eugenie),* created in 1994 for the roof of the Denver Art Museum. The large roof, with its industrial gray floor and thin walls of cutouts with rather jejune forms, has a distinctive feature: an inverted arc, like half a spyglass lens, that offers a view of the distant Rocky Mountains. Von Rydingsvard positioned her thirteen units in such a way that the viewer would register the borrowed mountainous elements in the first encounter with the piece. As in *Land Rollers,* the units, in their rhymed sequence, might go on forever, at least metaphorically. But a strange metamorphosis takes place as the massive individual units—fourteen feet long and well above knee height—become singly potent. Their enigmatic general shape resembles the venerable couch with shafts that once transported ancient nobility—an impression fortified by the vaguely anthropomorphic bulges from which the shafts emerge. But these litters, with their worn interiors, are fraught with ambiguities (are these extrapolations from the human figure? crafts to transport the dead? objects from some obscure cargo cult?). Moreover, although all thirteen units, like Plato's bed, are in the same general shape, each deviates enough to interrupt the smooth appraisal of uniformity and identity. Their

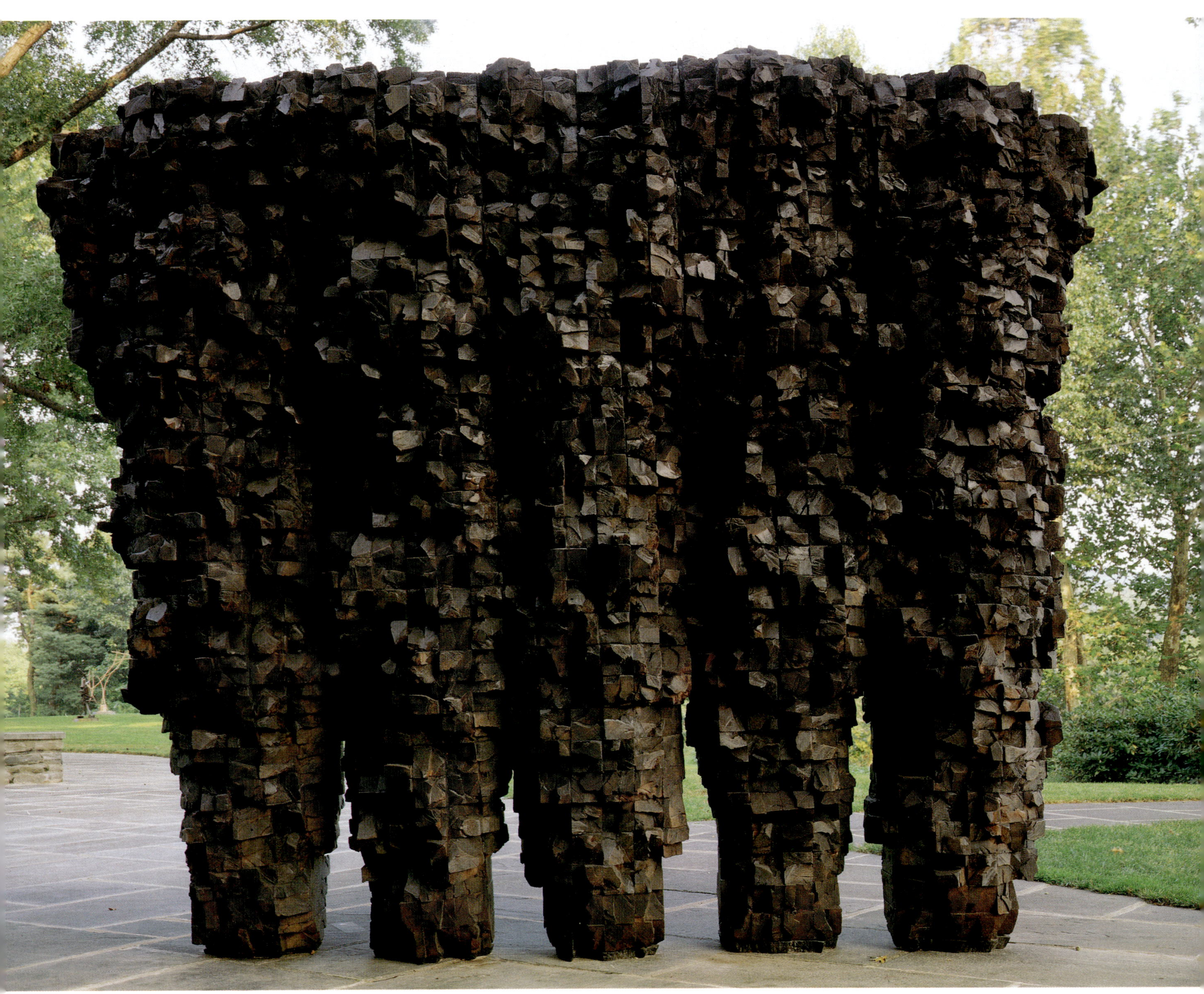

below and opposite:
Land Rollers 1992, cedar and graphite, 45 × 171½ × 670 inches.
Installation at Storm King Art Center, Mountainville, New York, 1992–93.
Collection of the artist, courtesy Galerie Lelong, New York.

pages 54–55:
Ene, Due, Rabe 1990, cedar and graphite, 22 × 523½ × 209 inches.
Installation at Storm King Art Center, Mountainville, New York, 1992–93.
Collection of the artist, courtesy Galerie Lelong, New York.

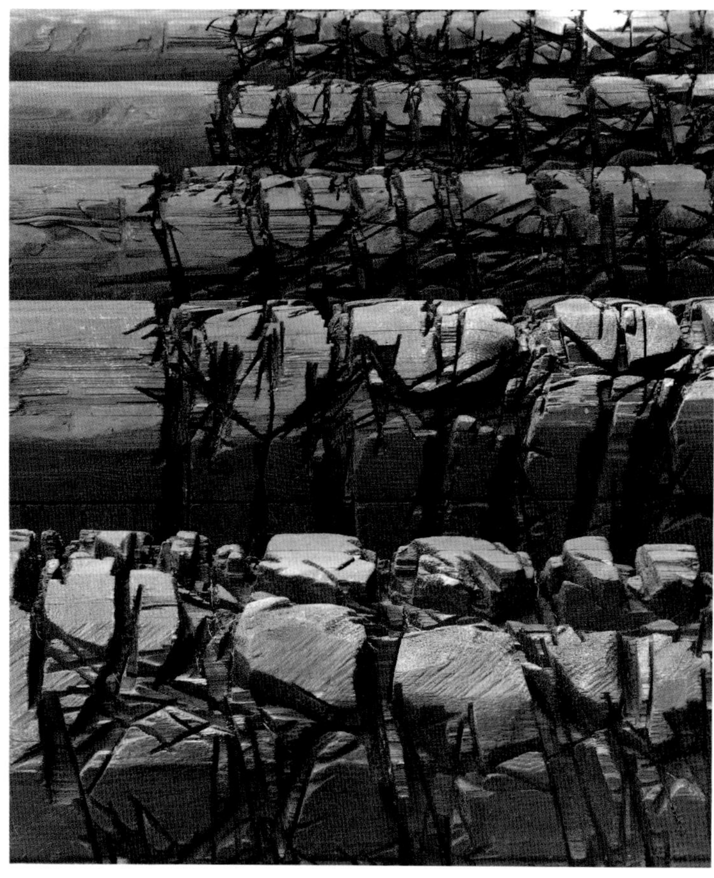

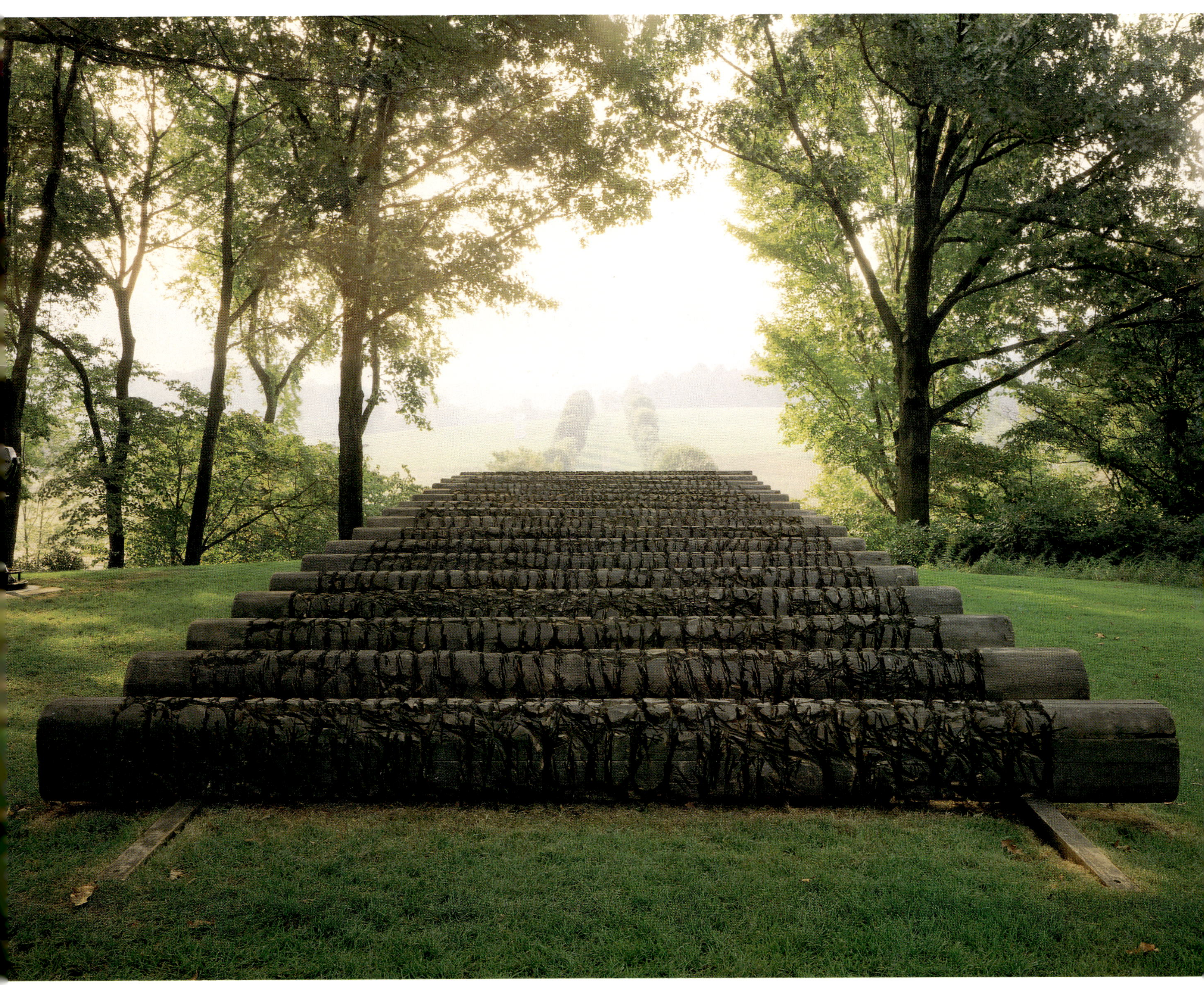

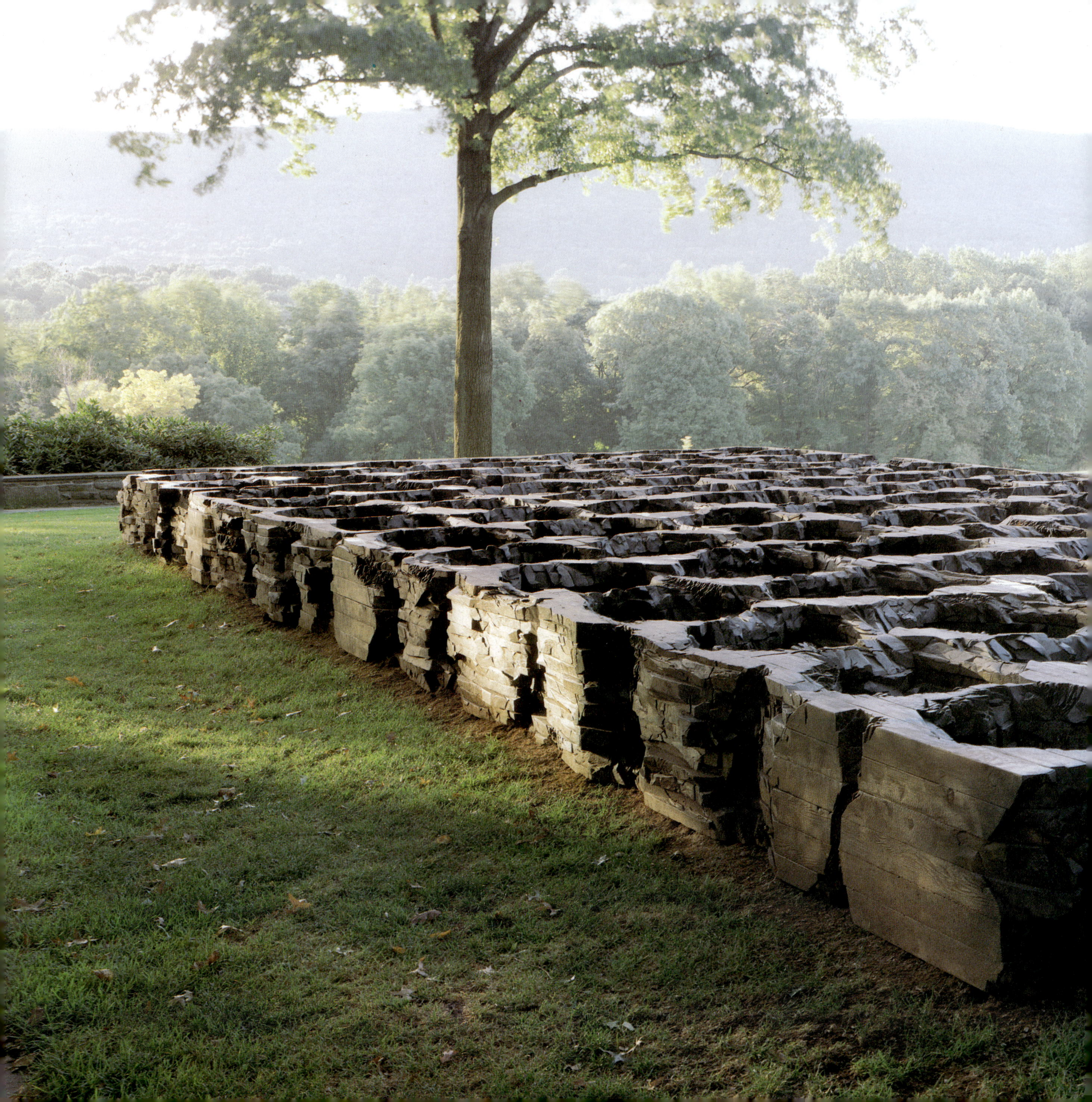

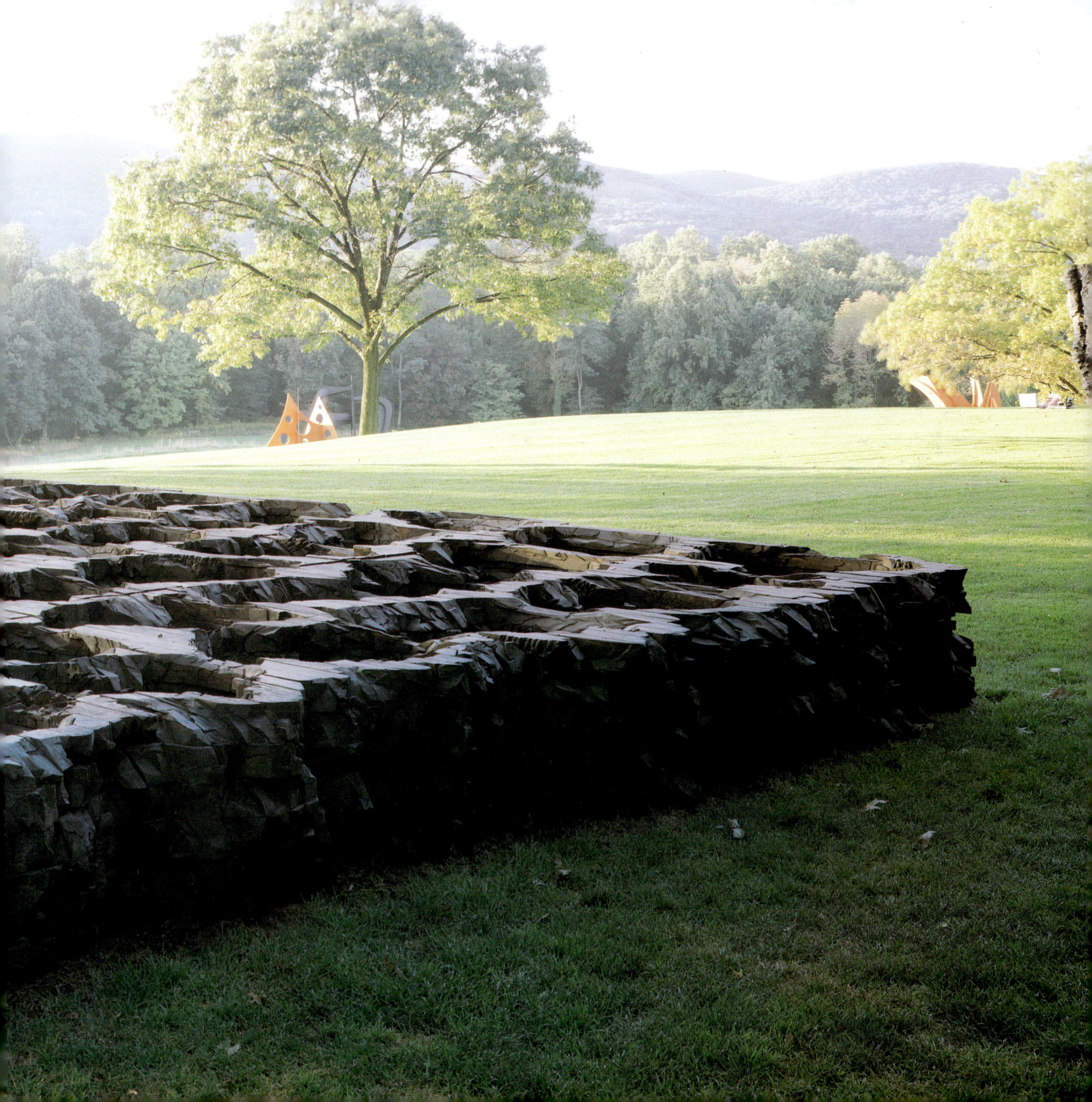

below and opposite:
Slepa Gienia (Blind Eugenie) 1994, cedar and graphite, 13 elements, 3 × 14 × 150 feet.
Outdoor installation at Denver Art Museum, Denver, Colorado, 1994.
Collection of the artist, courtesy Galerie Lelong, New York.

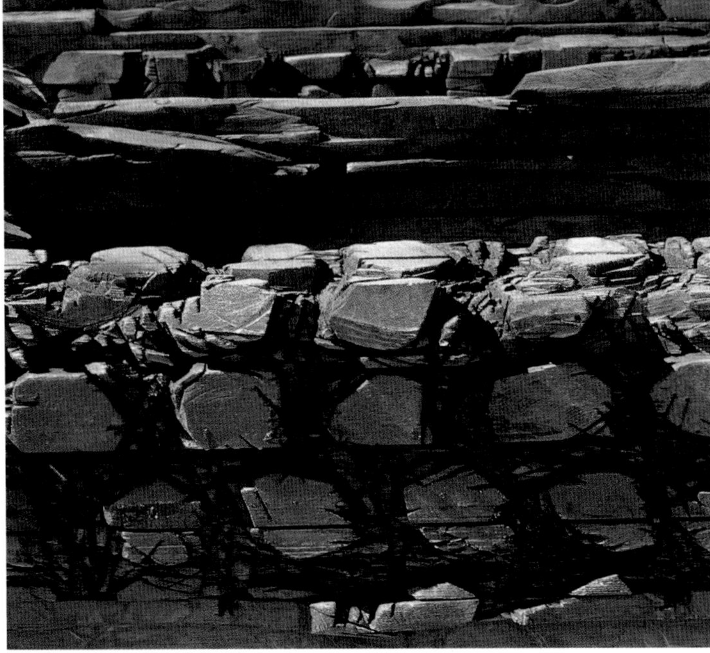

talismanic power resides precisely in their irregularity, their strangeness.

In von Rydingsvard's tradition, at least that part that derives from studies in modern art, the Surrealists hover constantly. It was the Surrealist group in the 1930s, led by the poet André Breton, that called attention to the potential magical properties of diverse objects they ordained as magical. Their decision to take ordinary objects out of ordinary contexts and lift them into the imaginative realm was arrived at through a long process of philosophical and anthropological inquiry. Breton had been swept up in the twentieth-century retrieval of magical objects from so-called primitive cultures. His admiration for Picasso, whose *Demoiselles d'Avignon* he early recognized as a singular departure from Western tradition, quickly led him to the acquisition of objects from non-European cultures. Eventually, their strangeness, their "otherness," springing from animistic sources, would be imaginatively posited in objects found in the quotidian activities of a modern man navigating the artificial byways of an urban metropolis. Von Rydingsvard is on the same path in *Slepa Gienia.* The acquired primitiveness of her imagery, arrived at through the cutting and gluing of industrially milled beams, deliberately aged by a patina of rubbed graphite, is a self-contained paradox, a challenge to habitual readings of objects in a given space. The title, which in Polish means "Blind Eugenie," is no doubt an afterthought, but contributes to the mysterious ambiance of the piece. It is a reminiscence of some childhood game, one of those children's games that are timeless, passed on for generations from untraceable sources, a game that is found in many differing societies and that no doubt relates to blindman's buff, as Francisco de Goya recalled it in his early tapestry designs. The only possible relationship between the title and the piece is in its air of ancientness, its inclusion of time as an element. And that again is an old Surrealist habit—distancing the name from the thing to create an utterly original other thing.

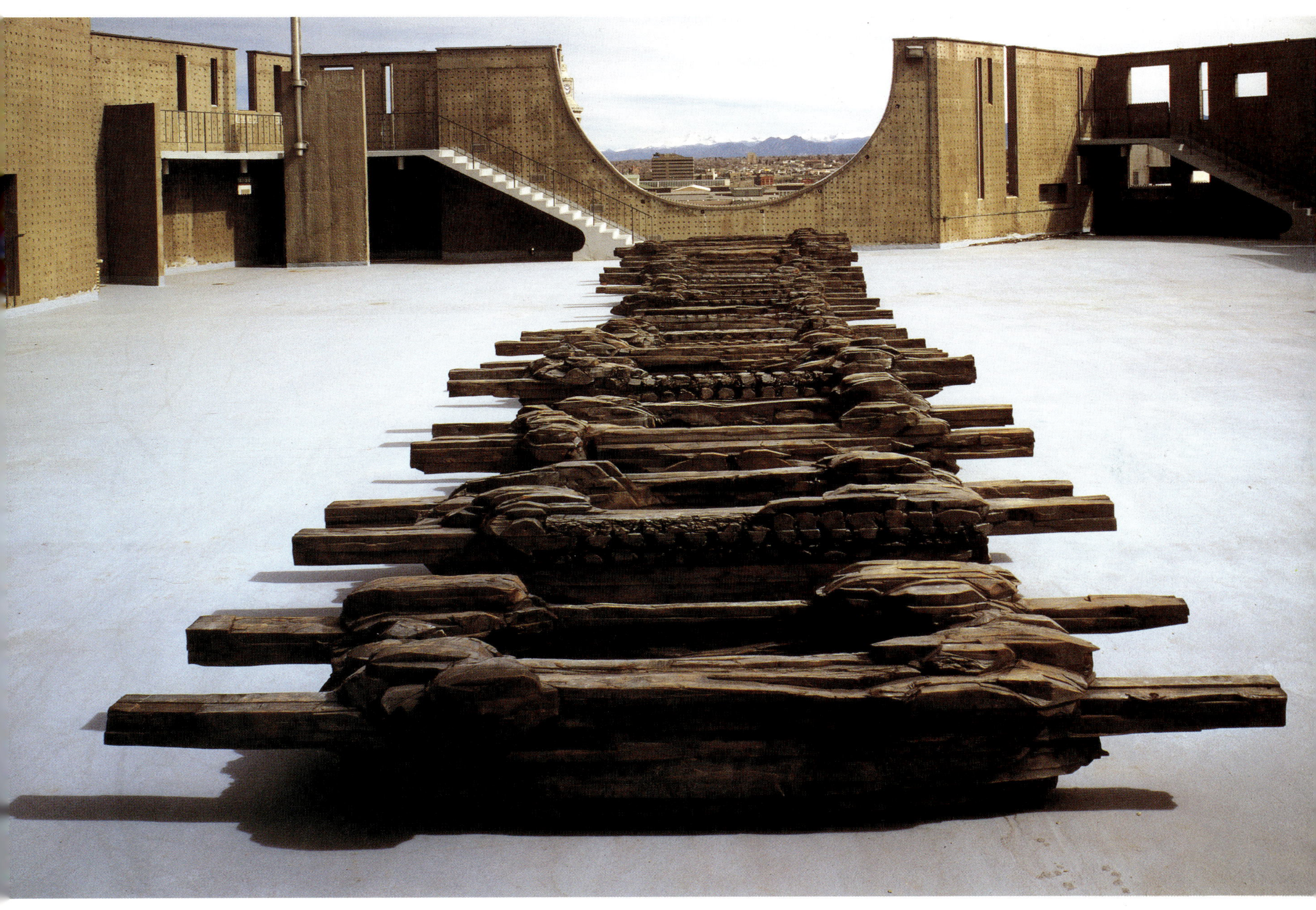

Woziwody Mur 1995, cedar and graphite, 74¼ × 75½ × 32 inches.
Collection of Sol Lewitt, Chester, Connecticut.

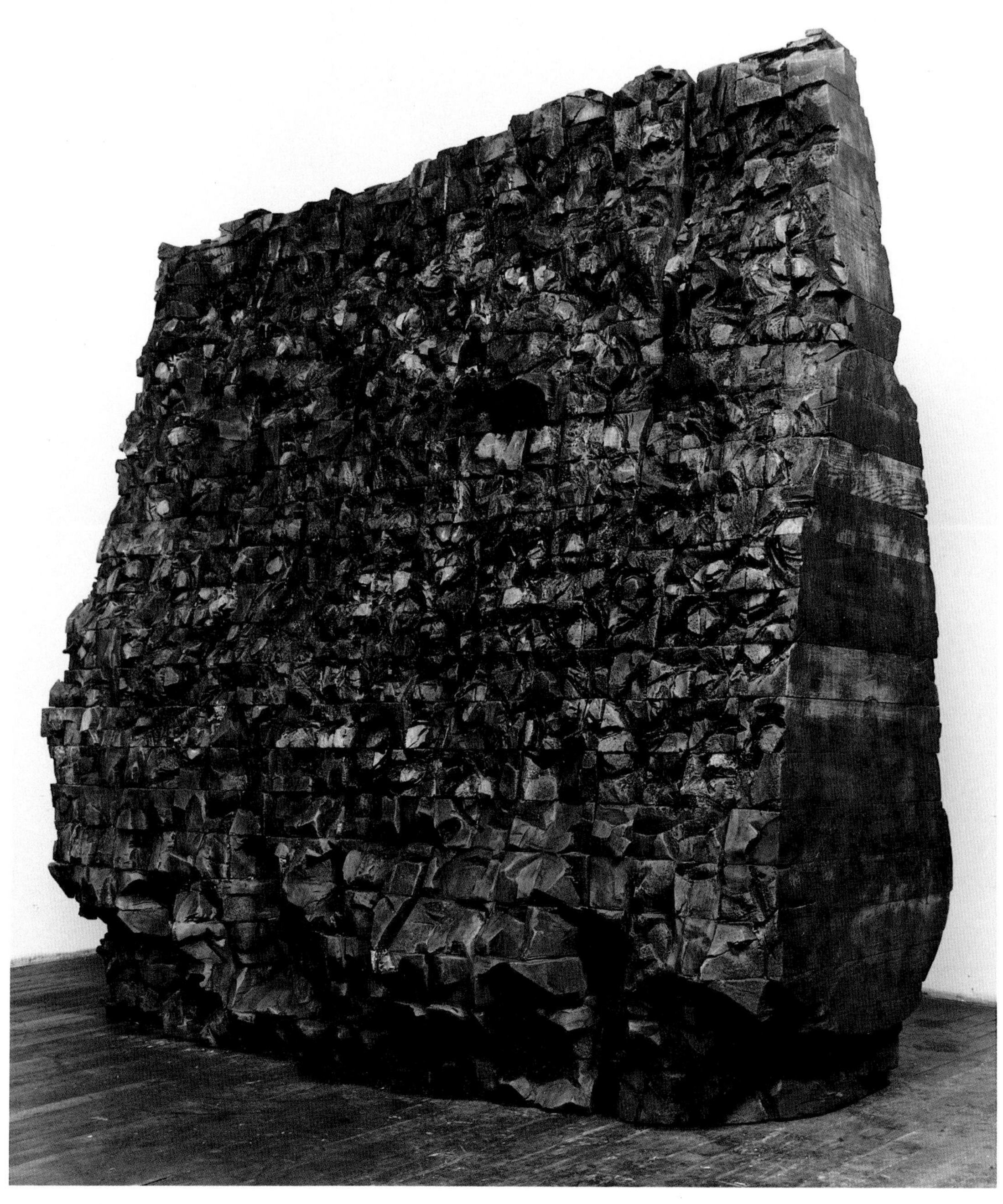

Krasavica 1993, cedar and graphite, 54 × 205¾ × 59 inches.
Collection of the artist, courtesy Galerie Lelong, New York.

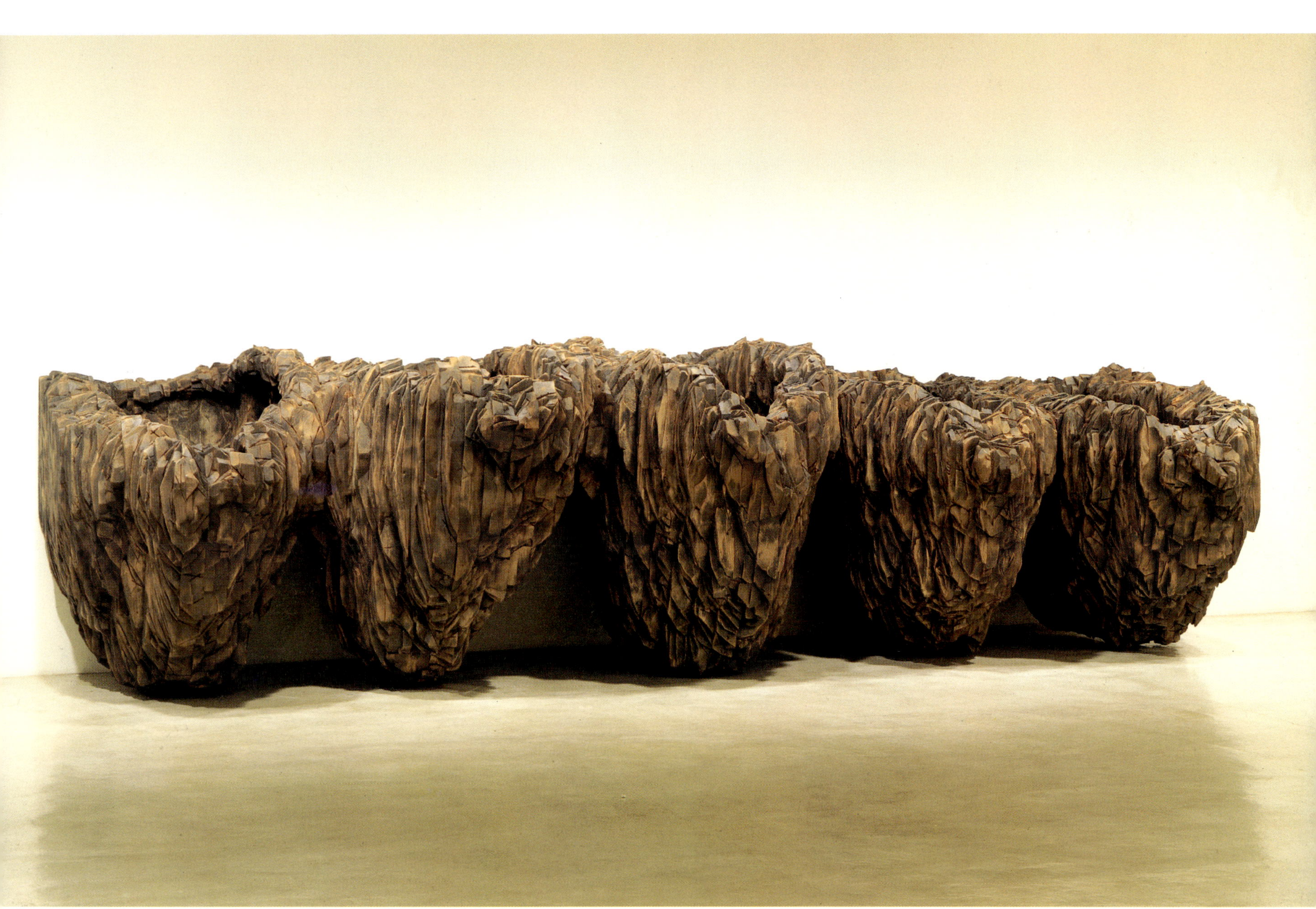

opposite:
Dla Gienka (For Gene) 1991–93, cedar and graphite, 88 × 53¼ × 31¾ inches. Collection of the artist, courtesy Galerie Lelong, New York.

Gravity is the sculptor's primary ally and foe, and tempers any of his creations—defiant or compliant. The word, with its etymological source in the quality of heaviness, also suggests seriousness, lack of levity. Von Rydingsvard's work is quintessentially grave, but there are occasional flashes of what may be taken as humor, as when she fashions balls that are lumpy like potatoes and thrusts them into receptacle shapes. Or when she carves what appear to be giant combs (which also resemble certain African musical instruments) that by their sheer size become caricatural, humorous. But basically hers is a grave enterprise, in which the symmetries of the human body and the laws of nature are of primary importance. Although she disclaims any sentimental attachment to wood, with its natural grains and irregularities, von Rydingsvard has nonetheless drawn from the yielding softness of cedar a kind of expressive subtlety that could only reside in an organic material such as wood, which, she admits, "*feels* like a humane material."

Much has been said about von Rydingsvard's additive method of work, but despite the use of power tools, clamps, industrial glues, and any technological help she can marshal, von Rydingsvard's approach to her sculpture has much in common with traditional methods. She begins with an indistinct general vision, just as a potter might with his wheel turning, and the work grows and changes as it moves upward. It can take many unexpected turnings. There is an openness to suggestion given in the process itself. It is not the joiner's calculated labor. The range of von Rydingsvard's expression is considerable, given the fixed routine her method requires. The gouging and scarring of the final surfaces, the lacerating jabs of the circular saw, invoke sensations of violence and disruption, usually subdued by the stable generosity of the interior form. But there is also a calm order throughout certain pieces, emphasized by the faceted regularity von Rydingsvard sometimes permits in the rectilinear terminals of her beams.

Basic to her technique—which she surely developed in answer to a deep and indefinable need—is the element of repetition, the implicit statement that there are situations in life that have no beginning and no end. The arts in human history are threaded through with the impulse to escape calendar time (surely the basis of much traditional Islamic art), and many of von Rydingsvard's routines suggest her need to enter the timeless universe of mythology. In casual remarks she has revealed her deep respect for ritual—the repetition of eternal gestures, always the same, in order to propitiate the gods who themselves are always the same. Her early quest for "grace" brought her to the iterated rituals of the Catholic Church. Her mature quest has brought her further afield, to Gregorian plain chant and to the writings of Julio Cortázar who, as she says, "has a way of not answering in a very fine way" and who "lives in the tangents and never comes to a conclusion."

Such tangents lure von Rydingsvard into increasingly complex sculptural adventures in which meanings are elusive. She addresses the imagination which first asks, in a troubled voice, what is it? And then she works furiously to invent a meaning. She often thinks in terms of generalized states of feeling. She has described spaces as "hemmed in, like a confessional, a coffin, a womb" and other kinds of spaces as expansive, like cultured fields or the sea. The actual three-dimensional objects she creates become lingering evidence rather than an overt declaration of the kind of feeling that only a visual artist, or a poet, can symbolize. That is why von Rydingsvard speaks of something so difficult to define as "psychological" space, and why she so often alludes to Giacometti, whose sculpture characterizes the pressures and actions of both time and space as they wear away at living things and, in their actions, shape them. When von Rydingsvard creates one of her gourdlike shapes, sometimes called bowls, she tends toward closure, but never achieves it. Her receptacles have an

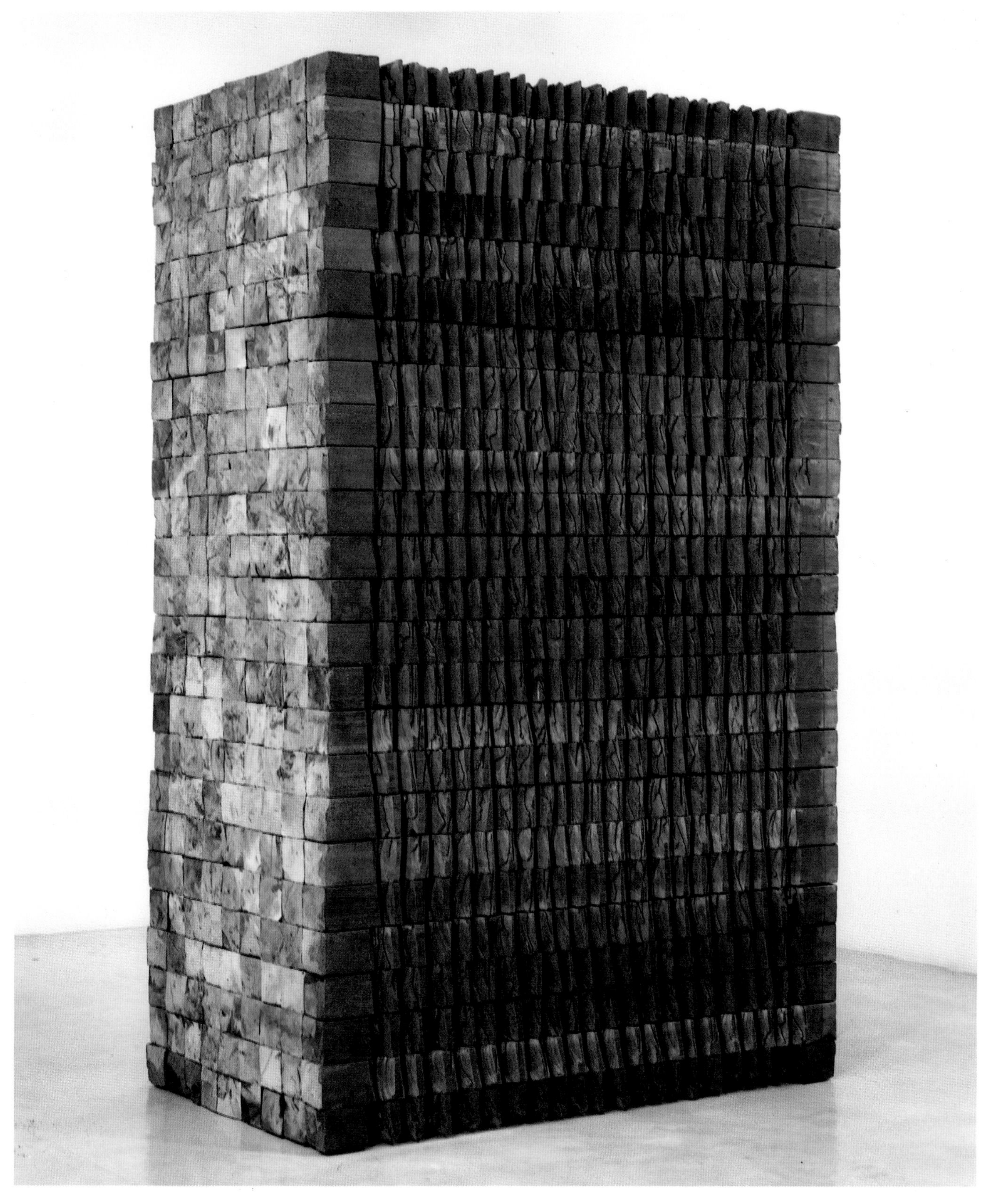

implied inner resonance, like a seashell, in which all sorts of hidden natural forces flow. Certainly this sense of contained energy is one of her most elusive, and yet most explicit meanings. It is not by chance that of all her memories of her first European journey, and particularly her introduction to Paris, what springs up first is the impression of the Pantheon.

Von Rydingsvard works with openness and closure instinctively, making use of all the emotional responses available to those tendencies, just as she works with man's complicated relation with the ground he stands on. Despite his ineluctable desire for flight, man is finally planted like the flora on the earth. Certain of von Rydingsvard's pieces proclaim that simple truth, such as an earlier work of 1983, *For Paul* (cedar, 5 elements, each 144 × 36 × 24 inches; collection of the artist), in which giant stanchions are endowed with exaggerated feet in much the way that Giacometti's figures rise as slender apparitions from enormously disproportionate feet nailed eternally to the ground. All the forces that work upon us, often without our awareness (including anxiety, to which she often refers as a prod and an endemic element in her work), are called into play as von Rydingsvard works her way up from the ground. As an oeuvre, von Rydingsvard's addresses what used to be called "the grand themes": birth, life, death, and as Levi Strauss aptly describes it, it is "an adding up to a wearing down."[8]

NOTES

Quotations, unless cited otherwise, are from conversations I had with the artist in recent years.

1. Interview with Judy Collischan Van Wagner, June 7, 1985, in Zimmer and Van Wagner, *Judith Murray: Painting, Ursula von Rydingsvard: Sculpture,* exh. cat. (Brookville, N.Y.: Hillwood Art Gallery, Long Island University, 1985), 43.

2. Cindy Nemser, "An Interview with Eva Hesse," *Artforum* 8, no. 9 (May 1970): 60.

3. Van Wagner, *Ursula von Rydingsvard: Sculpture,* 46.

4. Judd Tully, "Ursula von Rydingsvard," *Arts Magazine* 54 (May 1980): 22.

5. Giorgio de Chirico, "On Metaphysical Art," reprinted in Herschel B. Chipp, *Theories of Modern Art* (Berkeley: University of California Press, 1968), 452.

6. David Levi Strauss, ed., *Capp Street Project 1989–1990,* exh. cat. (San Francisco: Capp Street Project/AVT, 1991), 25.

7. Ibid.

8. Ibid.

Berek 1994, cedar and graphite,
107 × 14 × 32 inches.
Whitney Museum of American Art, New York,
gift of Linda and Ronald F. Daitz
and an anonymous donor, by exchange.

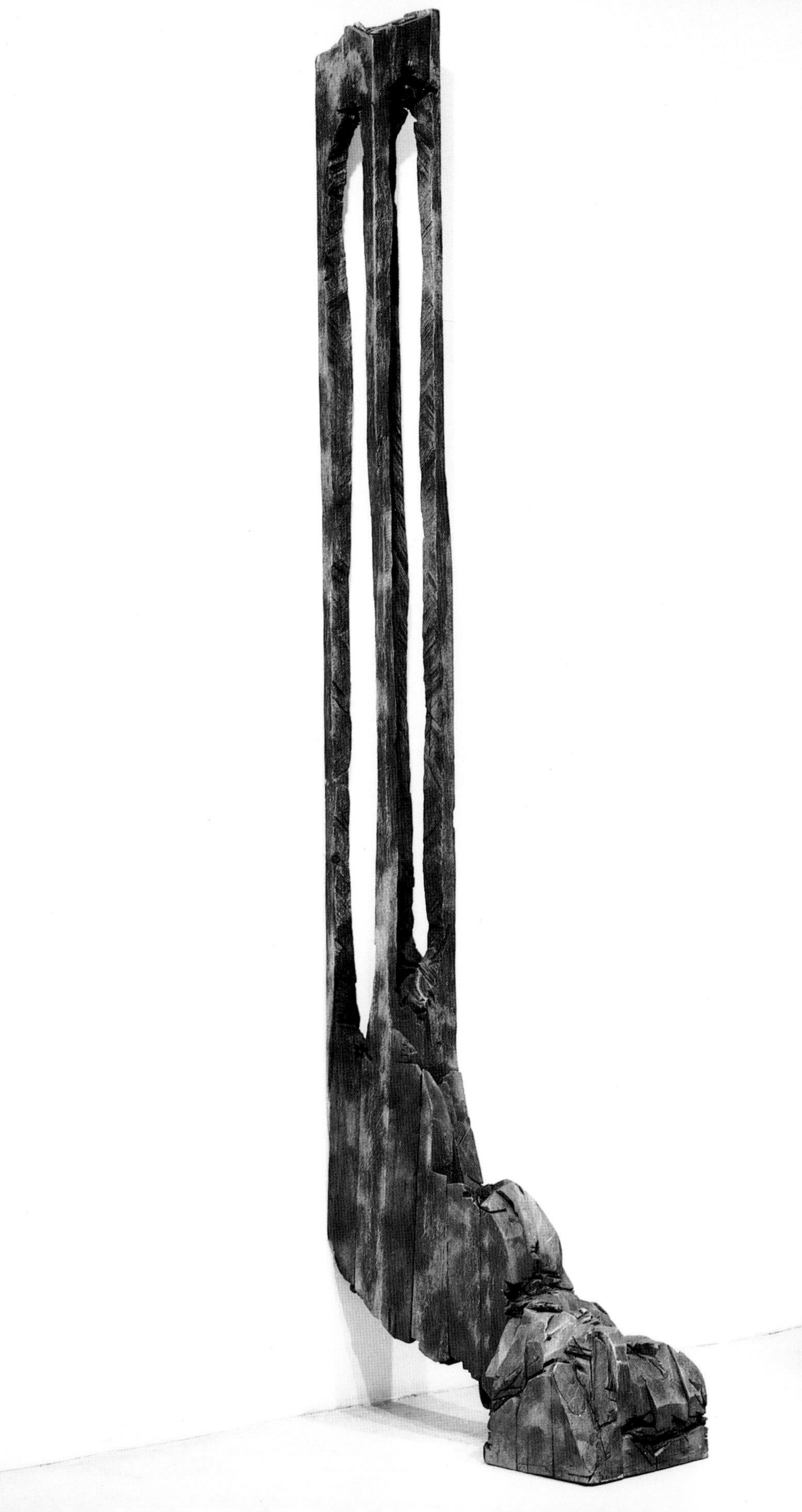

Five-Fingered Comb 1994, cedar and graphite, 47½ × 33 × 10 inches. High Museum of Art, Atlanta, Georgia, purchase with 20th Century Art Acquisition Fund.

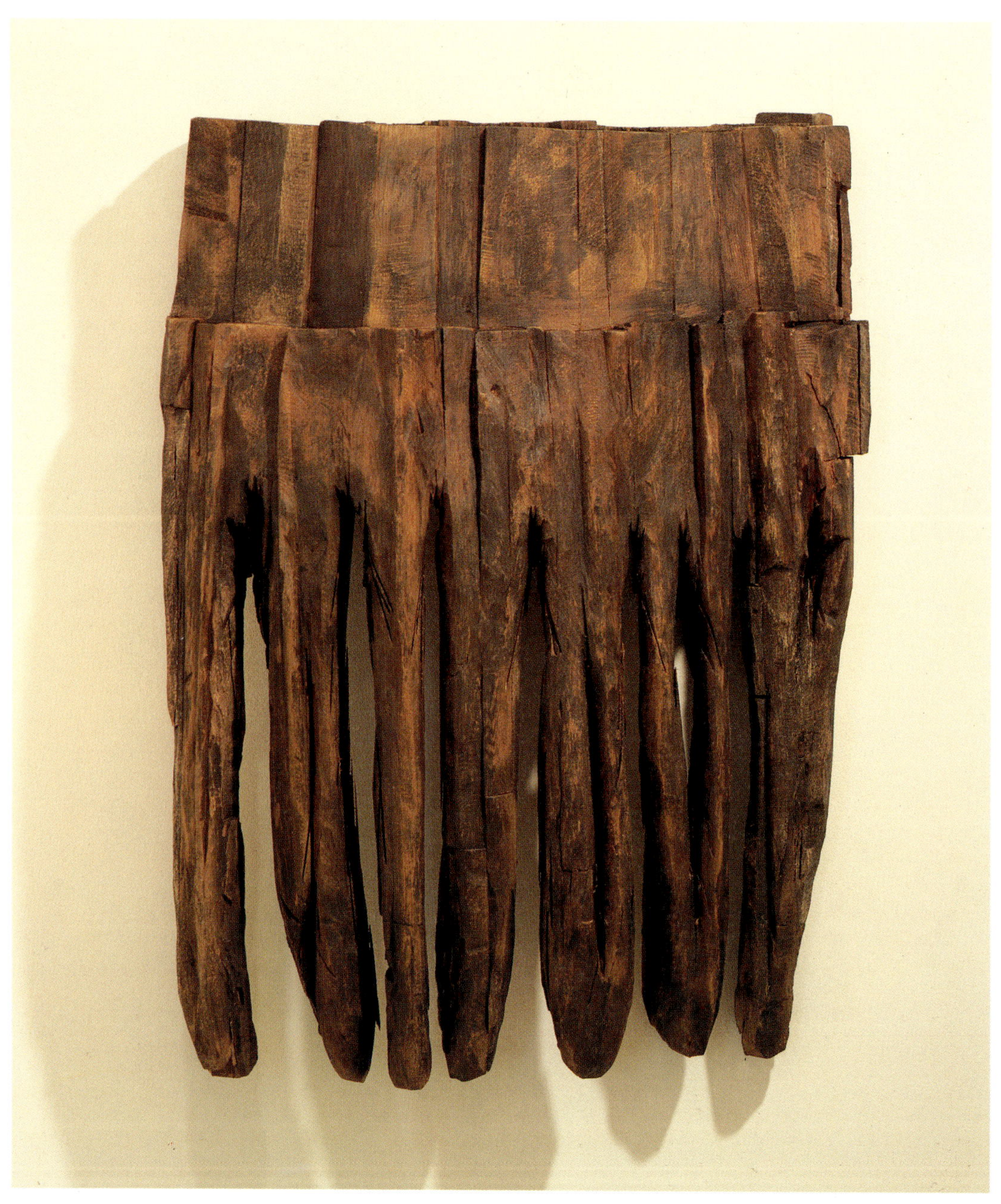

Untitled (Three Baskets) 1995, cedar and graphite, 40 × 103 × 47 inches.
Collection of the artist, courtesy Galerie Lelong, New York.

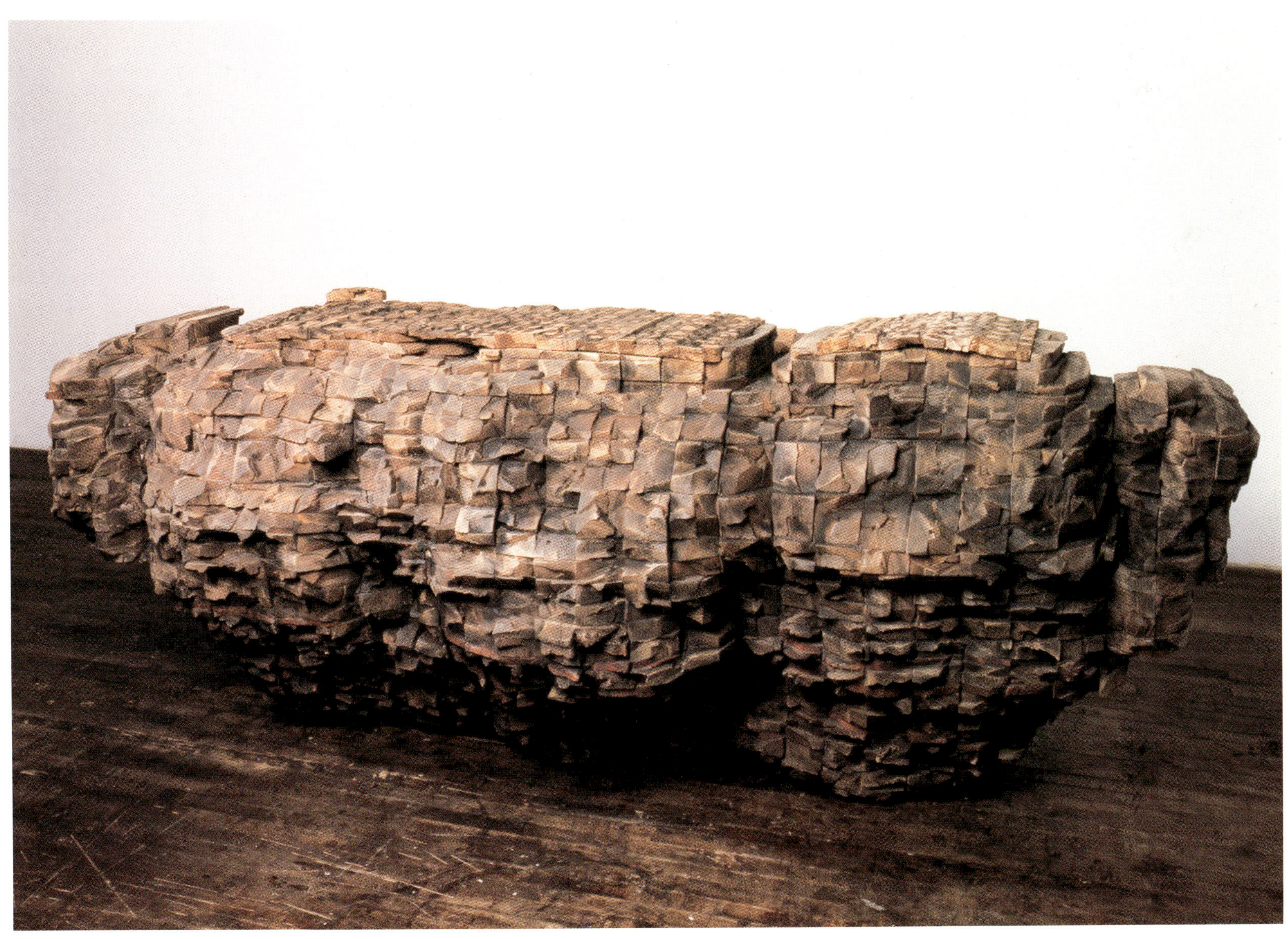

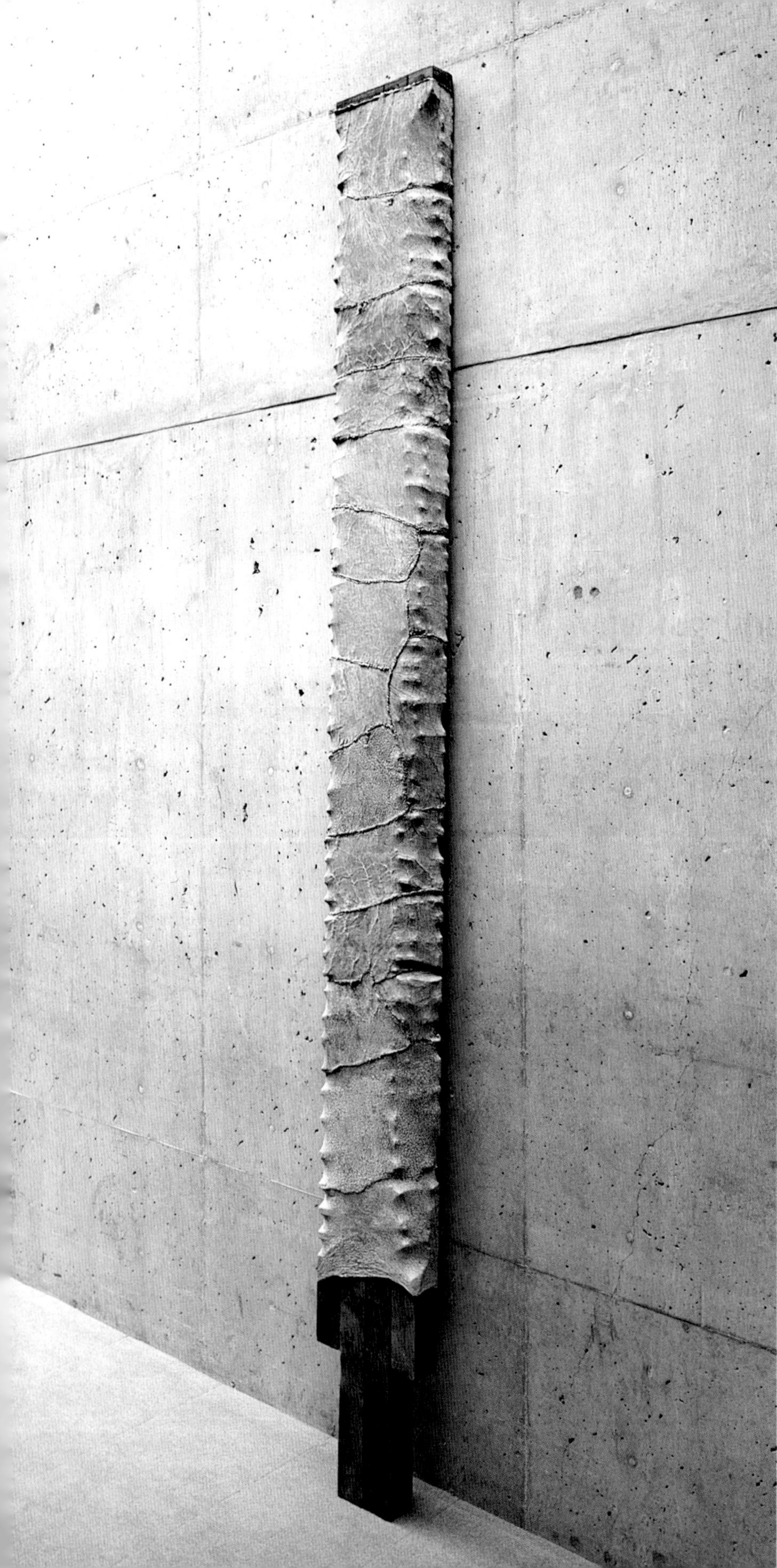

Maglownica 1995, cedar and cows' intestines, 148 × 14 × 3½ inches. Collection of the artist, courtesy Galerie Lelong, New York.

Vera's Collar 1995, cedar and whitewash, 44 × 72 × 4 inches.
Collection of Vera List.

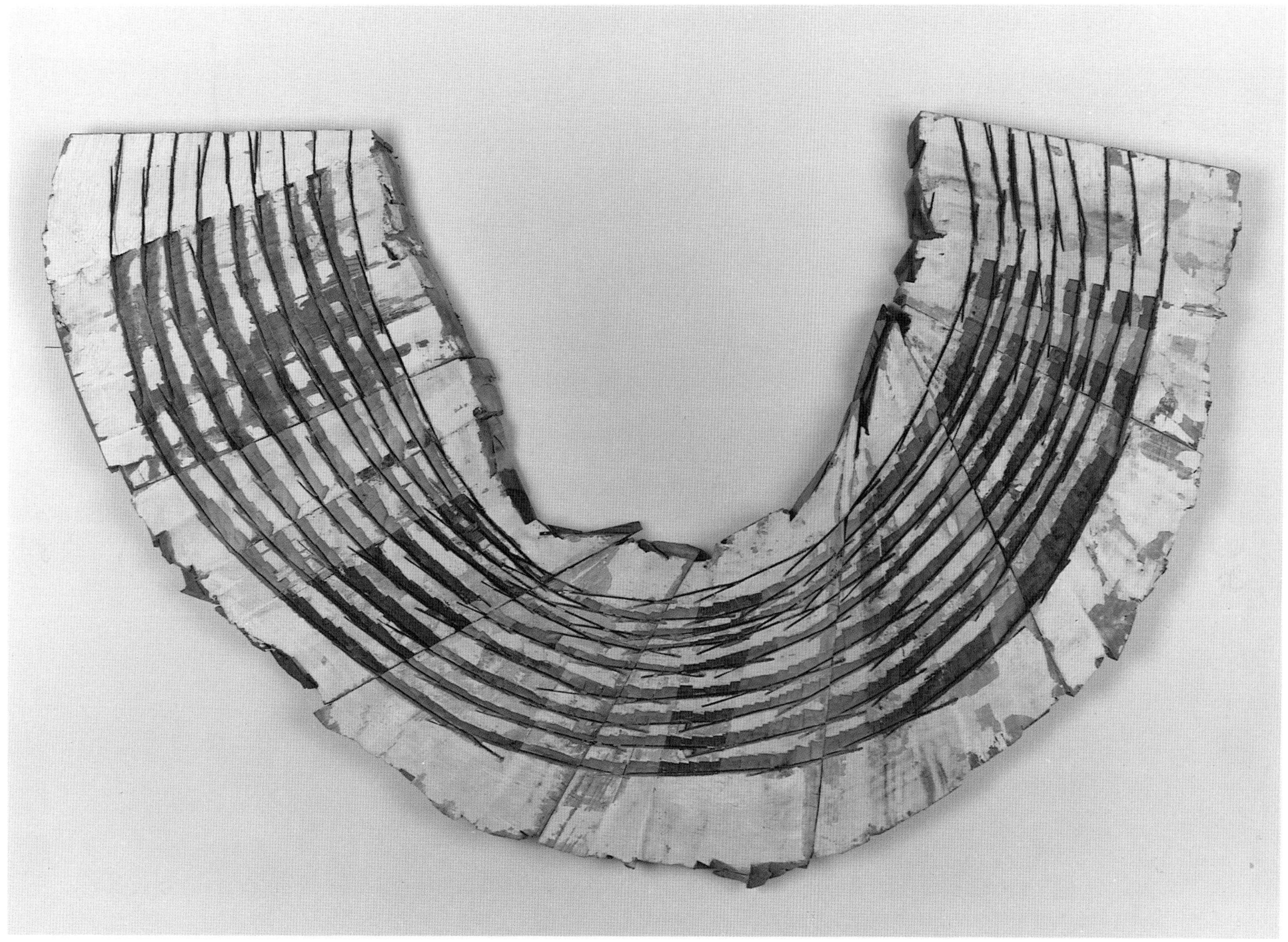

opposite:
Installation, "Socks on My Spoons," University Gallery, University of Massachusetts, Amherst, November 1995.

From left:

Untitled (Seventy Balls) 1995, cedar, 7 × 80 × 134 inches.
Collection of the artist, courtesy Galerie Lelong, New York.

Untitled (Two Plates) 1995, cedar and graphite, 12 × 264 × 126 inches.
Collection of the artist, courtesy Galerie Lelong, New York.

Untitled (Spoons with Soil) 1995, cedar, peat moss, glue, 122 × 130 × 16 inches.
Collection of the artist, courtesy Galerie Lelong, New York.

pages 70–71:
Untitled, work in progress at Museum of Art, Rhode Island School of Design, Providence, January 1996, courtesy Galerie Lelong, New York.

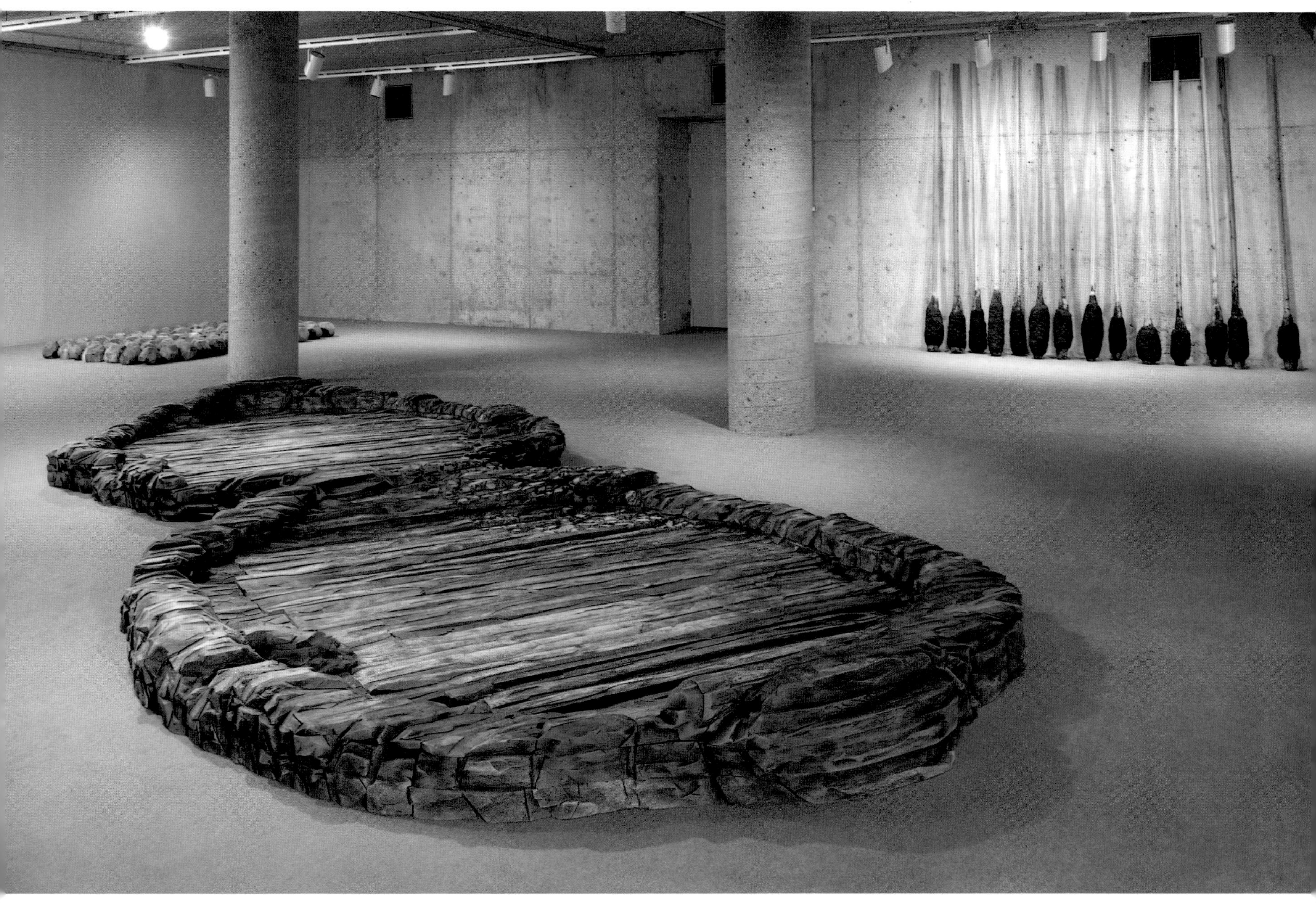

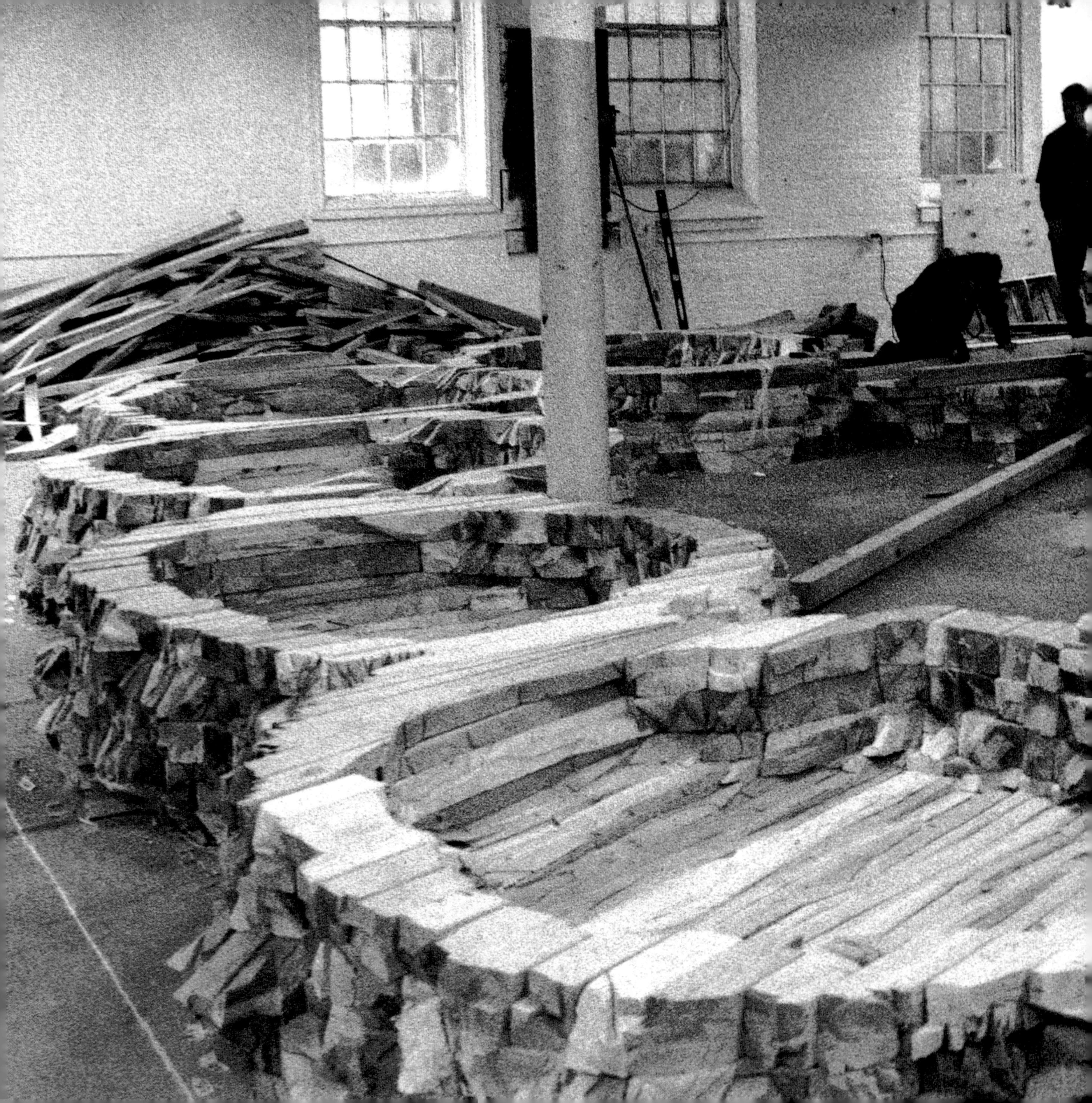

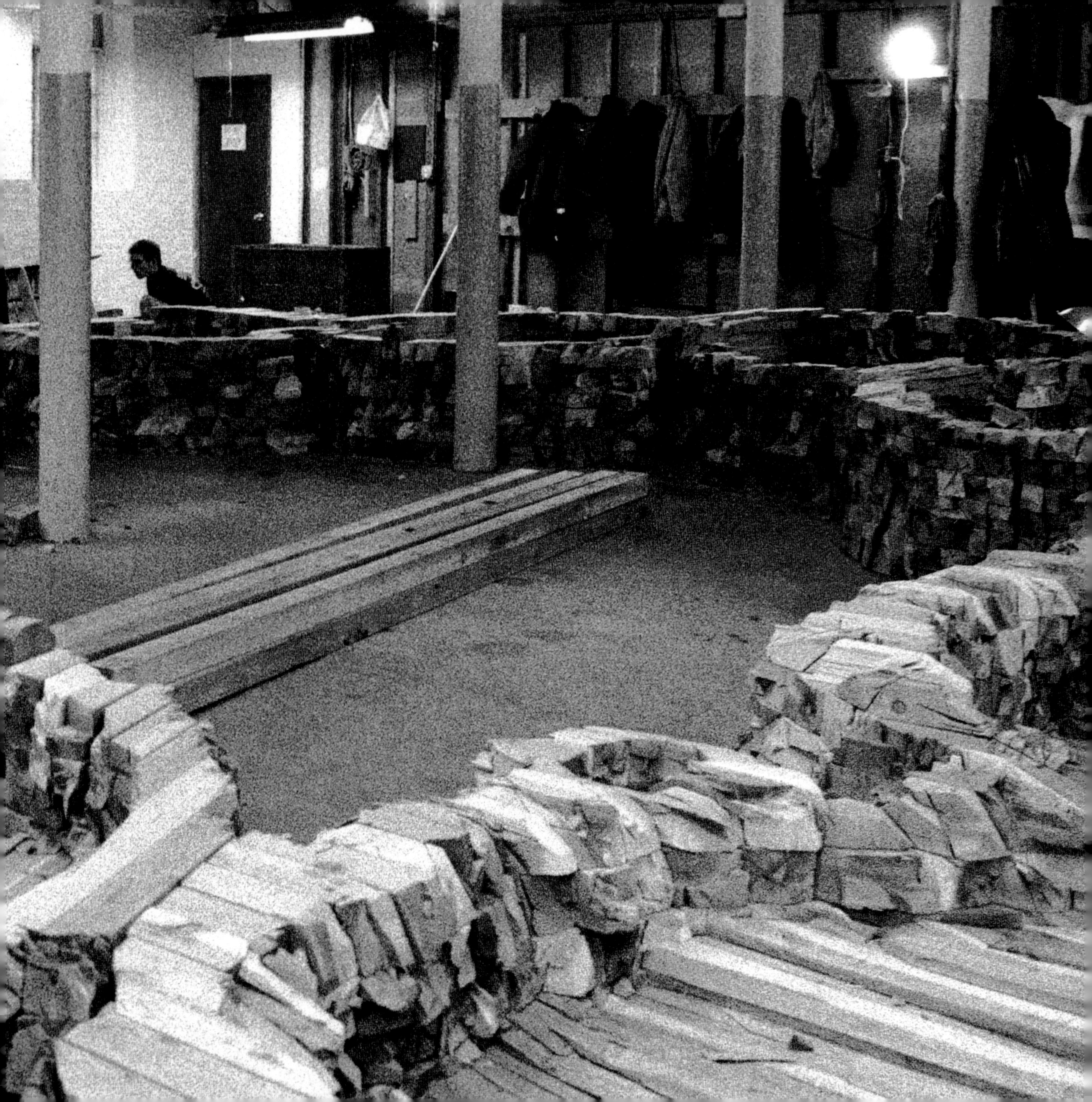

Page from the artist's journal,
May 1986.

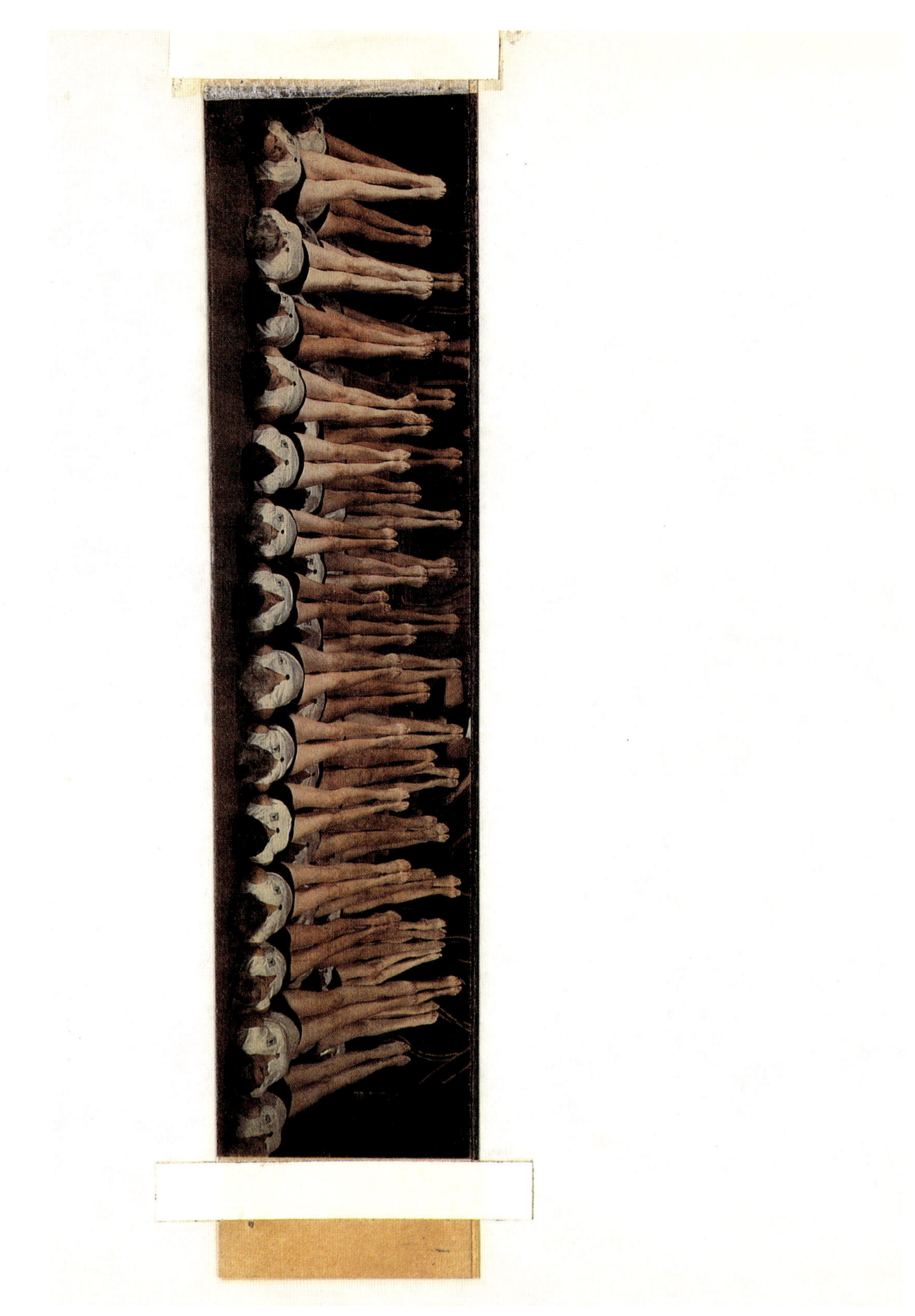

Marek Bartelik

RECLAIMING SPACES

. . . en Pologne, c'est-à-dire Nulle Part [1]

In a log she kept during a 1985 trip to Poland, Ursula von Rydingsvard wrote down several random dates from Polish history:

> 1241—Tartar attacks
> Tannenberg—Grunwald battle—Jagiello (king)
> leading
> July 1410
> . . . .
> early 1900s Paderewski = prime minister
> after WWI
> Poland fought Lithuanians & Ukrainians.[2]

An American with roots in Poland, von Rydingsvard was undertaking an open-ended voyage of self-identification common among American artists who seek to achieve further understanding of themselves by addressing their ancestral heritage. Born in Germany during World War II (her mother was Polish, her father Polish-speaking Ukrainian), the artist knew Poland only indirectly, through the re-creation of the environment and culture by Poles in exile. The 1985 trip—von Rydingsvard's first—provided her with an opportunity to apprehend Polish reality firsthand and to replace the fictive country created by her imagination with a realistic version of her family's native land.

Ursula von Rydingsvard is the fifth of seven children of Kunegunda and Ignacy Karoliszyn, peasant farmers who left their native village of Piaseczna, today in the southwest part of Ukraine, in 1939. They spent World War II working on a large farm near Deensen in the north central part of Germany. Born on the farm in 1942, von Rydingsvard describes it as "an ordered, bucolic place, where Polish and Russian workers were treated like slaves. Extreme disciplinary measures were taken if they broke rules." With the end of World War II, the artist's family was moved to a refugee camp, and for the next five years they awaited permission to emigrate to the United States. From 1945 to 1950 the Karoliszyns lived in eight different displacement camps, most of which were located on vacant military bases.[3]

The artist's recollections of the refugee camps are vivid and detailed, physical rather than pictorial, as her journal confirms: "The easiest way for me to recall my past is to examine the spaces in which the events took place."[4] A typical camp consisted of timber-made barracks; the most prominent structure was designated as the barrack-church and was usually recognizable only by a large cross placed in front of the building or on the roof. Homes were austerely furnished: large wood-burning stove, steel military cots, crude wooden table and chairs. To retain heat inside the house, the walls were covered with gray felt army blankets. A large watercolor of Christ on the cross, which the Karoliszyns carried with them from place to place, was a reminder of the family's deeply felt Catholicism. The Church played a crucial role in the lives of Poles in camps, cultivating a spiritual connection between the refugees and their predominantly Roman Catholic homeland. It maintained their faith in a better future and provided an orderly ritual in their unstable lives. Von Rydingsvard accompanied her mother to mass daily. During processions organized for major religious holidays, she and other children carried small religious statues or baskets full of flower petals to be dispersed in front of the priest. The earliest sculpture she remembers in her home was a plaster ram with a flag (a symbol of Christ's resurrection), used for Easter ceremonies.

As the artist evokes it, daily existence in the camps was thoroughly demoralizing: "If you can imagine men without jobs. What do they do with their lives? There were no laws, no police. Teenage children with no school to go to . . . they had no control over their future."[5] Although she played games with other children in the camp, von Rydingsvard discounts the role of interaction with peers in her early life. Instead, she stresses the significance of family within the context of the camps, a constant reminder that home and family could not be taken for granted:

> I did not play games nearly as much as other children did. When I did play them, they were in a style I recall as being serious. I often played with sticks, wooden balls, and other knife-carved wooden objects made with a child's will and awkward technical skills. I also played with crude, domestic objects in bombed-out brick buildings, the ruins of which were layered in ways that for me felt exciting. Those places provided a kind of landscape which I could easily transpose into anything I wanted.
>
> I remember mostly playing with my siblings, for the strongest emotional link was to my family, which I felt to be the last vestige of safety; my survival depended on my being wedded to that unit. I placed thick layers of idealization on parents and siblings, further fusing the bond. Much later, it took some hard peeling to find what in me was vital and mine.

In 1950 von Rydingsvard's family received an entry visa to the United States, and they traveled from Bremerhaven to New York City on board the ocean liner *General Bladford.* The Polish National Alliance of Brooklyn, USA, a life insurance company, assisted their settlement, in return for which they were asked to purchase a twenty-year life insurance policy for each family member. For the Karoliszyns America unfolded with a speed that drastically contrasted with the slow pace of their former refugee existence. After a short stay in the Polish National Alliance Home in Oak Ridge, New Jersey (used as a summer camp for the children of the company employees), the artist's family moved to Plainville, Connecticut, where her parents quickly got jobs and purchased a house. "No one would rent to [a family with] seven children," von Rydingsvard once recalled.[6] The family's settlement in Plainville was noted in the local newspaper, which considered the large immigrant family exotic enough to devote a front-page article to their arrival. It stated in a matter-of-fact way:

> The family of nine came to Plainville last night to move into their new home, and end a journey which started in Poland before World War II. . . . The house at 63 West Main Street was bought yesterday morning. . . . The PNA [Polish National Alliance] assured the Karoliszyn family that the mortgage will be fully covered for them until they can get established here. . . . The children range in ages from 18 months to 18 [17] years, but the mother intends to go to work. The older children can take care of the younger ones.[7]

The quickly achieved independence had its consequences. Von Rydingsvard remembers her first American home as being chaotic in the absence of parents who worked all day, holding down multiple jobs. During the week the artist's father worked in two factories; in one the workers spoke Polish almost exclusively. He had a job as a gardener on weekends. His wife worked cleaning a restaurant for a brief period of time and then as a baker. While their parents were preoccupied with making a living, the children made their own home. They lived in a two-story yellow-painted clapboard house, furnished with used furniture donated by the local community as a welcoming present. The family occupied the first floor and rented out the second for extra income.

Although Plainville had no Polish community, neighboring New Britain, Connecticut, had a large one. The artist's parents immediately established connections with Polish families, and the local Polish-American community provided them with emotional support. Von Rydingsvard, however, does not perceive the immediate impact of that community as particularly significant for her life:

> The effects of the Polish community of New Britain, Connecticut, were minimal on my life, though the parts to which I had been exposed have a familiar crudeness with frightening overtones. As a young child, I would sometimes feel sexually seedy undercurrents from the males of that community, and the females always seemed deeply immersed in their work, having an awareness that seemed never to go beyond their immediate families. But inside myself I nurtured another version of what it felt like being Polish. It was something pure and complex; it possessed a richness with its centuries of history, of grand gestures coupled with meticulous manners. This felt abstract, distant but important. I left Plainville with relief, anxious to break away from the stringent parameters of my life and my thinking.

For an American-raised artist traveling in Poland during the summer of 1985, nearly four years after the government's suppression of the Solidarity labor movement and four years before the demise of the Communist system, the country could offer only a gloomy picture of a nation bearing consequences of recent political turmoil. Von Rydingsvard visited major Polish cities, finding them submerged in quiet desperation. The trip took on a positive tone when she traveled to her mother's native village of Koszarawa in the southeast of the country, which she found rich in folklore and more picturesque than the cities of Poland, as if politics had exerted little influence on the rural landscape. She felt comfortable inside Polish homes, finding their interiors intimate in a familiar way. Her image of Poland was, however, overwhelmingly dark. Ultimately, the trip left her with a sense of sadness, not just because it gave her a depressing view of Poland, but, perhaps even more importantly, because it signified the collapse of the personal and idealized image that had been constructed over many years.

Although one could perceive this journey as another traumatic event in von Rydingsvard's life, it was liberating in that it released her from yearning for a place that did not exist. She had to wait four more years, until 1989, to return to Poland, and another three years to mount a large show at Warsaw's Centre for Contemporary Art (Centrum Sztuki Współczesnej), in the Ujazdowski Castle. With a less emotional eye and confronted by a different political situation, the artist was able to reconcile the present Poland with her imagined and idealized version (an intriguing coincidence with the discarding of Communism in Eastern Europe and Russia). This she achieved in part by choosing to look at the long-gone ancestral rural homeland in a manner somewhat close to Jean-François Millet's explorations of the mythic underpinnings of rural society. To say that von Rydingsvard has been simply romanticizing her biography means, however, not only to deny the power of her singular experience, but also to disregard the artist's awareness of those manifold aspects of her personal story that are more ambiguous and difficult to mythologize, such as her family's journey from Poland to Germany, their "buying" access to America by purchasing an insurance policy for each family member, the rather cynical welcome in Plainville by the local newspaper, or the artist's complex relationship with her parents. These "unstable" biographical moments, in fact, seem to form the crucial points of tension in von Rydingsvard's life and are a vital source of creative energy for her art.

Von Rydingsvard's first college years were at the University of New Hampshire, where she decided to become an artist. She left there for the University of Miami, where she received a B.A. and an M.A. In 1973 she enrolled in the master of fine arts program at Columbia University, where she studied sculpture with Ronald Bladen, George Sugarman, Jean Linder, and Sahl Swarz.[8] For her final project she presented a large work built of clay with protruding rusted steel pipes, along with several smaller sculptures made of stuffed muslin. Today the artist describes these early works as being sexually explicit, having fulfilled a need to "grapple with the psychosexual mark." Columbia's program offered opportunities to study art history with Meyer Schapiro and Theodore Reff. The mosaic of visiting artists and critics included Philip Guston, Brice Marden, Max Kozloff, and Dore Ashton. To expand her art education she audited lectures offered by the Whitney Museum of American Art's Independent Study Program. She gained further exposure to the New York art scene through visits to the Kitchen Center for Music and Dance, the Clocktower (Institute for Art and Urban Resources) in Long Island City, and 55 Mercer, a SoHo artists' cooperative to which her teacher Jean Linder belonged (von Rydingsvard worked for Linder as an assistant). She remembers Alberto Giacometti's 1974 retrospective at the Solomon R. Guggenheim Museum and cites it as an important influence on the art of her formative years. Recently discussing her interest in landscape, von Rydingsvard again mentioned the Swiss sculptor: "The most critical landscape to me is the psychological one. This is the landscape Giacometti fills his faces and bodies with. It is a form that is still in the process of evolving—perhaps not that clear about its destination."[9]

Among other sculptors whose work she studied closely were Constantin Brancusi and Richard Stankiewicz, attracted in part to those artists' Eastern European roots. Reflecting on a conversation with the sculptor and critic Sidney Geist, von Rydingsvard wrote in 1974: "Sidney said that Brancusi copied classical works at the beginning, copied his own pieces towards the end—there had to be a transitional period of his copying or being influenced by pieces of his environment or other pieces of his contemporaries."[10]

As a student, von Rydingsvard worked to formulate her artistic vocabulary, experimenting with different styles and media. On one occasion she noted in her diary that she would like to make steel sculptures that would "mimic handkerchiefs which were once neatly folded in 4, opened up and placed flatly on [the] ground with creases or folds still prominent."[11] Another time, she complained to herself in her diary that she could not find the right way to make steel sculptures: "metal forms are too often so rigid, serious and full of corners."[12] Ultimately she chose four-by-four-inch industrially milled cedar beams as her primary medium:

> Steel was hard to bend into a structure that felt humane and emphatic. When a friend of mine, named Michael Mulhern, brought me some cedar beams I felt ready for another material. I recall clearly how malleable and easy to bend cedar seemed, how easy it was to squeeze shims into openings, and how much I enjoyed the physical lightness of the wood. So that first cedar piece [*Untitled (Steel and Wooden Uprights)*, 1976] felt to me like imagery connected to teeth being held firmly by gums, celebrating my newly found ability to make a sculpture that felt organic.[13]

The technical process, which has remained basically unchanged from the early days, is crucial to understanding the making of von Rydingsvard's sculptures. It is labor intensive, often accompanied by the shrill sounds of cutting with the circular saw. The artist often begins a sculpture by tracing on the floor a sketchy outline of the bottom of the piece. She draws the lines on the four-by-four-inch beams, then makes cuts guided by the drawn lines and stacks the cut wooden elements from the bottom up. (Cedar being a soft wood, the artist has a high degree of freedom in making her marks.) Von Rydingsvard determines consecutive cuts by reacting

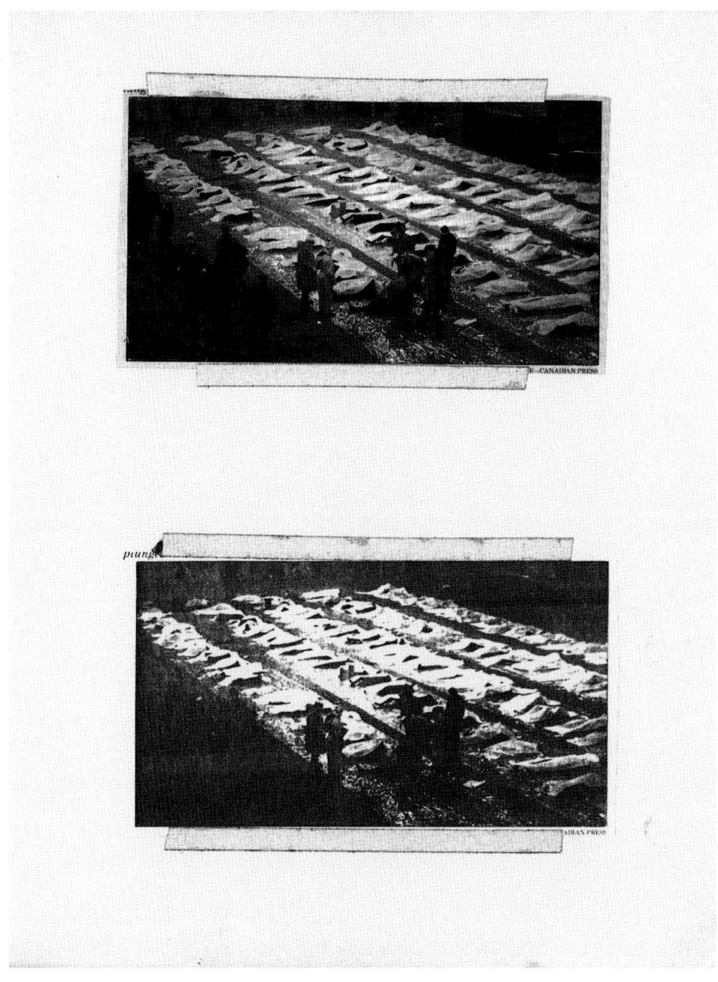

Page from the artist's journal, May 1986.

to the cuts on the beams that are already in place. After the sculpture is cut and stacked, it is marked to determine the exact location of each cut element, and then it is disassembled. Finally, the sculpture is laminated with the help of metal clamps that exert high pressure on the wood and, after the glue has dried, ground and chiseled.

Von Rydingsvard's choice of wood, originally dictated in large part by her frustration with the rigidity of steel and other materials, as well as by economic concerns, ultimately took on a more personal meaning as a cognate to her lingering memory of her early childhood spent in wooden barracks in refugee camps in Germany. At the time of moving to her first New York studio, located at 210 Spring Street in SoHo, she wrote in her diary: "I am going to start recording my dreams as I have been dreaming a lot. Also I can learn from them."[14] She has been recording her dreams (many of them about her childhood) ever since, writing them down in her journal next to observations on art, sketches, photographs, postcards, and personal notes.

Von Rydingsvard's anthology of artistic sources is vast, ranging from archaic Greek sculpture and Giotto's frescoes to African tribal art and the vernacular architecture of the many South American and European countries she has visited. It also consists of photographs from newspapers and magazines, which the artist collects, gluing them to the pages of her journal. Involved with the formulation of her own visual lexicon, the artist has attentively followed the current art scene:

> In the '70s the Minimalists seemed like kings—
> so in control, and with this powerful way of looking
> at things. It is one of the only times I felt there
> was a clear road between answers and forms.
> They reached for a kind of perfection that rebuffed
> the emotional content of my being. I was in awe of
> these Daddys who figured out such a clean mold.
> Their systems were too dry, hard-edged, and finally
> predictable. One could plug into the philosophy
> but not stay with the work visually.[15]

Although she condemns what she calls the Minimalists' omnipotence and their "ego of the architect,"[16] von Rydingsvard's connection to Minimalism should not be disregarded. In a 1985 interview the artist revealed an ambivalence shared by many 1970s artists toward their predecessors:

> I feel like a child of the minimalists. The regularity,
> the repetitive regularity. . . . There's a whole myth
> of perfection. My work is not sanitized and pure in
> terms of the kind of layering they did. . . . In some ways,
> I combine Abstract Expressionism and Minimalism.
> At one time, I was in awe of both. I got my mixture
> using some of the tools of both of these styles.[17]

The artist's debt to Minimalism is evident in her use of repeated modular units and their symmetry, in addition to her interest in industrial materials. Its influence is less visible, however, in her analytical approach to the issue of the symbiotic relationship between art and object, for she lacks the logocentric rigor associated with Minimalism that makes this relationship obvious.

Her relationship to the Abstract Expressionists is equally significant. She belongs to the artists from the 1970s who, as Clement Greenberg predicted, would see Jackson Pollock to be "essentially arbitrary and 'accidental'"—but who after all "consider this an asset rather than a liability."[18] Like the Abstract Expressionists, she believes in the power of—to borrow Goethe's expression—"des Handelns ew'ge Unschuld," the eternal innocence of action, as well as the Abstract Expressionists' paramount belief in the originality and the solitary ethos of work (in von Rydingsvard's case additionally reinforced by her peasant background).

Broadly defined, Minimalism and Abstract Expressionism served the artist principally as measuring rods or modifiers for the formulation of her own artistic vocabulary, as well as for the negotiation of "private" and "public" selves. Von Rydingsvard is also associated with the post-Minimalists, who borrowed from the Minimalists but reverted to an expressionistic vocabulary and a hands-on process with their materials. The differences between her works and sculptures generally identified as post-Minimalist are significant, however, for she seems to be satisfied with combining the nonsculptural, sexually connotative biomorphism and eccentric idiosyncrasies associated with post-Minimalism with a modernist equilibrium and sense of wholeness.

Von Rydingsvard's work shares some formal affinities with Louise Nevelson's wooden sculptures. Like Nevelson, von Rydingsvard favors a relieflike directness of frontality, monolithic qualities, and a Constructivist frame. Here again, however, differences override the similarities; not only do their sources differ—Nevelson's urban environment versus von Rydingsvard's vernacular—but Nevelson's works are more orderly and compartmentalized, descending from the Cubist tradition. On a biographical level, von Rydingsvard's focus on home and her father has been compared with Louise Bourgeois's preoccupation with phenomena of daily life overlaid with unspoken and unforgiven family relationships. Comparing the two artists' works, it is clear that the connection between von Rydingsvard and Bourgeois is tenuous, deriving perhaps from von Rydingsvard's statements, such as: "Also there were things in my life that are difficult to speak about, like the kind of drama between my father and myself. The menacing qualities of my work refer to it, perhaps; it's my secret way of stabbing, quietly."[19]

It is largely due to von Rydingsvard's insistence on artistic autonomy that, despite the fact that she is often included in all-women exhibitions, she resists being labeled a feminist or even a female sculptor. Genderizing her work is, in fact, extremely difficult. The artist's debt to the women's movement is evident in a more indirect way. Like most artists, both male and female, who began exhibiting in the 1970s, she benefited from the movement through its effort to unlock the emotional aspect of art and to restore belief in personal history. The critic Lawrence Alloway calls attention to another important result of the women's movement: as women's art "began to be accessible in quantity . . . women artists could begin to work knowingly in relation to the work of other women," and the differences between art of female and male artists "could be discussed again, but with adequate samples of women's art for the first time."[20]

In the 1970s the important arenas for radical departure from the artistic status quo were the so-called alternative spaces. Von Rydingsvard's sculpture, without claiming to be "alternative art," received support from 55 Mercer, the Institute for Art and Urban Resources (P.S. 1), and a number of nonprofit agencies specializing in the organization of outdoor art shows. In 1988 Exit Art presented a one-person show of von Rydingsvard's work that proved to be pivotal to her career.

An early outstanding piece by von Rydingsvard is *For Weston,* 1978, which was first shown at the "Indoor-Outdoor Exhibition" at P.S. 1 in 1978. It consists of seven forms clustered together and hovering against a wall, each resembling a hollow boulder with shell-thin walls. In making *For Weston,* the artist ground the laminated elements, leaving their surfaces carefully worked out. The natural fleshy pink color of cedar increases the piece's seductiveness. The organic elements abstracted to formal shapes, "fluted" by the lines of glued-together beams, evoke large, bottomless butter churns, haystacks, or perhaps abstracted, headless human bodies. The sharpness of the top openings' edges contrasts with the smooth surfaces of the walls, forming a clear demarcation between the interior and exterior of the cones, as if the edges guard entry to the hollow cryptic space inside, or perhaps testify to a decapitation. Although von Rydingsvard's vocabulary is highly abstracted, it is not devoid of subtle figural allusions. For instance, the artist's forms are usually proportioned to human scale and invested with individuality and uniqueness. Von Rydingsvard supports the dual figurative/abstract reading: "I feel that my most powerful pieces have [a] person hidden in them—in fact there are hints which make these forms feel like people—perhaps as people are felt as taken in through the peripheral vision."[21]

For Weston was dedicated to Weston McDaniels, whom von Rydingsvard met while she was working for Encore Community Services, a social-service organization, based in Saint Malachy's Church on West Forty-ninth Street, which provides food and assistance to the elderly, poor, and homeless of New York's Times Square and theater districts. McDaniels, an elderly man helped by Encore, referred to himself as a "major minor poet" and addressed one of his poems to von Rydingsvard: "Ursula: Upon Harness of Her Strength." *For Weston* commemorates the poet's death, while marking the beginning of von Rydingsvard's practice of suggestively naming sculptures after people who are close to her and influential for her work. The seven forms of the piece employ a number with biblical resonance and also allude to the number of children in the Karoliszyn family. The number seven reappears with an almost obsessive regularity in von Rydingsvard's art.

Apart from group shows, such as the "Indoor-Outdoor Exhibition," in the late 1970s and early 1980s von Rydingsvard had seven major individual shows in New York: three at 55 Mercer, one at the Robert Freidus gallery, two at Rosa Esman, and one at Bette Stoler. These shows generated a number of favorable but still circumspect reviews.[22]

As for many sculptors of her generation, outdoor, often site-specific sculpture has been a crucial aspect of von Rydingsvard's work, beginning in the late 1970s. This involvement serves as a reminder not only of her early interest in Earth art, but also of her participation in what Alloway calls the third stage of earthworks "linked to the sphere of play and leisure," following the earlier large-scale works by Robert Smithson, Michael Heizer, and Walter De Maria that were located in remote places, often isolated from the social sphere.[23] Commenting on the side effects of the "plein-air surge" in the 1970s, critic Sarah McFadden connects it to the growing number of institutions and programs involved with such works: from the federal government-sponsored Art and Architecture program to museums with sculpture gardens and not-for-profit arts organizations that specialized in finding sites for outdoor exhibitions.[24] Von Rydingsvard's sculptures appeared in a number of these important "peripheral" outdoor shows, which took place outside what was then considered the centers of artistic activity.

The artist's interest in Smithson's earthworks was far reaching. Not only was von Rydingsvard indebted to the author of the famous *Spiral Jetty* (1970, Great Salt Lake, Utah) in the realm of site specificity, he also helped her to approach art as a simile of the human condition equipped with a particular kind of mobility.

Page from the artist's journal, March 1986.

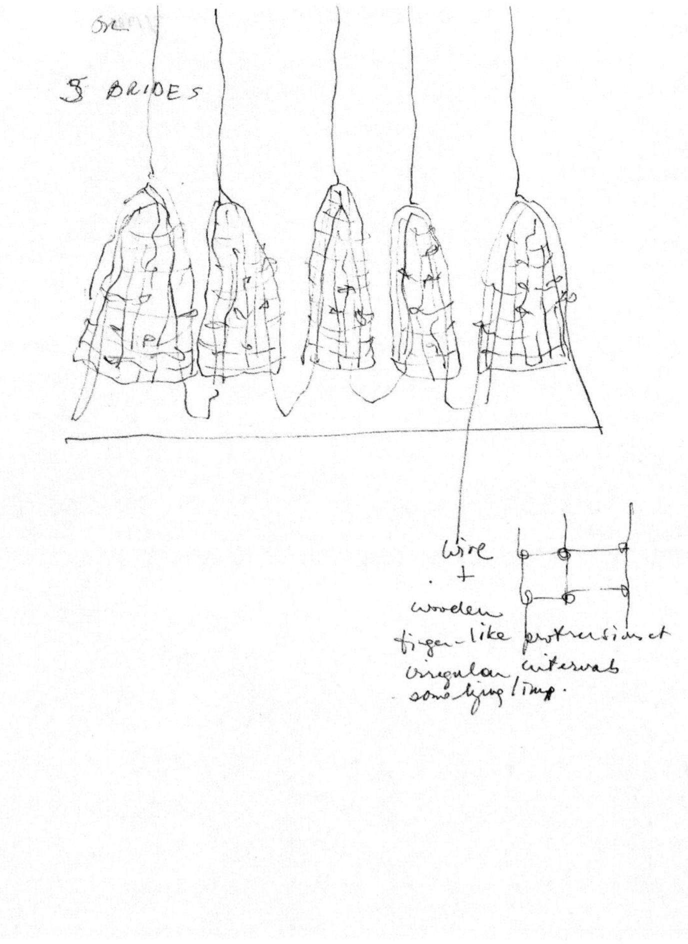

Associating art with the condition of displacement, von Rydingsvard followed Smithson in investing her work with inner exploration in conjunction with circumscribed sites. "You will always be faced with limits of some kind," Smithson once said. "There is no way you can really break down limitations; it's a kind of fantasy that you might have, that things are unlimited. . . . It doesn't matter where you are. So in a sense you are always expanding—the upper limits are always going out—like taking a larger and larger area or smaller and smaller area."[25] Indeed, in her site-specific projects von Rydingsvard has become involved with a specific type of artistic nomadism, which has served as a vehicle for the simulation of her own history. By actively connecting with her early displacement experience, neither denying its impact on her life nor politicizing it, von Rydingsvard has allowed herself to engage in a silent dialogue with her past.

In 1979 the artist made *Koszarawa* (destroyed), commissioned by the nonprofit institution Wave Hill in the Riverdale section of the Bronx and included in the outdoor exhibition "Wave Hill: The Artist's View." The exhibition took place on the grounds of Wave Hill's historic estate with some twenty-eight acres that have been transformed into a gigantic sculpture garden.[26] The 150-foot-long, 30-foot-wide, and approximately 2½-foot-high structure was made of five V-shaped forms that were composed of six interlocking oarlike elements. It had the presence of a semitransparent fence, a favored motif of many artists in the 1970s. While following the terrain, *Koszarawa* framed the manicured landscape. The work, whose title refers to the village in Poland where von Rydingsvard's mother was born, is a fantasy version of a "strength-in-weakness" structure, a structure that appears fragile, but at the same time serves to guard and protect. It is part sculpture, part architecture, and created from multiple ethnographic references as well as derived from the generic sculptural language of the late seventies.

Von Rydingsvard's insistence on creating semirustic forms from industrially processed materials might have resulted from realizing what critic Carter Ratcliff described in 1975 as the strong conditioning of drawing from other cultures: "We cannot make imaginative contact with non-Western or 'low' cultures except on terms provided by our own 'high culture.'"[27] In addition, that insistence might have been dictated by a decision to privilege a neutral vocabulary over a language that directly addresses current socio-political issues. Von Rydingsvard, whose art has distant roots in various folk cultures, would probably agree with H. J. A. Hofland, who writes in his essay for the 1991–92 "Wanderlieder" exhibition at the Stedelijk Museum in Amsterdam: "Every ideology—even when it evokes appearances to the contrary, even when for tactical considerations it is applied with folkloristic gimmicks—is the sworn enemy of the folk culture to which the Wanderlieder belong." [28]

Von Rydingsvard's next large environmental project, *Song of a Saint (Saint Eulalia),* 1979 (now dismantled), consisted of 180 12-foot-high vertical posts scattered over a 330-foot-long and 160-foot-wide area on a hillside. The piece was for a former chemical dump site located at the two-hundred-acre state-owned Artpark by the Niagara River Gorge, outside of Lewiston, New York. Organic vertical silver shapes (the wood turned silver due to exposure to the sun) with swollen "bellies" connote exotic buds, or—in the artist's more visceral description—"the thickening of a reed where there is an aberrant, round growth or a foamy mucus collection." [29] Although Artpark was once described by Barbara Baracks in *Artforum* as "a *paradis artificiel,* powered by political machinery geared to making the area's questionable status quo work," [30] von Rydingsvard expresses lack of interest in her work's political intent and voices the credo of symbiotic relationship with site that guides her entire artistic production. In a statement prepared for the Artpark project, the artist stresses a more sacred reading of her work:

> The sculpture creates a personal environment, a forest which can be seen from a distance, entered and wandered through. The sculpture is frontal as human bodies are and as architectural structures such as cathedrals are. The 180 modules of "Song of a Saint" face north giving the fragmented organic pod shapes laminated onto each of them optimal opportunity to take advantage of the light of the setting and rising sun. The regimented shadows of the beams stand more firmly and seriously. [31]

Around the time of working on *Song of a Saint,* von Rydingsvard wrote in her journal: "Time puts all back into an equilibrium, which is more in keeping with natural laws. I would like my work to be as though time acted on it—a very long time." [32] The artist named her work in Artpark after Federico García Lorca's poem "Song of a Saint," which refers to Saint Eulalia's suffering.

In 1980 *Saint Martin's Dream* was commissioned by Creative Time, another not-for-profit arts organization in New York, for the then uncompleted Battery Park City landfill in lower Manhattan. The work's site was a sandy ridge bordering the Hudson River. Following the configuration of the dune, von Rydingsvard's angular forms emerged from the sand, growing into fuller forms atop the dune, only to disappear in sand again. Arranged along an arching line, they mimicked the ridge's curvature. The piece once more connoted figurative associations, one of the most often mentioned being a flock of seagulls spreading wings in an attempt to detach themselves from the ground. Having problems with the piece's literary reading, the artist wrote: "Perhaps they do look much like seagulls. . . . Perhaps, too, my pieces need conditions which are specific for their survival—lighting conditions. That piece 'St. Martin's Dream' does look beautiful when the sun is setting or rising on it." [33]

According to the artist, the fact that the work's title refers to a saint holds little significance. The artist heard the name of the Academy of Saint Martin in the Fields Orchestra, and while listening to the music thought about Saint Martin dreaming in a field. But, as her journal reveals, von Rydingsvard, before giving the title to her work, studied closely Saint Martin's life. Naming her sculpture after a saint might, in fact, have to do with the artist's more general desire "to look at the people who surround me more abstractly."[34] Saints are, after all, often viewed as people with superhuman presence, but with "human scale for the human cry," as Barnett Newman would say.[35] By dematerializing the religious subject, while investing it with emotional qualities, von Rydingsvard indirectly followed, in fact, Newman's *Stations of the Cross,* 1958–66, which are often interpreted as the images that set standards for the abstract equivalents of artistic immaculate conception.

Von Rydingsvard's site-specific tour-de-force *Iggy's Pride,* 1990, is a monumental private commission for the Sonoma Valley ranch of Steven and Nancy Oliver. Looking for a "psychologically compatible place," the artist chose a site that she felt she "could sink into without loosing contact with the surrounding spectacular landscape." The sculpture consists of nine 17½-foot-long, 7-foot-high wooden wedges that touch each other in the back. They were placed into a cutout portion of the slope and boarded by concrete abutments on three sides, which prevent earth erosion. Due to their imposing presence, they can be seen from a great distance. Self-contained, heavy, impenetrable, they appear as bare geological formations, or perhaps as the "man-made islands" von Rydingsvard once wished to create.[36] Commenting on the work, the artist illuminates her approach to titling her sculptures:

> I had listed many titles that were possible, but none seemed right. It wasn't until I was on a plane returning to New York that I came up with the answer: *Iggy's Pride.* And I do know the source. It's my father. His name was Ignac. In the last years of his life, the staff at his nursing home called him Iggy. He was a man who understood concrete things, like floorboards, hinges on doors, beams.[37]

Recently von Rydingsvard elaborated on her statement, clarifying its reading:

> The Sonoma Valley piece is very concrete, but, more importantly, it has a spirituality that eases out of it gently. The name Iggy feels like a name used to call some kid next door one couldn't stand. In this title [*Iggy's Pride*], the word "Iggy" takes all the potency out of the name Ignac.

Von Rydingsvard herself feels that a close reading of her titles is unimportant. Nevertheless, her insistence upon choosing titles based on Polish words, or the names of friends and family members or of saints, is difficult to disregard. In titling her works this way, the artist seems to create her own code, which may be a way of expressing her need for safeguarding her status of an outsider by being equipped with a private language. With Polish titles, she also reenacts the practice of many immigrants of using their native language for private conversations. In referencing her works to her friends and family, the artist expresses the need for human ties and group solidarity with those close to her as a prerequisite for her survival. This bond is, however, a problematic aspect of von Rydingsvard's life, for it also involves certain tension with the rest of her family—"in order to separate, to be."

In 1988 von Rydingsvard was invited to participate in the group exhibition "Home Show: Ten Artists' Installations in Ten Santa Barbara Homes," organized by the Santa Barbara Contemporary Arts Forum (CAF), a nonprofit organization with a year-round program designed to promote contemporary art. The show, which was modeled on the 1986 exhibition "Chambres d'Amis" at the Museum of Contemporary Art in Ghent, Belgium, consisted of temporary installations created specifically for homes, or rather, *at* homes, thus moving beyond traditional modern exhibition space.[38] Von Rydingsvard chose a World War II bunker, built on the edge of a cliff for the purpose of surveying submarine activities. It was an unusual site for both a home and a "home show." The work had a more permanent character than any of the other installations in the show. It left no doubt as to which was the artist's creation and which the original house. As a result, one critic found the work "inappropriate" and "alien" to the exhibition, which he read as a postmodernist examination of the meaning of site specificity and the relationship between art and the viewer.[39] (Von Rydingsvard's refusal to overtly relate her works to current sociopolitical issues continues to unnerve her critics.) Instead of disrupting the living space, as most of the artists did, the artist reclaimed it by emptying the bunker of furniture and filling out the barren interior with her work. In a statement for the exhibition catalogue, von Rydingsvard disregarded the bunker's historic role and once again turned to a more sacred reading. She wrote:

> My first encounter with the view looking down from the World War II bunker in which I built the installation was one of awe. The Pacific Ocean washed the shore several hundred feet below. Apprehension followed in my trying to make a situation with any potency so close to the ocean. I was relieved that the bunker was a simple (single room 8 × 12 × 13 feet), intimate space stowed away in the highest part of the cliff. . . . I wanted the space to be a sanctuary, or a retreat, in which a kind of spirituality is touched on that is complemented by the sound of the waves.[40]

The piece's title, *Ursie A's Dream,* relates to von Rydingsvard's daughter's dream about walking through a row of confessional booths facing each other with open doors. As if to simulate the fatigue of a confession, the artist designed the booths to have the uncomfortable "height between altar and chair and a seat short in depth but normal width."[41] The sculpture is built of seven graphite-coated structures placed next to each other in a continuous form. Extended six feet high and thirteen feet wide, the work took over most of the back wall and the entire floor space, creating a claustrophobic feeling inside the bunker. As the photograph of the room prior to von Rydingsvard's installation reveals, the work parallels the position of a bed. The sanctuary-like interior indeed speaks of meditation; its quality of reverie evokes Etruscan tombs, arranged like houses with the dead presented as if asleep—to reassure the living as well as to maintain contact with the dead.

At the time of von Rydingsvard's 1988 exhibition at Exit Art, the gallery was providing individual shows to artists who the curators believed "had not received significant critical exposure or critical attention, despite having a solid body of work." Exhibitions were put together to illustrate "the hybrid state of contemporary art," perceived as a reflection of the nomadic experience of contemporary artists in sync with the current interest in exploring peripheral cultures.[42]

The Exit Art show established von Rydingsvard's reputation as an artist whose powerful, hard-labored art challenged the "anything goes" attitude of many artists in the eighties, while avoiding a return to the formal rigidity of Modernism. The critical response to the show confirmed that von Rydingsvard had found her unique place among contemporary American artists.[43]

The highlight of von Rydingsvard's show was the piece *Zakopane,* 1987, which attracted attention for its visual impact as well as for its enigmatic title. Zakopane, the name of a small town in the Tatra Mountains in the southeastern part of Poland (visited by the artist during her Polish trips), derives from the word "zakopać," which means hiding something in a ditch, covering it with earth.[44] Von Rydingsvard cites the image of pious women praying in the refugee camps as the piece's conceptual model.[45] The solemn structure, with its back to the wall, laminated and painted with whitewash, has an altarlike presence. Both accessible and private, it invites the viewer to dip a hand into the elongated vessels that line the sculpture's bottom, perhaps acting as simplified holy-water fonts (rather than as urinals—as one critic has recent ly suggested).[46] At the same time, access is discouraged by spiky beams that protrude from the top of the sculpture like barbed wire atop a prison or refugee-camp wall.

The visual impact of *Zakopane* is matched by *Dreadful Sorry,* 1987–88, and *Untitled (Seven Mountains),* 1986–87, both of which were in the Exit Art exhibition. *Dreadful Sorry* is von Rydingsvard's visualization of an act of suspended violence, in the process of happening but frozen in time. The work consists of five gigantic knives with whitewashed tops arranged as if on a kitchen rack, which has been "put up—after cutting straight," as the artist somewhat enigmatically describes it.[47] This work is elegant, yet also morbid and menacing, domesticated but brutal. The knives' shapes are echoed by carvings on the background wall, in a staged drama of action and reaction. *Untitled (Seven Mountains)* takes on a more Gothic presence, while retaining its archaizing rustic quality. The seven pyramidal forms look like small huts that achieve their apex some five feet above the ground with spectacular dignity. Von Rydingsvard shaped their tops like necks—"to resemble Brancusi's 'cock curve.'"[48] Dealing with the issue of how much she should reveal and how much conceal in her art, the artist wrote next to the preliminary sketches for *Untitled (Seven Mountains):* "somehow make them more inaccessible with layers over them or layers between them and the viewer."[49]

The Exit Art exhibition illuminated an important aspect of von Rydingsvard's work: her interest in the funerary and eschatological. *Umarles (you went and died),* 1987–88, is made of nine vertically placed rectangular boxes with gouged-out centers—6½ feet high, 11 feet wide, and 1 foot deep—combined in a freestanding vertical structure. The back of the sculpture is worked in a manner that evokes leather tanning. *Umarles* shares a coffinlike form with *Untitled (Felt Box),* 1986, which is a single coffer (2 × 4½ × 2 feet) with felt headrests. (While working on this piece, von Rydingsvard quoted Jean-Paul Sartre in her journal: "Peace came on velvet pads at nightfall in this great dark box, peace and the dead years."[50] She omitted the end of the sentence: "it was almost possible to believe that they had loved their lives."[51]) The work was later reincarnated in *Untitled (45 Tubs),* 1988–89, a site-specific installation of forty-five cedar chambers, each 23¼ × 53 × 21 inches, placed on a small clearing in a wooded area of Laumeier Sculpture Park in Saint Louis, Missouri. With reference to coffins or sarcophagi, these wooden tubs are almost rough hewn outside and expressively carved and patterned inside. Despite the claustrophobic aspect of the inner spaces, they generate warmth, suggesting places where one might crawl for security even at the price of physical discomfort. Next to one of her many journal sketches of the form, von Rydingsvard wrote: "It grows as though at least partially it is determining its own destiny."[52] Asked in 1985 about the cavernlike character of her numerous works, the artist responded:

> There is a dream that I have for a piece—that I've had for about a year and a half—of having a space that's a little smaller than my body—that feels as though there's a register on the surface as if somebody had just dug out a solid rectangle of wood through many, many years of effort. There are a number of these objects lined up next to one another. Visually, it's not a great thing to go on, but there is something very important to me about a space that's made as a result of the wearing down by time or human effort—by a hand or hand tool or by the elements, by the weather. I've had dreams of making spaces like a number of these cubicles and inside there would be marks while the outsides would be relatively neutral.[53]

Coinciding with the death of von Rydingsvard's father, *Umarles (you went and died)* has a title that employs the Polish verb "umierac" (to die) in the second person, its reflective quality somewhat colored by resignation with a tinge of the accusative tone. With its nine elongated coffinlike forms combined in one wall-like structure, it is von Rydingsvard's "do widzenia dziewięc razy" (nine times good-by).[54] The piece is an outstanding example of a memento mori that denies death by giving voice to both the deceased father and the mourning family. Suggesting a form of private devotion, the work touches upon von Rydingsvard's view of religion and death. During her 1987 trip to Italy the artist wrote:

> In some ways, I am glad I was brought up under my religion—the Catholic religion—during a time when it seemed my life depended on my embracing it so totally—really there was nothing else to embrace and it might have even been a matter of life or death for me to do that.[55]

More recently, she concluded:

> Religion had a tremendous hold on me at one time, to the degree that the goal of my life was to play with the rules of the Catholic Church and become a saint. . . . Today religion does not control my thinking any longer. But religious ceremonies still intrigue me, although they are from a vast range of religions. . . . As far as death is concerned, it is a deadline against which I bump myself every day. It's a real time limit, of my time, and I want to make sure that I do what I have to do before it comes. My works are not directly about death. When I worked on *Umarles,* I did not think about death. Instead, I thought about something being taken away from you, before you have a chance to figure out what you want to do. It is more about a feeling of incompleteness.

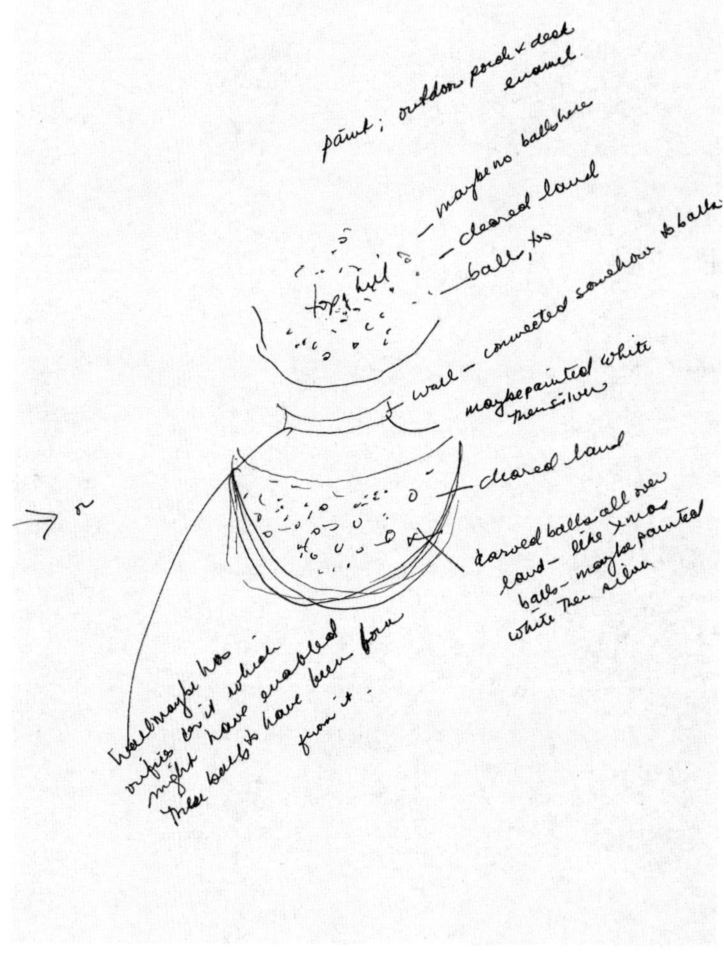

Page from the artist's journal, January 1987.

Page from the artist's journal, May 1994.

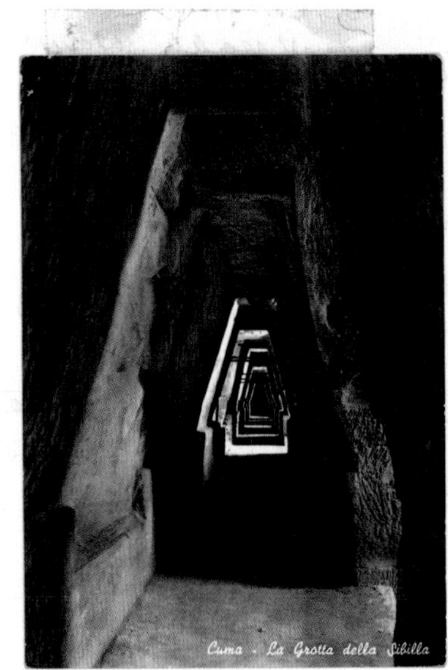

This is the image I looked at the night (just) before going to sleep & the chambers were small – irregularly rectangular, Thick walled & of heavy material like stone (painted on inside or cement.

By the time of her exhibition at Exit Art, von Rydingsvard's artistic vocabulary had undergone changes, taking a firmer direction toward unrefined spontaneity without losing its identifiable original character. As the artist became less hesitant in her use of tools, she was able to translate her anxiety into the working process by further relying on chance, or what she calls "the hazard of the self," which she considers a crucial force for her successful artistic production. Her carved striations achieved rhythmic, angry intensity as if executed in an act of violence. She also began to cover her works with rubbed-in graphite, an organic material that rather paradoxically allows her to downplay the natural aspect of the wood. While leaving a certain degree of transparency, the drab black-brown color gives her sculptures the edge of decay, or—as the artist describes it—"decomposition of an airy sort which has some life & vulnerability to it."[56] Von Rydingsvard continues, however, to explore familiar motifs derived from common farm tools, domestic implements, and vernacular architecture, and to approach them with the emphatically mechanical concerns of Minimalism.

While increasingly showing her works in museums and commercial galleries, von Rydingsvard continues to exhibit in nonprofit spaces. During a six-week residency at San Francisco's Capp Street Project in the winter of 1990, the artist built a large floor piece. It was laid out in a concrete garage that had been constructed in 1926 and was previously an auto detailing shop under the name Auto-Visual Techniques (AVT). The piece, untitled at the time, is a forty-three-foot-long visual fugue consisting of ninety-eight cuplike forms carved, chiseled, and finished with rubbed-in graphite and patterned in an irregular honeycomb configuration. Six layers of cedar beams were doweled and glued together into a solid platform structure. Covering almost the entire floor of the garage/gallery, the work left minimum space for walking around it, forcing the viewer to experience the sculpture as a restrictive place, best viewed from a balcony surrounding the room. It suggested a transcription of a natural place, in which, the artist wrote, "the earth opened itself up and revealed in a small rectangular section its most vulnerable parts."[57] In a statement provided for the Capp Street Project, von Rydingsvard digresses in a metaphorically veiled way:

> I recall in 1977 once seeing a moving maze of tiny insects surrounding a round rock. I recall an easy movement of separation and linkages that felt like the movement of the surface of the ocean. It wasn't possible to hold on or to keep track of its organic destination or even its parameters. With some force and determination it became possible to impose many kinds of orders, though they always felt too simplistic and really like lies as they cut out all the complexities and summarized them in a highly prejudiced or idealized way. This prejudiced summary of what I see perhaps has something to do with the particular style with which I make my images. I anchor heavily then on that which I understand and unconsciously fudge or let go of that which I don't.[58]

Two years later von Rydingsvard gave the Capp Street piece a more suggestive title—*Ene, Due, Rabe*[59]—and included it in the 1992–93 retrospective at the Storm King Art Center in Mountainville, New York.[60] Apart from its aspect of prestige, the exhibition was significant for two works specially produced for the location: *For Paul* and *Land Rollers*.

Land Rollers, next to *Ene, Due, Rabe,* is von Rydingsvard's attempt to create a horizontal sculpture that enters into a symbiotic relationship with the surrounding land. It was placed on the edge of a lawn, ending before the terrain begins to slope. Made of seventeen logs shaped from doweled and glued beams, positioned on a pair of wooden rails, the sculpture looks like a fragment of a fantastic ancient tract. Each log is calligraphically carved with looping grooves. Lined up with a colonnade of trees in the distance and suspended, as if about to tumble down, *Land Rollers* comes as close to whimsy as von Rydingsvard allows her sculptures to be.

With *For Paul* von Rydingsvard returned to one of her emblematic forms: an elongated, massive cylindrical shape. This monumental, robust sculpture, measuring roughly fourteen by fourteen by nine feet, looks like a gouged-out rock formation with an expressively hacked surface that shows an additional expressive level when placed outdoors, modeled by the natural effects of light and shade. The imposing structure generates a sense of seriousness, permanence, and equilibrium. It alludes to function while being obsolete. Although the richly sculpted exterior is all the eye can see, von Rydingsvard insists on the difference between the inside and the outside (absence and presence) despite the fact that the former is often invisible: "I have to be sure the inside is different from the outside," she noted next to a preliminary drawing.[61] The work has an elaborate twelve-chambered interior. *For Paul,* in fact, appears to have a supernatural dimension and suggests metaphysical power. Furthermore, sculpture's "primal domesticity" (to use Martin Friedman's expression)[62] conjures taut psychological resonance. One could argue that viewing this work is like putting oneself in the position of a child reconstructing his/her identity, mesmerized and frightened by the sculpture's coming to life, witnessing the process of merging reality with illusion, fears with fairy tales, transmuted into one.

In the same year that her retrospective opened at the Storm King Art Center and *Zygmunt* was installed at Cultural Space/The Laboratory in New York (a collaborative project with Judy Pfaff, accompanied by a performance by First World/El Primer Mundo, *Zygmunt* is another robust horizontal piece, with a bedlike presence, made of expressively hacked cedar), von Rydingsvard's works were put to a special test at the Center for

Page from the artist's journal, December 1995.

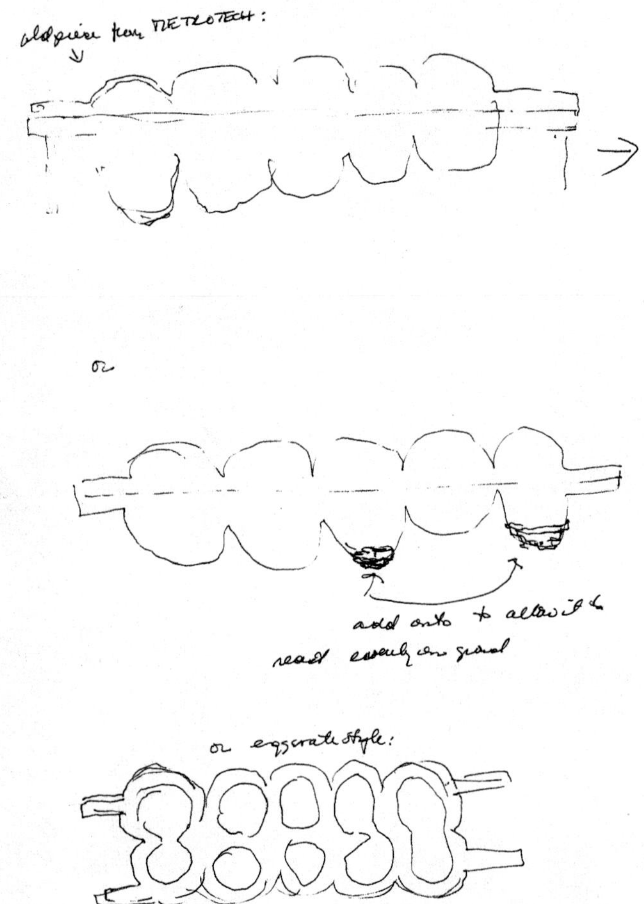

Contemporary Art in Warsaw. Although many of the artist's most important works were at the Storm King exhibition, nevertheless the show in Poland was enthusiastically received. It confirmed that though von Rydingsvard's artistic vocabulary does not have a Polish equivalent (neither in contemporary nor in past Polish art), she shares with many Polish artists (Magdalena Abakanowicz, Józef Szajna, Grzegorz Kowalski, Jacek Sempoliński, to name just a few) the need to anchor her art in the daunting memories of the World War II experience and its postwar psychological consequences, as both an important personal reference and a signpost historic event. Instead of directly alluding to the threat of destruction, or to the spirit of survival, these artists avoid direct translation of the past and connect their work to the Northern Romantic tradition of isolation of the individual in the nature, as a transhistorical way of encompassing both art and life and focusing on the darker psychological implications of art making in relation to the inner self.

Although von Rydingsvard is mostly known for her large indoor and outdoor sculptures, which with great ease take over the given space, as they did at San Francisco's Capp Street Project and in Warsaw, she has also proven that scale is not content in her work. Her small works (or rather, smaller works, for von Rydingsvard's sculptures are usually quite large in size) are like the entries in her journal: reflective statements, endowed with tenderness. They have the quality of found, "poetically humble" objects,[63] half-banal, half-totemic. They are eccentric and yet familiar, self-contained as if they belong to a private, fantastic universe-unto-itself—individual and independent.

These smaller, often single-form works elucidate von Rydingsvard's involvement with sculpture, which is informed by a set of complex, contradictory desires. She wants her works to look both industrial and organic. Interested in the coexistence of rational and irrational, the artist celebrates the monumentality of the everyday and inserts order into a stream-of-consciousness mode of expression. Von Rydingsvard emphasizes the ethos of work and subordination of "real objects" to her activity while insisting on being vulnerable. Searching for a visual sincerity that would allow her "to be anxious though quite in control"[64] (a sine qua non for her entire artistic production), the artist emphasizes the importance of craftsmanship, material, and the physical labor involved in her work. She incorporates her biography while insisting on being grounded in contemporary experience. Positioning her sculptures at the midpoint between metaphor and concreteness, she deliberately multiplies narrative possibilities through a *va-et-vient* of memory and action.

This practice is perhaps best illustrated by *Berek,* 1994, a recent work in which von Rydingsvard returns, via its title, to her childhood experience. *Berek* is a wall piece that looks like an awkward appendage with an exposed interior, extending off the wall like an organic yet deviant growth. The piece's title refers to the Polish name for tag, the popular game that is one of the few the artist remembers from her childhood. Thus here once again von Rydingsvard links the present to the past. But since the artist wishes her sculpture to be devoid of any specific reference to a place, person, or event,[65] the piece is also a finished artifice divorced from von Rydingsvard's personal story. During her 1990 trip to Poland the artist, seemingly thinking about the relationship between her art and her life, wrote:

> First day in Warsaw: I do not know what it is I really want from this trip. I keep shying away from the smart and intellectual. I am almost afraid that what I'm looking for is the human equivalent to my bowls, shovels—that is peasant, earth working types much like my parents but kinder. The object version of what I want I have considerably near figured out; the human version is not as clear.[66]

NOTES

If not otherwise indicated, quotations are from telephone conversations that I had with the artist on February 27, March 3, 7, 10, 15, and April 3, 1995.

I wish to thank Dore Ashton, Martin Friedman, and Michael Brenson for their important suggestions concerning von Rydingsvard's work; Rose-Carol Washton Long of CUNY Graduate Center for her warm interest in my essay; Jeanette Ingberman and Papo Colo of Exit Art, Mary Sabbatino of Galerie Lelong, Beej Nierengarten of Laumeier Sculpture Park, and the people at 55 Mercer for providing me with information about von Rydingsvard's shows; artists Michael Mulhern and Sylvia Netzer for sharing with me their memories of their school years at Columbia University; Susan Livingston for helping me with research at the Plainville Public Library; Sr. Elizabeth Hasselt for the information about Encore Community Services; and Julie Lasky, Deborah Frizzell, Claire Grandpierre, and Jamie Klainbaum for early editorial advice. Finally, I thank Ursula von Rydingsvard, who generously shared with me her journals, documents, and books, and the Polish critic Wiesława Wierzchowska, who first suggested the idea of a monograph on von Rydingsvard.

1. ". . . in Poland, that is to say, nowhere"; said in the introduction to the first performance, in Paris, of Alfred Jarry's *Ubu Roi,* 1896 (Alfred Jarry, *Oeuvres complètes* (Paris: Gallimard, 1972), 401.

2. Journal, December 1984–September 1985. Since 1973 von Rydingsvard has been keeping journals, which now consist of some forty large notebooks. Many of the entries are undated; these are cited by the inclusive dates given to the particular notebook.

3. Early dates in the artist's biography and the trajectory of the Karoliszyns during and after World War II (prior to their arrival in the United States) differ in various articles and catalogue essays devoted to von Rydingsvard's work. The present data, provided by the artist, is based on the recollections of her parents, her uncle Stanley Sternal, and her sister Jessica Hunt. The artist's father died in 1989, at the age of seventy-six. Her mother, now eighty-four, still lives in Plainville, Connecticut, where she has lived since she first came to America.

4. Journal, February 1981.

5. Interview with Judy Collischan Van Wagner in Zimmer and Van Wagner, *Judith Murray: Painting,*

Ursula von Rydingsvard: Sculpture, exh. cat. (Brookville, N.Y.: Hillwood Art Gallery, Long Island University, 1985), 44. In another interview the artist said: "I grew up in a situation where words did not count a lot. My parents were more or less illiterate. Spoken words were usually connected to basic existence. So the environment and objects were more my reality. I was tremendously attached to objects like butter tubs or washboards, wooden spoons and shovels—objects that had nothing to do with machinery and everything to do with the hand. Many of the buildings were very basic, built by the soldiers, often of a raw wood" (Marsha Miro, "Vulnerability and Ritual Live in Cedar Forms," *Detroit Free Press,* February 12, 1989, 3C).

6. Quoted in Michael Brenson, "Sculptural Theater," in *Ursula von Rydingsvard: Sculpture,* exh. cat. (Mountainville, N.Y.: Storm King Art Center, 1992), 28.

7. "Family of Nine Arrives Here from Germany," *Plainville News* 6, no. 3 (January 19, 1951), 1.

8. She calls her move to New York City "the new beginning." She had just divorced her first husband, Milton von Rydingsvard, a physician, with whom she has a daughter, Ursula Ann. In 1985 von Rydingsvard married Paul Greengard, a neuroscientist.

9. Unpublished artist's statement provided for the exhibition "Visions of America: Landscape as Metaphor in the Late Twentieth Century," held at the Denver Art Museum and the Columbus Museum of Art in 1994.

10. Journal, August 26, 1974.

11. Journal, January–September 1974.

12. Ibid.

13. Statement provided by the artist, July 28, 1995.

14. Journal, May 1975–January 1976.

15. Quoted in "A Rich, Redemptive Journey: Interview by Jill Viney," *Sculpture* 8, no. 8 (November–December 1989): 32–35. In another interview von Rydingsvard stated: "The parts that felt to me negative were things like the tremendous elegance with which they did their work. There was a kind of superiority, almost an elitism, about their imagery and almost a kind of cleanliness and antiseptic feel in their ideology. Antiseptic even to feelings . . . how contained it was, how sure of itself it was, and life feels very different. For me the most critical thing is that psychologically they feel hollow, emotionally they feel hollow. There's a feeling I get that they're so in control, and I don't believe it" (Brenson, "Sculptural Theater," 34).

16. Van Wagner, *Ursula von Rydingsvard: Sculpture,* 45.

17. Ibid., 43.

18. Clement Greenberg, "Recentness of Sculpture," in *American Sculpture in the Sixties,* exh. cat. (Los Angeles: Los Angeles County Museum of Art and Philadelphia Museum of Art, 1967), 24.

19. Ursula von Rydingsvard, "Thoughts about My Work," *Journal of Artists* 6 (Spring 1986): 46. Other women sculptors visible in the 1970s with whom von Rydingsvard's work can be connected are Jackie Winsor, Mary Miss, Jackie Ferrara, and Alice Aycock.

20. Lawrence Alloway, "Women's Art in the '70s," *Art in America* 64, no. 3 (May–June 1976): 64–72. The rather typical impulse of many female artists not to be closely associated with other women artists might in von Rydingsvard's case have personal overtones. Referring to her participation in the 1987 "Works by Women" National Sculpture Conference in Cincinnati, Ohio, she wrote: "What I felt today, I last time felt during my CETA [Comprehensive Employment Training Act, Title 6] days. A depressing congregation of a great number of artists, except there were all women. All seemed like lost artists. The air seemed filled with what I am so afraid of—a kind of pathos. I am always afraid that my pieces have it. I am afraid, too, that I have it in me as well" (Journal, May 10, 1987).

21. Journal, March 8, 1991.

22. Reviewing the first show at the Rosa Esman Gallery, Grace Glueck, in the *New York Times,* while wondering whether von Rydingsvard's *Stations for Santa Clara,* 1981, were designed to focus our attention on the wood or on the form ("matter over mind"), concluded that "they succeed handsomely" ("Ursula von Rydingsvard," *New York Times,* November 5, 1982, C18). William Zimmer, in the *Art Gallery Scene,* commented in relation to the same exhibition: "It's always a mystery to me how she achieves such an emotional pitch by such maneuvers as a seemingly casual stacking of lumpish forms in one bay" ("Von Rydingsvard at Rosa Esman," *Art Gallery Scene,*

November 16, 1982, 26). Susan Harris, in *Arts Magazine,* noted: "The pieces work on both formal and psychological levels," with some replete with the "emotional repercussions of personal experience" ("Ursula von Rydingsvard," *Arts Magazine* 57, no. 4 [December 1982]: 46).

Reviews of the early shows confirmed the slowly but steadily growing interest in von Rydingsvard's sculpture. By the early 1980s her work had attracted the critical attention of John Russell of the *New York Times,* who called von Rydingsvard "one of the best young sculptors around" ("Invitational Exhibition at Rosa Esman Gallery," *New York Times,* June 27, 1980, C24) and referred to her as an artist with a particular place among living sculptors in wood who "can work on a very large scale in the open air, and . . . also make house pieces" ("Ursula von Rydingsvard [Rosa Esman Gallery . . .]," *New York Times,* April 3, 1981, C23). Harold Olejarz in *Arts Magazine,* commenting on her *Wind Catchers,* 1978 (cedar, 32 × 132 × 48 inches; collection of Stanley Karoliszyn), exhibited at the Robert Freidus Gallery, was impressed by von Rydingsvard's "personal synthesis of minimalism and primitivism" ("Ursula von Rydingsvard," *Arts Magazine* 53, no. 5 [January 1979]: 17). Referring to *Untitled,* 1976 (cedar, 29 × 26 × 96 inches; destroyed), Lucy Lippard wrote in *Art in America:* "Ursula von Rydingsvard's untitled studio work in which a crowd of rounded posts, originally meant to huddle together at the end of a stark, low corridor, are transposed to the outdoor vastness quite successfully" ("'Wood' at the Nassau County Museum," *Art in America* 65, no. 6 [November–December 1977]: 136–37).

23. Lawrence Alloway, "Public Sculpture for Post-Heroic Age," *Art in America* 67, no. 6 (October 1979): 9–11.

24. Sarah McFadden, "Going Places, Part II: The Outside Story," *Art in America* 68, no. 6 (June 1980): 51–61.

25. Said at the symposium "Earth" at the Andrew Dickson White Museum of Art, Cornell University, 1970, in *Writings of Robert Smithson,* ed. Nancy Holt (New York: New York University Press, 1979), 164–65.

26. The exhibition, curated by Linda Macklowe and Suzanne Randolph, included sculpture by Alice Adams, Siah Armajani, Donna Byars, Tom Doyle, Robert Lobe, Roelof Louw, Martin Puryear, Ned Smyth, John Willenbecher, and von Rydingsvard.

27. Carter Ratcliff, "On Contemporary Primitivism," *Artforum* 14, no. 3 (November 1975): 64.

28. H. J. A. Hofland, "A Skeptical Voice," in *Wanderlieder,* exh. cat. (Amsterdam: Stedelijk Museum, 1991), 8.

29. Unpublished artist's statement provided for the exhibition "Visions of America: Landscape as Metaphor in the Late Twentieth Century," held at the Denver Art Museum and the Columbus Museum of Art in 1994.

30. Barbara Baracks, "Artpark: The New Esthetics Playground," *Artforum* 15, no. 3 (November 1976): 29.

31. The artist's statement, 1979 (unpublished), provided to Artpark for the project.

32. Journal, May–September 1980.

33. Journal, June 14, 1980.

34. Journal, January–December 1984.

35. Thomas B. Hess, "The Stations of the Cross," in *Barnett Newman* (New York: Museum of Modern Art, 1971), 100.

36. Journal, July 3, 1986.

37. Quoted in Paul Gardner, "Do Titles Really Matter?" *Artnews* 91, no. 2 (February 1992): 97.

38. Artists who participated in the show were Kate Ericson and Mel Ziegler, Ann Hamilton, Lisa Hein, David Ireland, Jim Isermann, Joseph Kosuth, Erica Rothenberg, Norie Sato, Ilene Segalove, and von Rydingsvard.

39. Referring to the piece *Celebrity Stimulator* by the Los Angeles artist Erica Rothenberg, Ron Graziani wrote in *Santa Barbara Magazine:* "Rothenberg notes a growing convergence between the public and private sectors; with this installation she seems to be saying that the public sector is winning. Although she is able to give public—or advertising—imagery a new bite, her method of communicating with a streamlined smoothness depends on selling an artificial construction that denies the awkwardness in the real world. Postmodern images often buy into this premise and rarely work with an object's materiality—the objects are merely placed, not shaped. What is often left out or repressed in the marketing or packaging of a product is concern for the object itself." Then he comments on von Rydingsvard's work: "It was this concern for individual objects that made the piece by the New York artist

Ursula von Rydingsvard worthwhile despite its inappropriateness to the theme of the show. . . . The mere fact that she worked the wood with such confidence made this piece the most traditional and alien project in the show. The image had a certain academic look; it was almost Cézanne-like in workmanship" (Ron Graziani, "The Home Show: Public Art in Private Places," *Santa Barbara Magazine* 14 [November 1988]: 58).

Later, Robert Mahoney, reviewing von Rydingsvard's 1990 show at Lorence Monk, complained that she "has responded with a bit too much assumption (religiously speaking) in her heart to the clean light and cleaner flooring of Lorence Monk SoHo Valhalla. The work looks very neat and clean here, all dressed up for the benefit of a museum" ("Ursula von Rydingsvard [Lorence Monk, March 3–31]," *Arts Magazine* 64 [Summer 1990]: 94). One could argue, however, that this concern about the work's symbiotic relationship with the commercial gallery and the museum in fact applies as much to contemporary art in general as to von Rydingsvard's work, for no matter how subversive it seems to be, at the end the artist always has to comply with the rules dictated by the institutionalized system of exhibiting.

40. Von Rydingsvard's statement in Dore Ashton, *Home Show: Ten Artists' Installations in Ten Santa Barbara Homes,* exh. cat. (Santa Barbara, Calif.: Santa Barbara Contemporary Arts Forum, 1988), 31.

41. Journal, August 1987–August 1988.

42. Interview with Jeanette Ingberman, Exit Art, March 14, 1995. The artists presented in Exit Art individual shows were later included in a group exhibition called "The Hybrid State" (November 2, 1991–January 25, 1992), curated by Ingberman and Papo Colo. Participating artists included, among others, Ida Applebroog, Jimmie Durham, Guillermo Gómez-Peña, David Hammonds, and Krzysztof Wodiczko.

43. In the late 1980s critics responded to von Rydingsvard's art in a more attentive way than they had previously. William Zimmer in *Sculpture* wrote: "With the sculptures of Ursula von Rydingsvard we always see the blood, sweat and tears. But in conjunction with the evident toil we get memorable shapes of great poise and elegance. Her recent exhibition at Exit Art offers these qualities in spades, not only with large works of repeating elements, but in several smaller, single images as well" ("Ursula von Rydingsvard, Exit Art, New York City," *Sculpture* 7, no. 4 [July– August 1988]: 26). Michael Brenson found von Rydingsvard's reliefs "the least successful" but called *Untitled (Seven Mountains)* "as menacing and enchanted as a Central European fairy tale" ("Setting Free in Images in Big Beams of Wood," *New York Times,* April 1, 1988, C32). The review of the Exit Art show in *New York Magazine* concluded: "A decade ago, everybody (it seemed) was hacking away at wood. It's not what the artist does, it's what she makes of it. Von Rydingsvard took many years to merge her instincts with her control of technique. The medium doesn't offer much latitude of expression, but she has made it her own by finding a private link with the past" (Kay Larson, "Ursula von Rydingsvard," *New York Magazine* 21, no. 19 [May 9, 1988]: 81). Avis Berman in *Artnews* observed: "Von Rydingsvard has plainly earned the right to an art unsparing in its expression of trauma, an art that bluntly exposes raw nerves. Yet her sculptures, while brooding and somber, are oddly domestic and comforting—haunting rather than despairing, stoic rather than sentimental. It is her discovery of stability amid uncertainty and misery, and her presentation of structures that speak more of sanctuaries, hearths, and plows than of tombs and torture chambers, that make von Rydingsvard's sculpture so compelling" ("Ursula von Rydingsvard: Life under Siege," *Artnews* 87, no. 10 [December 1988]: 97–98).

Although a few reviewers (see Mahoney, "Ursula von Rydingsvard [Lorence Monk, March 3–31]") have been critical of von Rydingsvard's work, the response has been overwhelmingly favorable. Eric Gibson's "Decade in Review" is typical. Calling the 1980s the decade of "Beuys and Koons," when "the utopian assumptions of the public art establishment were brought sharply down to earth," Gibson called von Rydingsvard a sculptor who "remained within a recognizable tradition but used it creatively" to produce "original variations on traditional methods of carving and modeling" (*Sculpture* 8, no. 3 [May–June 1989]: 21, 23).

44. My definition of "zakopać" is based on *Słownik języka polskiego,* vol. 3 (r–z), ed. Mieczysław Szymczak (Warsaw: Państwowe Wydawnictwo Naukowe, 1981), 913.

45. Von Rydingsvard also links this work with a more recent experience: "For me, Zakopane has conceptual and emotional connections with a search I just carried out [in 1989] through the

northern parts of Poland to find people who still sing the oldest folk songs known to that region of the country. I felt as though, through hearing these songs, a gift was given to me with earnestness and simplicity, a gift describing the person singing, his or her history and that part of the physical world with its never ending forests and their echoes, and a culture where intimacies within a family unit count for so much. The songs' themes of love, yearning and harvest are repeatedly sung in rhythmic cadences; a kind of litany whose verbal phrases and tones are repeated over and over again, occurs" (artist's statement in John Yau, *Diverse Representations 1990,* exh. cat. [Morristown, N.J.: Morris Museum, 1990], 45).

46. Describing *Zakopane,* Peter Clothier wrote: "Here, the architectural suggestion is of a rough, labor camp dwelling, a long barn wall, or perhaps a row of chancery pews. Under its dark, protective overhang and its baffling row of thigh-high, primitively carved (are they mangers? or udders? Praying figures? Wombs heavy with pregnancy, or urinals? Baptismal fonts?) our role becomes that of habitation, utilization, or the fulfillment of some unspecified ritual" ("Ursula von Rydingsvard," *Artspace* 16, no. 5 [September–October 1992]: 59).

47. Journal, October 30, 1987.

48. Journal, August 27, 1990.

49. Journal, March 22, 1986.

50. Journal, September 1985–May 1986.

51. Jean-Paul Sartre, *Troubled Sleep,* trans. Gerard Hopkins (New York: Alfred A. Knopf, 1951), 342.

52. Journal, August 1987–August 1988.

53. Van Wagner, *Ursula von Rydingsvard: Sculpture,* 48.

54. Journal, September 1985–May 1986.

55. Journal, August 1987–August 1988.

56. Journal, March 9, 1985.

57. Journal, August 27, 1990.

58. David Levi Strauss, ed., *Capp Street Project 1989–1990,* exh. cat. (San Francisco: Capp Street Project/ AVT, 1991), 24.

59. "Ene, due, rabe" refers to a Polish children's rhyme, similar to the English "eeny, meeny, miney, mo."

60. Critical response to von Rydingsvard's retrospective was again favorable, largely confirming what had been stated previously about her art. Patricia C. Phillips in *Artforum* saw the artist's work in relation to "classical tradition, Modernist monumentality, and the accretive, additive, and movable art of today," and stated that "spanning both time and place, von Rydingsvard's sculpture is a tribute to the idea of work—both psychical and intellectual" ("Ursula von Rydingsvard: Storm King Art Center," *Artforum* 31, no. 1 [September 1992]: 101). In *Art in America,* David Levi Strauss complimented the artist for combining seeming contraries: "the geometric and the organic, the abstract and the representational, the formally rigorous and the emotionally expressive," resulting in a "balance between evocative and the literal" ("Sculpture as Refuge," *Art in America* 81, no. 2 [February 1993]: 89–92, 125). Vivian Raynor said of von Rydingsvard that "hers is labor intensive art delivered with tremendous conviction" and that "this 14-year survey contradicts its neo-ness by suggesting that a true sense of history comes from within and is not something to be acquired" ("Sculptures of Wood in a Wooden Setting," *New York Times,* September 20, 1992, C26). Commenting on von Rydingsvard's art, Peter Clothier found the artist's work related to the Central European landscape, which, unfortunately, he could compare only with its rather formulaic descriptions in Jerzy Kosinski's *Painted Bird* ("Ursula von Rydingsvard," *Artspace* 16 [Sept.–Oct. 1992], 58–59).

61. Journal, 1990.

62. Conversation with Martin Friedman, March 20, 1995.

63. Journal, September 1974.

64. Ibid.

65. Von Rydinsgvard once proclaimed: "Knowing a thing intellectually—either its name, exact psychical location, philosophical sources of its becoming or being what it is etc., is a cause for the dismissal of that object, event, or place" (Journal, 1990).

66. Ibid.

Matti Megged

INSIDE, OUTSIDE

In the spring of 1990 I visited the studio of Ursula von Rydingsvard to see her sculptures in the environment in which they grow, to witness the process of their being molded by the artist's hands. I could see several of the sculptures in various stages of development in a place that was natural for them to be in. Although they clearly demonstrated human scale, that they were made by human hands, I could not escape the sense that they were striving, even threatening, to break through the walls or the roof of the house. Even those sculptures whose forms alluded to their belonging inside the house—those that referred to a chair, a kitchen wall, a spoon, or a comb—demonstrated this dramatic aspiration to break out of their confinement. This sense of forceful growth, of expansion, was yet stronger when I looked at the larger sculptures that von Rydingsvard was working on at the time of my visit, such as the big cones that are taller than any human.

I don't know whether von Rydingsvard intends to endow her sculptures with this quality, this inclination to break out of their space, or if it is inevitable, caused by the mere force of their creation. This conflict between "inside" and "outside" manifests itself in all of von Rydingsvard's works, whether they are confined inside the walls of a room or are in an outdoor space, free of physical constraints.

I later discovered this inner drama at work in the opposite sense when I saw von Rydingsvard's sculptures out of doors at her 1992 retrospective at Storm King Art Center in Mountainville, New York. The works exhibited there—*Ene, Due, Rabe,* 1990; *Five Cones,* 1990–92; *For Paul,* 1990–92; *Land Rollers,* 1992; to name several—were larger than the ones I had seen in her studio. Not confined inside the walls of a house, they were apparently more free and did not immediately testify to the process of their making. They were objects, things that existed by their own force, seemingly comfortable in the natural landscape that surrounded them. Yet they demonstrated no less than the domesticated indoor objects the same dramatic conflict between inside and outside. They belonged to the open landscape, while they yearned for the inner landscape of the creative imagination, of the hands that made them.

This inner conflict, always present in von Rydingsvard's work, is manifested in various ways. At first sight *Land Rollers* resembles a group of railroad ties, unmoving on the ground, yielding to the force of gravity. But as one observes them, their power becomes apparent and it seems possible that they can release themselves from the law of gravity that binds them to the earth. At any moment they might move and roll off to the abyss, or possibly to confront the landscape that is all around them.

Like many of von Rydingsvard's sculptures, the elements of *Land Rollers* appear on the surface to resemble each other, to all be similar. They have an innate tendency toward rhythmical repetition, and yet they are different from each other. For each is engraved with the artist's personal handwriting, a sort of hieroglyphics, which endows them with a sense of mystery and allows them to speak about themselves, about the drama they contain, in a language known only to the artist.

This conflict between rhythmical, almost ritualistic repetition and the enigmatic uniqueness of each element of the piece is perhaps yet more obvious in *Five Cones.* At first glimpse the five cones appear to resemble one another, to repeat each other. Yet under longer observation the inner tension between the cones becomes apparent. At first the cones seem to be one solid body, as if the artist had cut them out of a single immense tree trunk. But each was actually modeled separately, and the hand or the will of the artist forces them to cling to one another. Thus the means of making the sculpture becomes essential to its meaning.

This is true also of *Untitled (Nine Cones),* 1977; *Untitled (Seven Mountains),* 1986–87; and *Three Bowls,* 1990. Each of these sculptures encompasses several seemingly similar elements, bonded together as a group, but with each piece bearing the mystery endowed on it by its creator, in her singular language. These sculp-

overleaf:
Von Rydingsvard's Brooklyn studio, 1995.

tures have a further layer of mystery hidden deep inside them. When one stands before the bowls and the cones, it is not possible to see what is inside them, just as the mountains yield no clue as to their interior spaces. Each one of these mountains seems to me as if it is pregnant, as if it covers the secrets of the cones and the bowls.

A sculpture that von Rydingsvard made in 1990 for the San Francisco Capp Street Project, now titled *Ene, Due, Rabe* after a Polish children's game, reminds me of sheep troughs. This work too embodies the conflict between the rhythmical repetition of shape and the unique character of each of the troughs. The handwriting of the artist on the walls of each trough conceals the meaning of these vast shapes, perhaps even to the artist herself. Again and again von Rydingsvard hints in her sculptures of the mysteries behind seeming sameness.

Also common to von Rydingsvard's oeuvre is that her objects, though integrated in the landscape, are never really part of it. *Song of a Saint (Saint Eulalia),* from 1979, for example, looks as if it is a row of artificial trees in a landscape. Again, there is the conflict between "inside"—in this case, inside nature—and "outside"—the alienation of humans from nature. The artist's love of nature is attested by her material, the wood of the cedar tree, yet she refuses, deliberately, I believe, to repeat or imitate the forms of nature.

In a similar vein, she refers to her childhood, to her family and to her roots in Poland, to the rites of the Catholic Church, always alluding to these experiences, but with few direct sources from them in her imagery. Some of the titles she assigns to her works evoke these memories, such as *Ignatz Comes Home* (her father's name was Ignacy); *Koszarawa* (after a town in Poland); *Oj Dana Oj Dana* (a Polish children's game); *Polish Wing; Umarles* (from the Polish verb "umierac," to die); and *Zakopane* (also a Polish town). But these titles are given as an afterthought and are not intended to tell a story or to explain the work. Rather, they evoke a store of memories, thereby providing a clue to the artist's creative process.

I believe I have found at least one of the keys to von Rydingsvard's story in her sculpture *Tunnels on the Levee,* 1983 (now destroyed), with its three tunnels that hint at graves or tombs or bunkers. Each one reveals and simultaneously conceals its secrets. The artist has referred to the notion of "contained anxiety" in these tunnels (conversation with the author, 1990). Likewise, one can see this "contained anxiety" in *16 Handrests,* 1984, which too might be a metaphor for a place of refuge or a sanctuary—in von Rydingsvard's words, "from a hardcore city feeling, a place into which a person could enter and quietly let go in a form of meditation." *Confessor's Chair,* 1989 (cedar and stain, 66 × 18 × 42 inches; collection of the artist), also may serve as a refuge, or a place for meditation. Its secret meaning is both closed and open, exposed to our eyes but hidden.

Von Rydingsvard has spoken about some of her sources, about her pilgrimage to Assisi, about returning to the environment of her childhood, about the inspiration she got from a poem by Lorca or from looking at Mexican clay huts. But in the end there is no need for answers to the questions "why" and "what for," or for the theories and speculations that follow such questions. The sculptures exist. They are present, real. They contain inside them the secrets of their maker's past, the history of their creation. But in spite of their mystery, or perhaps because of it, they allow us to participate in their presence, to be both inside and outside what we are viewing.

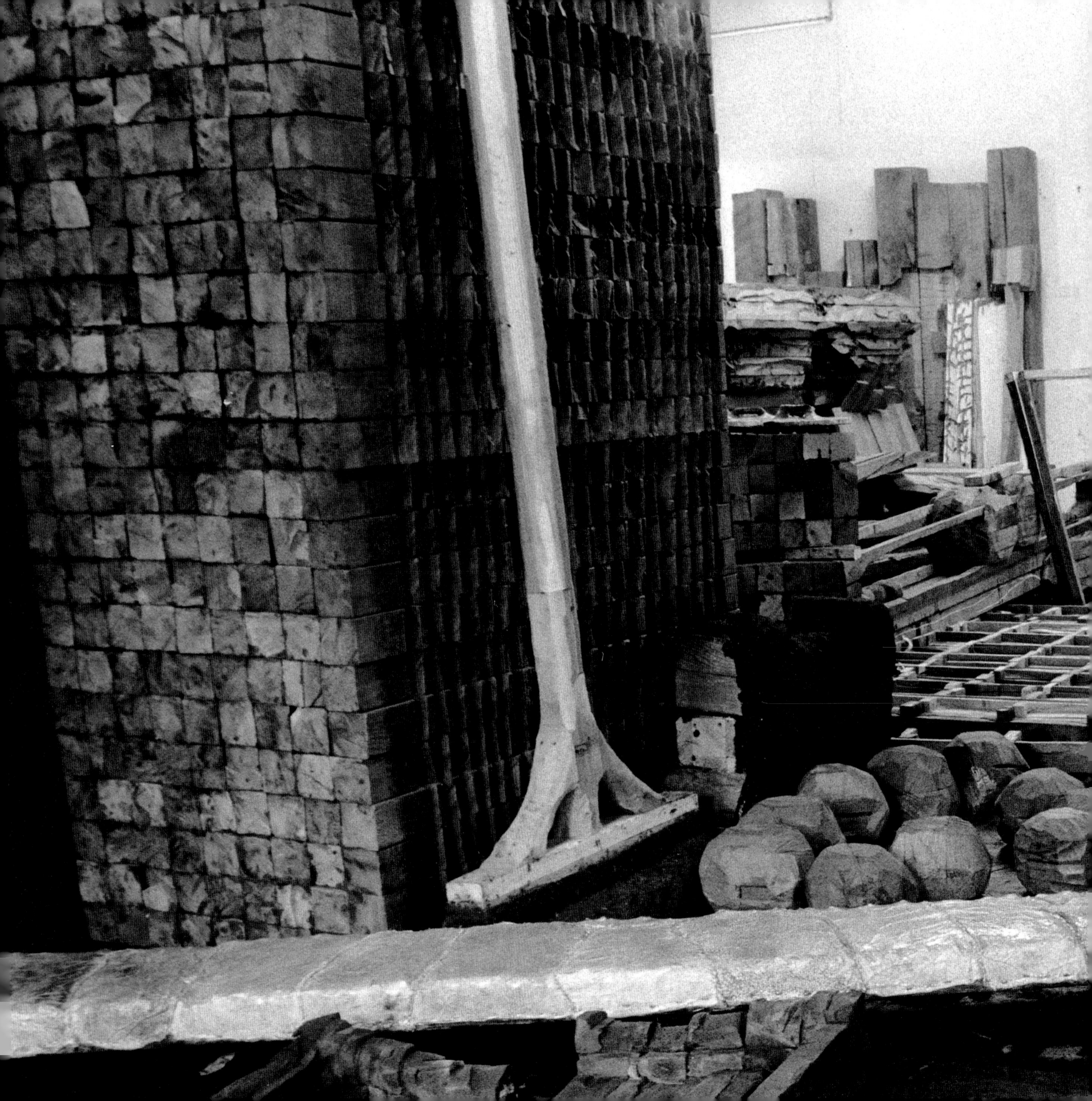

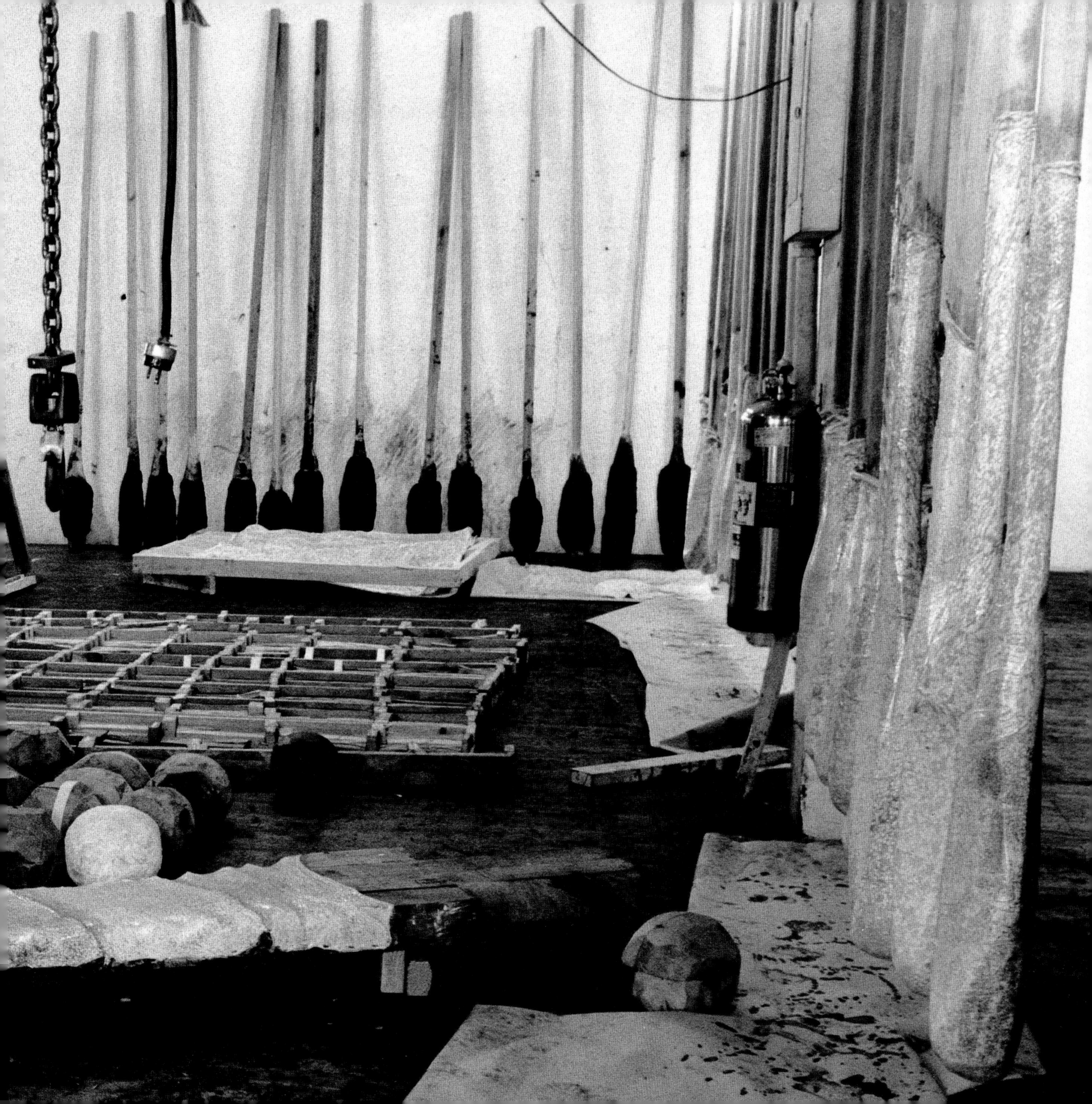

CHRONOLOGY

top:
The artist's family at Camp Seedorf, Seedorf, Germany, 1949.
From left: brother Henry, sister Christine, sister Jessica, mother Kunegunda holding brother Stanley, father Ignacy, brother Eugene, Ursula, brother John.

bottom:
The artist's family en route to the United States aboard the liner *General Bladford* in 1950.
From left, front row: brother John, sister Christine, Ursula; back row: uncle Stefan Haczka, sister Jessica, aunt Rose Haczka, mother Kunegunda, unidentified man.

1942: Ursula Karoliszyn born July 26 in Deensen, Germany, to Ignacy and Kunegunda (née Czarniecka-Sternal) Karoliszyn; she is the fifth of seven children.

1945–50: The Karoliszyns live in Germany in eight different post–World War II refugee camps for displaced Poles.

1950: The family emigrates to the United States; they travel from Bremerhaven to New York on board the ocean liner *General Bladford.*

1951: The family settles in Plainville, Connecticut.

1960–62: Undergraduate study at the University of New Hampshire, Durham. Studies drawing and painting with Christopher Cook and art history with Jim Fasanelli.

1962–65: Receives B.A. and M.A. from the University of Miami, Coral Gables, Florida. In 1963, marries her first husband, Milton von Rydingsvard.

1969–70: Studies at the University of California, Berkeley. Daughter, Ursula Ann, is born.

1971–73: Lives in New Britain, Connecticut. In the summer of 1972, takes classes in painting and drawing at the New School for Social Research, New York. Admires the paintings of Willem de Kooning, Arshile Gorky, and Mark Rothko.

1973–74: Divorces Milton von Rydingsvard and moves to New York City. Enters master of fine arts program at Columbia University. Studies with, among others, Ronald Bladen, Jean Linder, Meyer Schapiro, George Sugarman, and Sahl Swarz. Attends lectures by Tricia Brown, Philip Guston, Lucas Samaras,

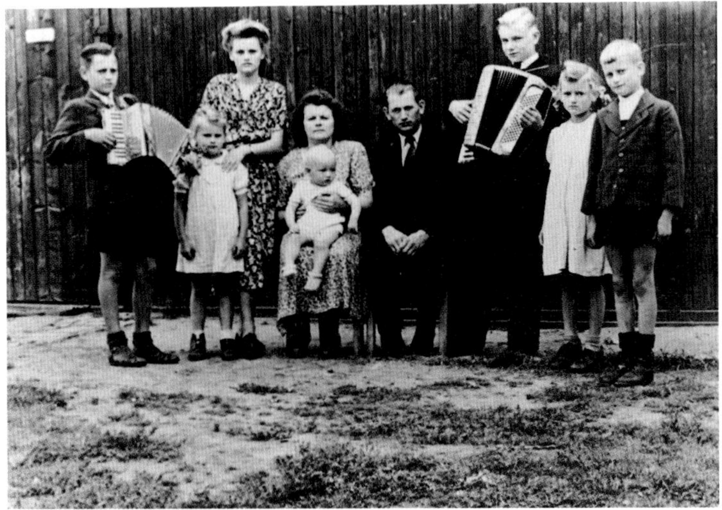

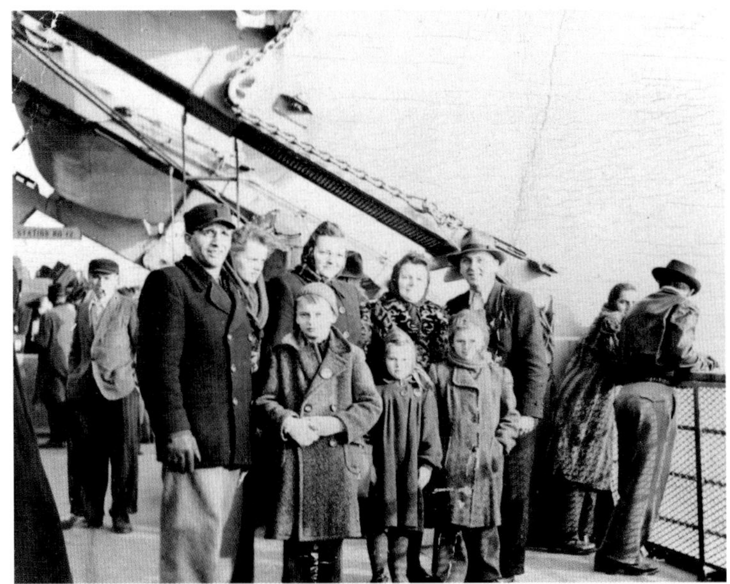

Von Rydingsvard in her Spring Street studio, 1979.

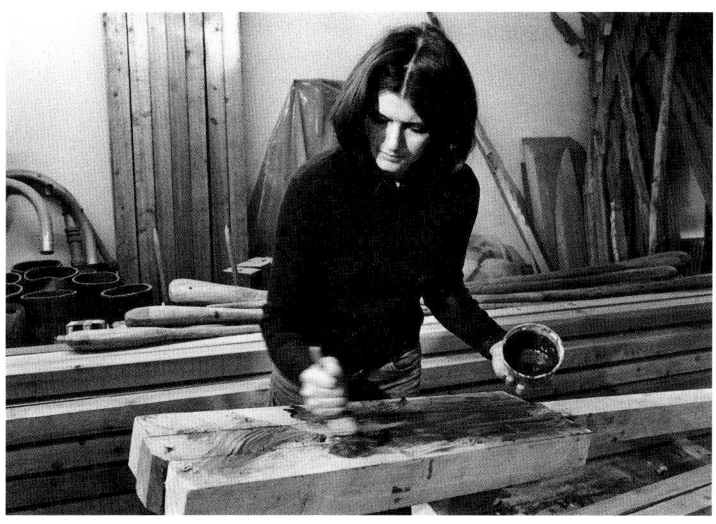

and Leo Steinberg. Summer job at the Museum of Modern Art (spends lunch hours studying the museum's collection). Sees Giacometti retrospective at the Solomon R. Guggenheim Museum. Works in welded steel. Begins to keep a journal.

1975: Graduates from Columbia University with M.F.A. in sculpture. Audits classes taught by Dore Ashton at Cooper Union. Begins to work in cedar, which becomes her principal material. Moves to her first New York studio at 210 Spring Street in SoHo, where she lives and works. Receives Fulbright-Hays Travel Grant to visit Poland, but is not able to travel there due to the political situation.

1976: Works for Encore Community Services, a social-service organization based in Saint Malachy's Church on West Forty-ninth Street.

1977–78: Exhibits *Untitled,* 1976, in "Wood," Nassau County Museum of Fine Arts, Roslyn, New York (curated by Jean Feinberg). Becomes member of 55 Mercer, an artists' cooperative in SoHo. *For Weston,* 1978, included in "Indoor-Outdoor Exhibition" at the Institute for Art and Urban Resources (P.S. 1), Long Island City, New York. Appointed assistant professor at Pratt Institute, Brooklyn, New York (until 1982). Grant from New York State Council on the Arts. Works for Comprehensive Employment Training Act, Title 6 (CETA). Meets artists Carl Andre, Sol LeWitt, and Robert Ryman.

1979: *Koszarawa,* 1979 (now destroyed), included in "Wave Hill: The Artist's View," organized by the nonprofit organization Wave Hill in the Riverdale section of the Bronx, New York (curated by Linda Macklowe and Suzanne Randolph); later displayed at the Neuberger Museum, State University of New York, Purchase. *Song of a Saint (Saint Eulalia),* 1979 (now destroyed), commissioned by Artpark, outside of Lewiston, New York. Grant from the National Endowment for the Arts.

1980: *Saint Martin's Dream* created for "Art on the Beach" program, sponsored by Creative Time for the Battery Park City landfill, New York. Grant from Creative Artists Program Service (CAPS). Appointed assistant professor at Fordham University, Bronx, New York (until 1982). Travels to Guatemala and Mexico, visits Tikal and Palenque.

1981: Appointed instructor at the School of Visual Arts, New York (until 1982). Travels to Europe for the first time since emigration in 1950; visits France and Italy; studies works by Giotto.

1982: Appointed assistant professor and, then, associate professor in the Sculpture Department, Yale School of Art, New Haven, Connecticut (until 1987). *Stations for Santa Clara,* 1981, exhibited at Rosa Esman Gallery, New York. Meets artist Judy Pfaff.

1983: Receives Guggenheim Fellowship. *Tunnels on the Levee* (now destroyed) commissioned by "Dayton City Beautiful Project," displayed in Deweese Park, Dayton, Ohio.

1984: Moves to her current studio in the Williamsburg section of Brooklyn, New York. Exhibits *16 Handrests,* 1984, in "Contemporary Art at One Penn Plaza," One Penn Plaza, New York (curated by Dore Ashton). Receives the Mark di Suvero Athena Foundation Grant.

1985: Marries Paul Greengard, a neuroscientist. First trip to Poland on a Grisward Travel Grant from Yale University; visits Koszarawa, the native village of her mother located in the southeast of the country.

1986: Teaches in the Graduate Division at the School of Visual Arts, New York (until the present). Individual Artists Grant from the National Endowment for the Arts. Travels to Lapland in northern Scandinavia. Starts using graphite on her cedar surfaces.

1987: Works included in "Sculpture of the Eighties: Aycock, Ferrara, Frank, Lasch, Miss, Pfaff, Saar, Sperry, von Rydingsvard, Zucker," Queens Museum of Art, Flushing, New York, and "Standing Grounds," Contemporary Arts Center, Cincinnati, Ohio. Participates in "Works by Women" National Sculpture Conference, Cincinnati, Ohio. Second Individual Artists Grant from the National Endowment for the Arts. Travels to Italy.

1988: *Ursie A's Dream* created for "Home Show: Ten Artists' Installations in Ten Santa Barbara Homes," organized by Santa Barbara Contemporary Arts Forum (CAF), Santa Barbara, California. Metropolitan Museum of Art, New York, buys *Untitled (Seven Mountains),* 1986–87; on display in the museum from 1989 to 1995. Brooklyn Museum, Brooklyn, New York, purchases *Umarles (you went and died),* 1987–88; on display from 1989 to 1996. Travels to Loire Valley, France.

1989: *Untitled (45 Tubs),* 1988–89, installed at Laumeier Sculpture Park in Saint Louis, Missouri (permanent installation). Participates in "Encore: Celebrating Fifty Years," at the Contemporary Arts Center, Cincinnati, Ohio (curated by Sarah Rogers). Ignacy Karoliszyn dies.

1990: *Untitled* (later renamed *Ene, Due, Rabe*) made and shown at San Francisco's Capp Street Project, San Francisco, California. *Three Bowls,* 1990, installed at the Walker Art Center, Minneapolis, Minnesota (curated by Peter Boswell and Martin Friedman). Included in "Out of Wood," Whitney Museum at Philip Morris, New York (curated by Josephine Gear). Second trip to Poland.

1991: *Iggy's Pride,* 1990, installed on the Sonoma Valley ranch of Steven and Nancy Oliver, Geyserville, California. Included in "The Hybrid State," Exit Art, New York, and "Jestesmy," Zacheta Gallery, Warsaw, Poland. Receives honorary doctorate from Maryland Institute College of Art, Baltimore.

1992: Installation *Zygmunt* at the Cultural Space/The Laboratory, New York (collaboration with Judy Pfaff). *Girlie Girl,* 1991, purchased by the Virginia Museum of Fine Arts, Richmond. The American section of the Association of International Art Critics cites the Storm King Art Center ten-year retrospective as best small-museum exhibition of the 1991–92 season. Joins Galerie Lelong, New York. Travels on a freighter along the coast of Norway.

1993: Travels to Ireland.

Iggy's Pride in progress,
Oliver Ranch, California, 1991.

Von Rydingsvard in her Brooklyn studio, 1996.

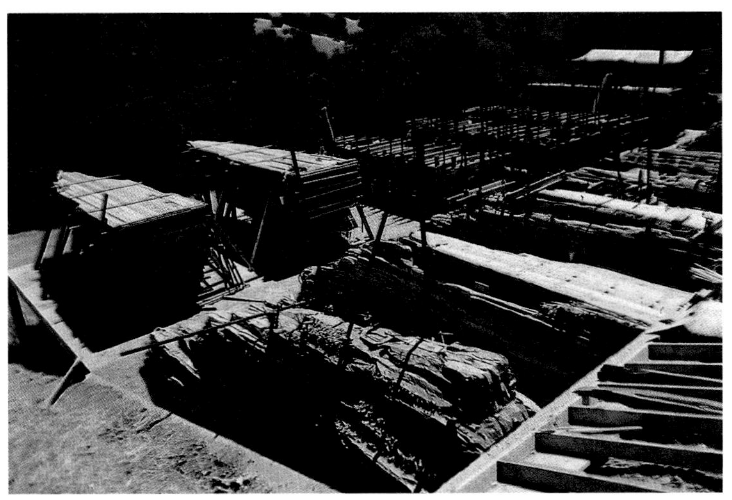

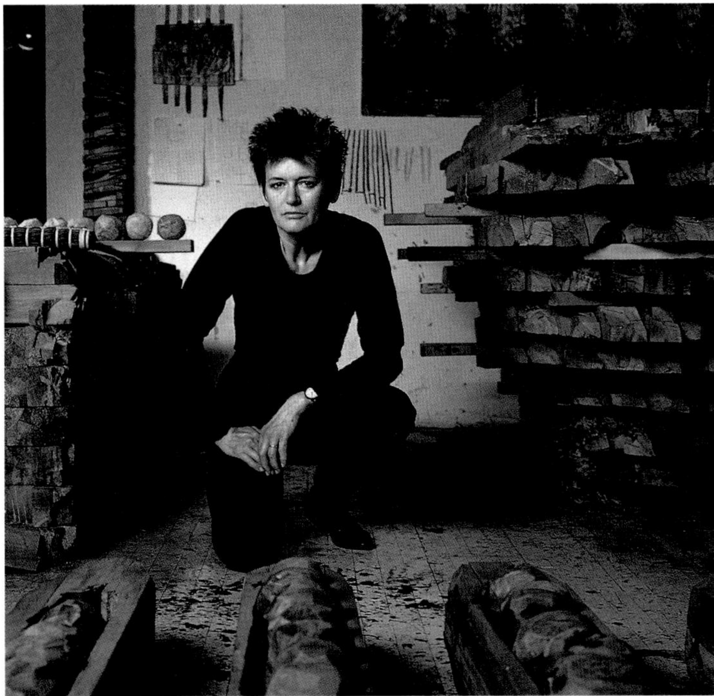

1994: *Corrugated Rollers,* 1994, displayed at the Three River Festival, Pittsburgh, Pennsylvania (curated by Sarah Rogers), and at Metro Tech Plaza, Brooklyn, New York, commissioned by Public Art Fund of New York (curated by Jim Clark). Included in "Visions of America: Landscape as Metaphor in the Late Twentieth Century," at the Denver Art Museum, Denver, Colorado, and the Columbus Museum of Art, Columbus, Ohio (curated by Martin Friedman); and "Beyond Nature: Wood into Art," Lowe Art Museum, University of Miami, Coral Gables, Florida. *For Paul* purchased by Storm King Art Center, Mountainville, New York. Receives Sculpture Award from the American Academy of Arts and Letters. Builds a country studio in Accord, New York. Travels to Italy (Tuscany and Umbria).

1995: *Berek,* 1994, purchased by the Whitney Museum of American Art, New York. *Five-Fingered Comb,* 1994, purchased by the High Museum of Art, Atlanta, Georgia. *Untitled (Five-Fingered Bowl),* 1995, purchased by the Orlando Museum of Art, Orlando, Florida. Travels to Ukraine and Poland. Hood Museum of Art, Dartmouth College, Hanover, New Hampshire, acquires *Untitled* drawing. *Krasivica* exhibited in "Beyond Gender" at Snug Harbor Cultural Center, Staten Island, New York.

1996: Receives the Alfred Jurzykowski Foundation Award in Fine Art.

SOLO EXHIBITIONS

1977
55 Mercer, New York

1978
Robert Freidus Gallery, New York

1979
55 Mercer, New York

1980
55 Mercer, New York

1981
Rosa Esman Gallery, New York

1982
Rosa Esman Gallery, New York

1984
Bette Stoler Gallery, New York

1988
Laumeier Sculpture Park, Saint Louis, Missouri

Exit Art, New York

1989
Cranbrook Academy of Art Museum,
Bloomfield Hills, Michigan

1990
Capp Street Project, San Francisco, California

Fabric Workshop, Philadelphia, Pennsylvania

Lorence Monk Gallery, New York

1991
Lorence Monk Gallery, New York

1992
Center for Contemporary Art
(Centrum Sztuki Wspołczesnej), Warsaw, Poland

1992–94
Storm King Art Center, Mountainville, New York
(ten-year retrospective)

1994
Galerie Lelong, New York

Weatherspoon Art Gallery, University of North Carolina,
Greensboro

Metro Tech Plaza, Brooklyn, New York

1995
Art Museum, University of Wyoming, Laramie

University Art Gallery, Fine Arts Center, University of
Massachusetts at Amherst

1996
Galerie Lelong, New York

Museum of Art, Rhode Island School of Design, Providence

Exhibition Catalogues

Alloway, Lawrence. *Ursula von Rydingsvard.* New York: Bette Stoler Gallery, 1984.

Ashton, Dore. *Home Show: Ten Artists' Installations in Ten Santa Barbara Homes.* Santa Barbara, Calif.: Santa Barbara Contemporary Arts Forum, 1988.

Brenson, Michael. *Ursula von Rydingsvard: Sculpture.* Mountainville, N.Y.: Storm King Art Center, 1992.

Collischan Van Wagner, Judy K. *Lines of Vision: Drawings by Contemporary American Women.* New York: Hudson Hills Press, 1989.

Feinberg, Jean E. *Ursula von Rydingsvard: Sculpture.* Storrs: Jorgensen Gallery. University of Connecticut at Storrs, 1980.

Friedman, Martin. *Visions of America: Landscape as Metaphor in the Late Twentieth Century.* New York: Harry N. Abrams for the Denver Art Museum and the Columbus Museum of Art, 1994.

Onorato, Ronald. *Ursula von Rydingsvard and Vito Acconci: Sculpture at Laumeier.* St. Louis: Laumeier Sculpture Park, 1990.

Ostrow, Saul. *Ursula von Rydingsvard.* New York: Lorence Monk Gallery, 1990.

Phillips, Patricia. *Ursula von Rydingsvard: Sculpture* (in Polish). Warsaw: Ujazdowski Contemporary Art Center, 1993.

Sims, Lowery S. *Sculpture of the Eighties.* Flushing, N.Y.: Queens Museum, 1987.

Strauss, David Levi, ed. *Capp Street Project 1989–1990: Artists in Residence and Experimental Projects.* San Fransisco: Capp Street Project AVT, 1991.

Varnedoe, Kirk, Linda Macklowe, and Suzanne Randolph. *Wave Hill: The Artist's View.* Bronx, N.Y.: Wave Hill, 1979.

Yau, John. *Ursula von Rydingsvard.* New York: Exit Art, 1988.

Yau, John. *Diverse Representations 1990.* Morristown, N.J.: Morris Museum, 1990.

Zimmer, William, and Judy Collischan Van Wagner. *Judith Murray: Painting, Ursula von Rydingsvard: Sculpture.* Brookville, N.Y.: Hillwood Art Gallery, Long Island University, 1985.

Articles

Atkins, Robert. "Ursula von Rydingsvard." *7 Days* 1, no. 4 (April 20, 1988): 51.

Baker, Kenneth. "Landscape That Fills a Room." *San Francisco Chronicle,* December 13, 1990, E3.

Bartelik, Marek. "Ursula von Rydingsvard, Galerie Lelong." *Artforum* 33, no. 2 (October 1994): 102–3.

Berman, Avis. "Ursula von Rydingsvard: Life under Siege." *Artnews* 87, no. 10 (December 1988): 97–98.

Brenson, Michael. "Sculptors Find New Ways with Wood." *New York Times,* December 2, 1984, sec. 2, 29.

———. "Setting Free in Images in Big Beams of Wood." *New York Times,* April 1, 1988, C32.

———. "Wood." *New York Times,* June 7, 1985, C24.

Clothier, Peter. "Ursula von Rydingsvard." *Artspace* 16, no. 5 (September–October 1992): 58–59.

Cotter, Holland. "Sculpture under the Sky: Free, Daring and Soon Departed." *New York Times,* August 26, 1994, C1, C25.

Gardner, Paul. "Do Titles Really Matter?" *Artnews* 91, no. 2 (February 1992): 97.

Gibson, Eric. "Decade in Review." *Sculpture* 8, no. 3 (May–June 1989): 21, 23.

Glueck, Grace. "Ursula von Rydingsvard." *New York Times,* April 18, 1980, C22.

———. "Ursula von Rydingsvard." *New York Times,* November 5, 1982, C18.

Graziani, Ron. "The Home Show: Public Art in Private Places," *Santa Barbara Magazine* 14 (November 1988): 52–61.

Harris, Susan. "Ursula von Rydingsvard." *Arts Magazine* 57, no. 4 (December 1982): 46.

Kimmelman, Michael. "Intonations in Wood of Ritual and Refugee Camps." *New York Times,* July 17, 1992, C21.

Larson, Kay. "Inside Out." *New York Magazine* 25, no. 24 (June 15, 1992): 100–101.

———. "Ursula von Rydingsvard." *New York Magazine* 21, no. 19 (May 9, 1988): 81.

Levi Strauss, David. "Sculpture as Refuge." *Art in America* 81, no. 2 (February 1993): 89–92, 125.

Lippard, Lucy. "'Wood' at the Nassau County Museum." *Art in America* 65, no. 6 (November–December 1977): 136–37.

Lubell, Ellen. "Ursula von Rydingsvard." *Arts Magazine* 52, no. 1 (September 1977): 38.

Mahoney, Robert. "Ursula von Rydingsvard (Lorence Monk, March 3–31)." *Arts Magazine* 64 (Summer 1990): 94.

McFadden, Sarah. "Going Places, Part II: The Outside Story." *Art in America* 68, no. 6 (Summer 1980): 51–61.

Miro, Marsha. "Vulnerability and Ritual Live in Cedar Forms." *Detroit Free Press,* February 12, 1989, 3C.

Newhall, Edith. "Ursula von Rydingsvard, Galerie Lelong." *Artnews* 93, no. 7 (September 1994): 167.

Olejarz, Harold. "Ursula von Rydingsvard." *Arts Magazine* 53, no. 5 (January 1979): 17.

Phillips, Patricia C. "Ursula von Rydingsvard, Bette Stoler Gallery." *Artforum* 23, no. 1 (September 1984): 111.

———. "Ursula von Rydingsvard: Storm King Art Center." *Artforum* 31, no. 1 (September 1992): 101.

Princenthal, Nancy. "Six Sculptors." *Artnews* 82, no. 7 (September 1983): 194, 198.

Raven, Arlene. "Double Bed (Judy Pfaff and Ursula von Rydingsvard: Zygmunt)." *Village Voice* 37, no. 10 (March 10, 1992): 91.

Raynor, Vivien. "Art: Seven Sculptors at Penn Plaza." *New York Times,* June 15, 1984, C23.

———. "Changes at a Sculpture Park." *New York Times,* August 22, 1993, sec. 13NJ, 15.

———. "Sculptures of Wood in a Wooden Setting." *New York Times,* September 20, 1992, C26.

Russell, John. "Invitational Exhibition at Rosa Esman Gallery." *New York Times,* June 27, 1980, C24.

———. "Review." *New York Times,* November 26, 1976, C16.

———. "Ursula von Rydingsvard (Rosa Esman Gallery . . .)." *New York Times,* April 3, 1981, C23.

Tully, Judd. "Ursula von Rydingsvard." *Arts Magazine* 54 (May 1980): 22.

Viney, Jill. "A Rich, Redemptive Journey: Interview by Jill Viney." *Sculpture* 8, no. 8 (November–December 1989): 32–35.

von Rydingsvard, Ursula. "Thoughts about My Work." *Journal of Artists* 6 (Spring 1986): 45–47.

Zimmer, William. "Art on the Beach." *SoHo Weekly News* 7, no. 39 (June 25–July 1, 1980): 39.

———. "Ursula von Rydingsvard, Exit Art, New York City." *Sculpture* 7, no. 4 (July–August 1988): 26.

———. "Von Rydingsvard at Rosa Esman." *Art Gallery Scene,* November 16, 1982, 26.

PUBLIC COLLECTIONS

Aldrich Museum of Contemporary Art
Ridgefield, Connecticut

William Benton Museum of Art
University of Connecticut, Storrs, Connecticut

The Brooklyn Museum
Brooklyn, New York

Center for Contemporary Art
Ujazdowski Castle, Warsaw, Poland

The Detroit Institute of Arts
Detroit, Michigan

High Museum of Art
Atlanta, Georgia

Hood Museum of Art
Dartmouth College, Hanover, New Hampshire

Laumeier Sculpture Park
St. Louis, Missouri

The Metropolitan Museum of Art
New York

Neuberger Museum of Art
State University of New York at Purchase

Orlando Museum of Art
Orlando, Florida

Storm King Art Center
Mountainville, New York

Virginia Museum of Fine Arts
Richmond, Virginia

Walker Art Center
Minneapolis, Minnesota

Whitney Museum of American Art
New York

INDEX

Page numbers in *italics* refer to illustrations.

PHOTOGRAPH CREDITS

Jesse Alexander, 37
David Allison, 14, 15, 17, 19 right, 20, 21, 27–32, 34, 35, 39–41, 43–45, 47, 49, 59, 61, 63, 64
Ben Barnhart, 66, 69
Del Bogart, 70–71
Vincent Dante, 58, 65, 67
© 1996 Sigrid Estrada, 101 bottom, jacket flap
R. Hensleigh, 6
Charles Juhasz, 101 top
Elka Krajewska, 4, 96–97
Larry Lame, 33
Bob Laruch, 38
Marbeth, 19 left, 24, 99
James Milmore, 56, 57
Jennifer Reiss, 18
George Scarna, 22
Lee Stalsworth, 13
Jerry L. Thompson, jacket front, 8, 51–55, endleaves
John Townsend, 2
Ursula von Rydingsvard, 11, 36, 42
Greg White, 23

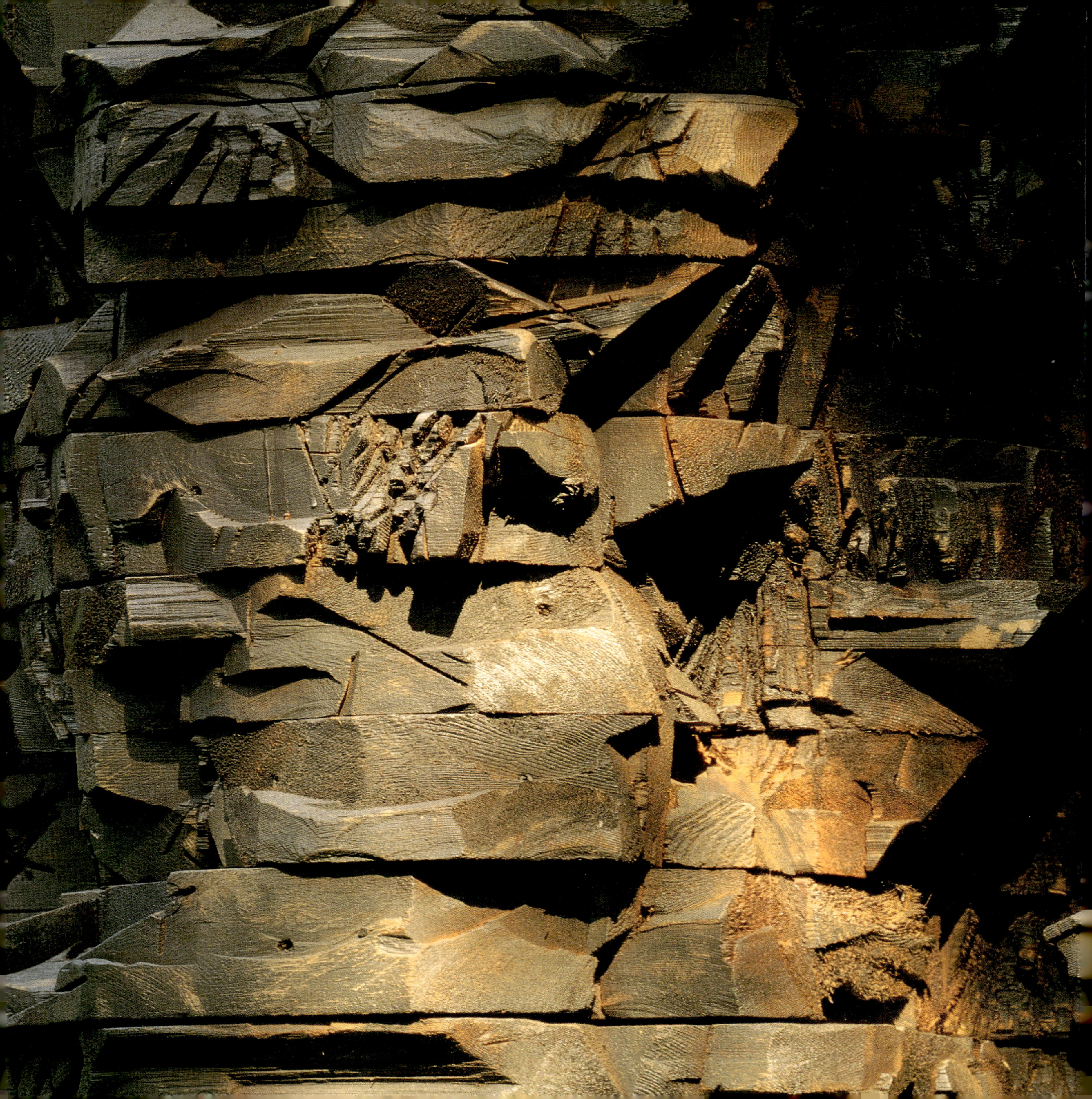